Keeping Kids Safe, Healthy, and Smart

Kimberly Williams and Marcel Lebrun

Rowman & Littlefield Education
Lanham • New York • Toronto • Plymouth, UK

Published in the United States of America
by Rowman & Littlefield Education
A Division of Rowman & Littlefield Publishers, Inc.
A wholly owned subsidiary of The Rowman & Littlefield Publishing Group, Inc.
4501 Forbes Boulevard, Suite 200, Lanham, Maryland 20706
www.rowmaneducation.com

Estover Road
Plymouth PL6 7PY
United Kingdom

British Library Cataloguing in Publication Information Available

Library of Congress Cataloging-in-Publication Data
Williams, Kimberly.
  Keeping kids safe, healthy, and smart / Kimberly Williams and Marcel
Lebrun.
       p. cm.
  Includes bibliographical references.
  ISBN-13: 978-1-57886-971-8 (cloth : alk. paper)
  ISBN-10: 1-57886-971-4 (cloth : alk. paper)
  eISBN-13: 978-1-57886-973-2
  eISBN-10: 1-57886-973-0
  1. Children's accidents—United States—Prevention. I. Lebrun, Marcel. II.
Title.
  HV675.72.W55 2009
  371.7—dc22   2008035564

∞™ The paper used in this publication meets the minimum requirements of
American National Standard for Information Sciences—Permanence of
Paper for Printed Library Materials, ANSI/NISO Z39.48-1992.
Manufactured in the United States of America.

To Whitney and Dalton and all the world's children—may you grow up safe and healthy.

Kim Williams

To all the members of my family who have encouraged me to be the best I can be. It is only with your support, enthusiasm, and belief in my abilities that I have been able to achieve what I have. Thank you

Marcel Lebrun

Contents

Part III: Keeping Kids Safe in All Spaces

Foreword

David Hyerle

Most parents feel that they know what is best for their children and how to protect them from harm. Most teachers feel they know how best to keep children safe in schools and to nurture their unique capacities to learn. Yet, as both a parent and an educator, I have come to believe that my decisions are too often based on *intuitions* from my "in-the-moment" reactions rather than *informed* by "up-to-date" information from the field. In the back of my mind, I also think that if I need information about a child-safety or health issue, I can just talk to a friend or colleague or Google the topic and download information in my search for solutions. But in this age of way too much poorly organized information—often grounded in questionable sources and expertise—going to the Web can be like being caught in a maze.

So I am thankful for this book, as should be *every* parent and teacher responsible for children in this new world. Within this comprehensive resource by Kim Williams and Marcel Lebrun, we are offered the best of both worlds: well-organized information for decision making *and* high-quality Web-based references in order to access more information as needed. This book will certainly save all of us time and save us from our fears of the unknown, but, most importantly, it may actually save the lives of children in our communal care.

With the turn of the century, daily life is rapidly changing for us and for our children. Parents, grandparents, extended families, and caregivers of diverse backgrounds must become aware of the dangers across the public, private, and cyberspaces in which our twenty-first-century children are maturing. And we must learn how to work together and resolve conflicts.

But we have no need to be mystified. Whether it is bullying and violence on the playground and sports teams, drugs and nutrition, or the social network of cyberspace, Williams and Lebrun address each area with clarity and straightforward writing—and statistics. Too many times over my years of parenting and working in schools I have witnessed parents and teachers feeling the need to overprotect children for fear of potential dangers . . . and I have felt the same need within myself. An isolated story of a harmed child can now circulate like a virus around the community, then race into the spin cycle of cable news and immediately network through the Web. Out of fear alone, we may jump to protect our children, rather than thinking through our options. Williams and Lebrun support us by presenting a range of information that often reveals that we must be careful, thoughtful, and proactive, but not *reactive.*

The gift that these authors offer us is a middle path for working through health and safety concerns. We can make better decisions using the "*A, B, C*" process that gives structure to each chapter of the book: *A*sk, *B*ring together, *C*onsider the options, *D*o what you can, *E*valuate your successes, and *F*ind out more. This "*A* to *F*" process creates a balanced, holistic frame through which we can see our children. The authors could have simply focused their research only on hot-button topics, such as ADD/ADHD, nutrition and childhood obesity, drug use, violence, and Internet dangers (which they do address in detail). Williams and Lebrun do more by expanding our understanding of the well-being of children. They guide us into the range of the emotional, social, and intellectual lives of children, giving us the context for thinking through problems when we and our children must face them in the moment.

In the long run, we want our children to be safe and healthy so that *they* become independent actors in this rich and complex world—thinking through problems just as we do—and not carrying our fears along with them as they step out on their own.

David Hyerle, EdD
Founding Director, Thinking Foundation
Former National Board Chairperson, Educators for Social Responsibility

Introduction

Nothing is more important to Americans than the safety of their children.

> —U.S. Education Secretary Margaret Spellings,
> October 31, 2007, press release on www.ed.gov

This book addresses the most important goals of all adults in all societies—keeping our children healthy and safe. As U.S. Department of Education Secretary Margaret Spellings correctly states above, "Nothing is more important to Americans than the safety of their children." How can we as parents, teachers, caregivers, administrators, doctors, policy makers—adults in a democratic society—keep our children safe from harm? What poses the greatest risk to children? What can we do to address these risk factors?

As responsible adults we must seek to reduce risks that young people face by examining the sometimes hidden dangers children face and invoking strategies for keeping them safe—not only in schools but online and in other places children work and play. We will cover the key threats to children's safety and well-being and examine strategies that adults can use to *prevent*, and if necessary *intervene*, in dangerous or harmful situations. And finally, if children engage in harmful, dangerous, threatening, or hurtful activities, we address possible ways to address the needs of these children while continuing to protect others.

To gather some personal anecdotes in addition to our own from our decades of experience as educators, we used Survey Monkey (www.surveymonkey.com) to solicit responses to open-ended questions about

1

safety experiences from our undergraduate and graduate students. A variety of students responded, reflecting on their experiences with topics covered in this book—from car accidents to mental health to learning problems.

What poses the greatest harm for our nation's children? Perhaps surprisingly to some people: car accidents, drowning, fires, homicide, suicide, and poisoning. The U.S. government, through the Centers for Disease Control and Prevention (CDC), keeps statistics on the leading causes of death and injury for children and adolescents, and these key statistics from the CDC have informed the topics included in this book.

The leading cause of death the CDC reports for ages one to forty-four is "unintentional injuries"—in other words, accidents. Car accidents are the leading cause of unintentional accidents, with 40 percent of adolescent deaths attributable to automobile accidents. The second leading cause of death for adolescents (aged fifteen to twenty-four) is homicide, followed by suicide.

The second leading cause for children aged five to fourteen is cancer; third for ages five to nine is congenital abnormalities, and third for those in the ten to fourteen age group is suicide. This book targets those accidents that are preventable, as well as issues of homicide/violence and suicide (see table I.1).

For more information go to the CDC's "10 Leading Causes of Death by Age Group, United States—2003," at ftp://ftp.cdc.gov/pub/ncipc/10LC-2003/PDF/10lc-2003.pdf).

Table I.1.   Centers for Disease Control and Prevention's Top 10 Leading Causes of Injury Death by Age Group

	Age Group				
Rank	*<1 year*	*1–4 years*	*5–9 years*	*10–14 years*	*15–24 years*
1	Unintentional suffocation	Unintentional MV traffic	Unintentional MV traffic	Unintentional MV traffic	Unintentional MV traffic
2	Unintentional MV traffic	Unintentional drowning	Unintentional fireburn	Suicide suffocation	Homicide firearm
3	Homicide unspecified	Unintentional fireburn	Unintentional drowning	Unintentional drowning	Suicide firearm
4	Homicide classifiable	Unintentional suffocation	Unintentional other land transport	Homicide firearm	Unintentional poisoning

Adapted from the CDC report "10 leading causes of injury death by age group highlighting unintentional injury deaths, United States" ftp://ftp.cdc.gov/pub/ncipc/10LC-2003/PDF/10lc-unintentional.pdf

Sections are organized around the following three different themes of major threats and hidden dangers to children in our country: threats in *school spaces* (e.g., in classrooms, on buses, on playgrounds, and on sports teams), threats in *cyberspace* (e.g., bullying/harassment and child predators/child pornography), and threats out in *other spaces* where children work and play (e.g., intrapersonal and interpersonal violence, including self-mutilation, choking, suicide, and bullying; accidents; poisoning; physical, sexual, and psychological abuse/violence; environmental threats; drugs; and mental illness, such as depression, bipolar disorder, and posttraumatic stress disorder).

The format of the chapters will use the following structure:

+ *Ask*: What Is Potentially Dangerous or Problematic for Children? What Can I Do (or What Can Be Done) to Make This Child (or These Children) Safer or Healthier or More Successful in This/These Situation/s (or Similar Ones)?
+ *Bring* Together All Advocates Who Can Assist in Making Children Safer in These Situations
+ *Consider* the Options (Particularly Ones with Demonstrated Success)
+ *Do* What You Can
+ *Evaluate* Your Success
+ *Find* Out More

Each chapter will provide an overview of different threats and hidden dangers for young people, followed by strategies for keeping children safe. There will be checklists of ideas to consider when addressing these issues with a child. And resources for more information will also be provided. This book is designed to be a practical guide for parents, educators, care providers, and any adult concerned with the welfare of children. The very survival of our species depends on keeping our children healthy and safe.

Part I

KEEPING KIDS SAFE IN SCHOOL AND SCHOOL-RELATED SPACES

Chapter One

Playground Safety

As my five-year-old daughter came home crying from her first days of kindergarten, I asked, "What's the matter?" Through her sobs, she replied, "Amy was mean to me. . . . She said she didn't want to be my friend anymore and told the other girls not to play with me on the playground or talk to me. . . . I thought she was my friend." I felt like crying myself—I had no real answer for her.

—Mother of two

Cruel behavior starts early in schools. The above example of a kindergartener learning this very early on in school shows how children are exposed to this hurtful, harmful, painful cruelty at a young age. They learn to cope as best they can, or they continue to struggle in school, at home, and in life. Most of this kind of mean treatment in schools happens out of the view of adults, but some of it happens within their gaze—without response or protection.

Unfortunately, like the mother in this example, adults in schools don't know what to do. Some say, "Would you like someone to treat you that way?" Or some don't respond and say to themselves and others, "It's just the way kids are." Or, as we have also heard, "It toughens them up for the *real world.*"

Does it have to be the way kids are? If we as parents, teachers, and other adults in society believe that this kind of cruel peer treatment is unacceptable, we are in a position to prevent it. We do not tolerate this kind of behavior in adult spaces. Why should children have to endure it nearly every day?

The next few chapters examine the potentially harmful school spaces for children—not just emotionally but also physically: playgrounds, classrooms, buses, sports teams, and other school spaces. Within each topic are red flags to attend to as a teacher and/or parent and ways to improve these situations for children.

PLAYGROUNDS

Each year in the United States, emergency departments treat more than 200,000 children ages 14 and younger for playground-related injuries. . . . About 45% of playground-related injuries are severe—fractures, internal injuries, concussions, dislocations, and amputations. . . . About 75% of nonfatal injuries related to playground equipment occur on public playgrounds (Tinsworth 2001). Most occur at schools and daycare centers (Phelan 2001).

Between 1990 and 2000, 147 children ages 14 and younger died from playground-related injuries. Of them, 82 (56%) died from strangulation and 31 (20%) died from falls to the playground surface. Most of these deaths (70%) occurred on home playgrounds. (Tinsworth 2001, CDC 2007)

Children need exercise and free play during school hours. There is irrefutable of evidence supporting the benefits of physical activity—it is healthy not only for a child's growing body (with some research advocating sixty minutes of cardiovascular activity for children each day) but also for the child's developing brain. Many schools invest money in playgrounds and playground equipment to enhance children's play—but playgrounds have a host of hidden dangers for youngsters and need careful supervision and regular maintenance.

> **ASK: WHAT IS POTENTIALLY DANGEROUS OR PROBLEMATIC FOR CHILDREN? WHAT CAN I DO (OR WHAT CAN BE DONE) TO MAKE THIS CHILD (OR THESE CHILDREN) SAFER OR HEALTHIER OR MORE SUCCESSFUL IN THIS/ THESE SITUATION/S (OR SIMILAR ONES)?**

In our online survey, there were several personal examples of breaking limbs, mostly arms, on playground equipment. Also, some mention head injuries (described in a later chapter) from falling off and landing on heads. Some injuries, like this one, are difficult to predict or avoid, but we need to try to think ahead about what could be problematic.

> During elementary school my friends and I were playing tag at recess. Our elementary school was made of bricks and one of the walls was our safety net, or "goo." One of my friends was running to goo and ran into the wall, breaking his nose. An ambulance came, and we were no longer allowed to use the walls at recess time. (College sophomore)

Playground accidents are the number one cause of injury for children in day care and children aged five to fourteen. As the mother of a two-year-old who broke her arm at day care playing on playground equipment (KW), I know all too well how important it is to pay attention to young children in these spaces. Also, caretakers need to take falls seriously, because often when youngsters break bones, they don't know it until long afterward. For example, when my daughter broke her arm at day care at age two, nobody knew her arm was broken—she went nearly ten hours before being taken to the emergency room. Very young children can disassociate the pain in these kinds of extreme cases—and often as a parent or caregiver, the only clue you have of serious injury is the child's failure to use a body part when he or she normally would.

In addition to the physical and emotional costs, there are also economic ones; for example, the Office of Technology Assessment (1995) reported that playground accidents/injuries cost about $1.2 billion. In our online survey, there were examples like this one that were a blend of playground accidents and bullying. Another reason for adult vigilance is to be on the lookout for bullying behaviors, such as in this example (more in later chapters on bullying):

> When I was in 1st grade a 5th grader pushed me off the monkey bars and I fractured my arm in several places. (Twenty-year-old college student)

Hidden dangers and who is most at risk. Most parents and teachers are aware of the dangers of falling and inappropriate use of playground equipment, but perhaps fewer are aware of the hidden dangers of playgrounds. For example, strangulation is the number one cause of death of children on playground equipment. Parents and educators need to be extra vigilant about the clothing children wear when on the playground—particularly scarves, necklaces, or any article of clothing that could get caught and strangle a child. On home play equipment, swings are the most dangerous and responsible for the most injuries, whereas on public and school playgrounds, climbers (monkey bars, climbing walls, ladders) are most dangerous (Tinsworth 2001).

In addition to the equipment, adult caretakers need to pay attention to the material on the ground of the playground—that is, is it cement, chips, rocks, or some other material. Impact-absorbing substances are recommended for areas where there are play structures. Consider the following examples from our survey:

> There was a lot of falling down and getting hurt. The playground was all cement so if you fell down you were much more likely to get hurt. (College junior)

> My sister had a wood chip go into her eye when she was playing on a playground once. It didn't come out so my mom took her to the ER where they put drops in her eye to see the chip with a black light and took it out. (College sophomore)

Children between the ages of five and nine tend to be at the highest risk (Phelan 2001); that is, they have the highest rates of emergency room visits for playground injuries, and girls tend to be at slightly higher risk than boys (55 percent versus 45 percent, respectively) (Tinsworth 2001).

Suecoff (1999) found that low-income neighborhoods' playgrounds had maintenance hazards and other dangers, such as garbage and rusty and damaged equipment. The same is true for high-poverty schools. Adequate funding and adult volunteers should be available to maintain playground equipment and determine which pieces are unsafe or developmentally inappropriate. Consider the case of dangerous large slides:

> My sister actually fell off of the steps of a huge slide, she was only 3 steps up, and when she fell she ruptured her ear drum and is now deaf in one of her ears. And later on they finally had taken the slide out because I'm sure many other kids got hurt by it as well. (College sophomore)

For more information: the Centers for Disease Control keep track of statistics and dangers and create recommendations for helping children stay safe on playgrounds (see CDC 2007).

The National Safe Kids Campaign (NSKC) has researched playground safety and created the following fact sheet for parents and school personnel:

When and Where Playground Deaths and Injuries Occur

- It is estimated that one-third of playground equipment-related deaths and 75 percent of playground equipment-related injuries occur on public playgrounds.
- Playground injuries are the leading cause of injury to children in child-care and to children ages 5 to 14 in schools.
- Lack of supervision is associated with 40 percent of playground injuries. A recent study found that children play without adult supervision more often on school playgrounds (32 percent of the time) than playgrounds in parks (22 percent) or childcare centers (5 percent).
- Strangulation resulting from entanglement and entrapment is the primary cause of playground equipment-related fatalities, accounting for nearly 56 percent of the deaths. Falls to the surface are responsible for an additional 20 percent of the deaths.
- Approximately 70 percent of playground equipment-related injuries involve falls to the surface, and 10 percent involve falls onto equipment.
- Falls are the most common mode of playground injury and account for approximately 80 percent of all playground equipment-related injuries. Head injuries are involved in 75 percent of all fall-related deaths associated with playground equipment.
- Nearly 40 percent of playground injuries occur during the months of May, June, and September.
- The majority (53 percent) of injuries that occur on public playgrounds involve climbing equipment, while the majority (67 percent) of injuries that occur on home playgrounds involve swings.

Who Is at Risk

- Female children have a slightly higher risk of sustaining playground-related injuries than males.
- Children ages 5 to 9 account for more than half of all playground-related injuries.
- Children ages 4 and under are more likely to suffer injuries to the face and head, while children ages 5 to 14 are more likely to suffer injuries to the arm and hand.
- A young child is at increased risk of injury when playing on equipment designed for older children. Only 42 percent of U.S. playgrounds have

separate play areas for children ages 2 to 5 and children ages 5 to 12, and
only 9 percent have signs indicating the age appropriateness of equipment.
- The risk of injury is four times greater if a child falls from playground
  equipment that is more than 1.5 meters (approximately 5 feet) high than
  from equipment that is less than 1.5 meters high.
- The risk of injury in a fall onto a non-impact-absorbing surface such as
  asphalt or concrete is more than twice that of falling onto an impact-absorbing surface. It is estimated that only 9 percent of home playgrounds
  have appropriate impact-absorbing surfacing around stationary equipment. (NSKC 2004, para. 4-5)

BRING TOGETHER ALL ADVOCATES WHO CAN ASSIST IN MAKING CHILDREN SAFER IN THESE SITUATIONS

A number of concerned adults and groups are interested in making playgrounds safe havens for children. The following groups would be potential advocates:

- parent organizations
- teachers and administrators and organizations
- adult staff in schools who monitor playgrounds
- community organizations
- corporations that sell playground equipment
- local law and policy makers
- school boards
- neighborhood organizations
- playground equipment manufacturers and installers

Consider all the stakeholders in preventing accidents on school, home,
and public playgrounds. When possible, try to get a group of volunteers
willing to do playground safety audits, provide additional supervision,
and engage in routine maintenance tasks. Most adult caregivers and con-
scientious community members will volunteer their time to keep children
safer. One concerned teacher, parent, or community member (or even the
local parent-teacher organization) can oversee this important series of
tasks to prevent playground injuries.

CONSIDER THE OPTIONS (PARTICULARLY ONES WITH DEMONSTRATED SUCCESS)

The NSKC has researched the effectiveness of different strategies to keep kids safe on playgrounds.

Playground Injury Prevention Effectiveness

- Protective surfacing under and around playground equipment can reduce the severity of and even prevent playground fall-related injuries. According to a 2002 national survey, 75 percent of public playgrounds lack adequate protective surfacing.
- A recent study found that the rate of playground-related injuries at North Carolina childcare centers dropped 22 percent after a law was passed requiring new playground equipment and surfacing in childcare facilities to conform to U.S. Consumer Product Safety Commission guidelines.

Playground Laws and Regulations

- Playground equipment guidelines and standards have been developed by the U.S. Consumer Product Safety Commission [CPSC] and the American Society for Testing and Materials. At least seven states have enacted some form of playground safety legislation.
- The CPSC has issued voluntary guidelines for drawstrings on children's clothing to prevent children from strangling or getting entangled in the neck and waist drawstrings of outerwear garments, such as jackets and sweatshirts. Children are at risk from strangulation when drawstrings on clothing become entangled in playground equipment.

Health Care Costs and Savings

- The total annual cost of playground equipment-related injuries among children ages 14 and under was estimated to be $1 billion in 1998.

Prevention Tips

- Avoid asphalt, concrete, grass and soil surfaces under playground equipment. Acceptable loose-fill materials include shredded rubber, hardwood fiber mulch or chips, and fine sand. Surfacing should be maintained at a depth of 12 inches and should extend a minimum of 6 feet in all directions around stationary equipment. Depending on the

height of the equipment, surfacing may need to extend farther than 6
feet. Rubber mats, synthetic turf and other artificial materials are also
safe surfaces and require less maintenance.

- Ensure that a comprehensive inspection of all playgrounds is conducted by qualified personnel. Abide by daily, monthly and annual
  playground maintenance schedules. Ensure that schools and child-
  care centers have age-appropriate, well-maintained playground
  equipment and that trained supervisors are present at all times when
  children are on the playground. Report any playground safety hazards
  to the organization responsible for the site (e.g., school, park authority, city council).
- Always supervise children when using playground equipment. Maintain visual and auditory contact. Prevent unsafe behaviors like pushing,
  shoving, crowding and inappropriate use of equipment. Ensure that
  children use age-appropriate playground equipment.
- Maintain separate play areas for children under age 5.
- Remove hood and neck drawstrings from all children's outerwear. Never
  allow children to wear helmets, necklaces, purses, scarves or clothing
  with drawstrings while on playgrounds. (NSKC 2004, para. 6-10)

DO WHAT YOU CAN

Children are at risk of injury on playgrounds. Adequate adult supervision and age-appropriate playground equipment are critically important. As adult caregivers and playground supervisors, examining children's clothing for strangulation hazards can prevent children from
choking on playground equipment. In addition, because playgrounds
are spaces that are often undersupervised, bullying, harassment, and
fighting more often occur there (more on these topics will be discussed
in later chapters).

Ideally, adults will work together to keep public playgrounds in good
repair, and adults will supervise young children on these public playgrounds. On school playgrounds, adult supervision should be sufficient
given the number of children being supervised. Supervisors should be
trained to handle conflicts as they arise and work to resolve these conflicts
peacefully. Home playgrounds should be developmentally appropriate
with adults close by to help children navigate equipment.

Highlighted Recommendations

- Supervisors need to be closely monitoring children's interactions with one another as well as the ways they use playground equipment.
- Adult supervisors need to be trained in conflict resolution and mediation and trained to intervene.
- Supervisors must have adequate adult backup.
- Schools should encourage teacher and administrator participation on playgrounds.
- As most playground fatalities (56 percent) are a result of strangulation, entanglement, or entrapment, parents and adult supervisors should be on the lookout for this and pay close attention to drawstrings on children's clothing. Do not allow children to wear scarves or necklaces or to have drawstrings exposed.
- Playgrounds (both at home and schools) can be made safer by adding softer surfaces on the ground.
- Playground equipment should have regularly scheduled routine maintenance.

EVALUATE YOUR SUCCESS

Playground audits. Perhaps the best way to evaluate success is to do a playground assessment or audit to determine whether or not equipment is safe and in good repair. The audit should also include an examination of the supervision; that is, are adult supervisors trained, engaged, and vigilant? Are students made aware of the rules and possible dangers? Are there signs posted warning of the dangers for children? Are adults intervening in meaningful ways when conflict or bullying arises? Playground audits should be completed by an adult observer during the peak playground usage times to determine the answers to the aforementioned questions on a routine basis.

Student surveys. Designing an anonymous survey that asks children to rate how safe they feel on the playground is another strategy to determine if children are being bullied or harassed or injured by their peers on the playground. Surveys can use simple language and be read to preliterate groups; for example, have students agree ☺ or disagree ☹ with the statement "I feel safe on the playground." Students may not always report injuries or fears to adults.

We need to ask children direct questions—never assume that no news is good news. For example, only when I asked my third-grade daughter about the playground did she tell me that she had some kind of minor injury nearly every day. On the day I asked her, she showed me a bruise where she was kicked as someone crashed into her on the slide, and a bump on her head where she and someone else bumped heads on another piece. She would not have even mentioned these "minor" infractions to me, as they are seen as a matter of course on the playground. We need to prevent these kinds of minor infractions to avoid even more dangerous ones. However, we also need to balance children's need for fun and free, unstructured play with safety.

FIND OUT MORE

Centers for Disease Control and Prevention (CDC). 2007. Playground injuries: Fact sheet. CDC. www.cdc.gov/ncipc/factsheets/playgr.htm (accessed August 30, 2008).

National Safe Kids Campaign (NSKC). 2004. Playground injury fact sheet. NSKC. www.preventinjury.org/pdfs/playground_injury.pdf (accessed November 18, 2007).

Tinsworth, D., and J. McDonald. 2001. Special study: Injuries and deaths associated with children's playground equipment. Washington, DC: U.S. Consumer Product Safety Commission.

Chapter Two

Classroom Spaces

Abusive Teachers, Fires, and Bomb Threats

> I know a few people that have gotten in physical fights in the school. There was hair pulling, hitting, etc. These usually occurred during lunch or break where there was less supervision.
>
> —Twenty-year-old college student

Although classrooms are perhaps the safest spaces within a school building and schools are among the safest places for children, there are still ways that teachers, parents, and other school personnel can contribute to creating safer classroom and other school spaces for all children. Bullying, fighting, and harassment still happen in classrooms, and children still feel victimized in these spaces. Teachers need to be aware of teasing, taunting, and other hurtful behavior and to encourage children to tell an adult if someone is making them feel sad or uncomfortable. Teachers need to have a plan of action for responding to such behavior. Sometimes, sadly, children fall victim to bullying and abusive behavior at the hands of teachers and administrators. For example, one young woman wrote of a negative experience she had with teacher behavior toward students:

> A negative experience I had in school was when my teacher would put frown faces to any answer I got wrong on papers in second grade. I still remember how embarrassed I felt when I would see my paper sitting on my desk face up with frowns, I would flip it over as quickly as I could.

Adults can hurt, but they can also help. One way that adults can make a difference in improving the quality of life children have in schools is to intervene early and often. Consider this example of an elementary school teacher:

> I was on supervision in the elementary cafeteria when a child dropped his tray of food with a loud bang on the floor. Several of the 2nd and 3rd grade students laughed and clapped when this happened. I blew my whistle and the room went silent. I explained that clapping when someone dropped a tray was disrespectful and that at our school we show respect for ourselves and for each other. I told the crowd that we don't clap and cheer when a friend drops a tray and that I never wanted to see that happen again. The room remained quiet for another minute and I know each one of them was thinking about how they would react next time.

Adults need to pay attention to problem behavior, explain to children why it is problematic, and give them a chance to think about how to react better next time. If we fail to respond, then we send the message that the behavior is acceptable. It's the same with adult behavior—if we allow problematic adult behavior toward children to continue, we create a tacit agreement that the behavior is okay.

ASK: WHAT IS POTENTIALLY DANGEROUS OR PROBLEMATIC FOR CHILDREN? WHAT CAN I DO (OR WHAT CAN BE DONE) TO MAKE THIS CHILD (OR THESE CHILDREN) SAFER OR HEALTHIER OR MORE SUCCESSFUL IN THIS/THESE SITUATION/S (OR SIMILAR ONES)?

Protection from adults. Sometimes teachers can be downright hurtful to students, such as in the first example. They can intimidate, harass, bully, and abuse. Students should feel comfortable reporting such behavior to other adults at home or at school and feel that their concerns are heard and taken seriously. Consider the following example:

> I have had a few teachers that get so angry that they lose control and start yelling. Seeing that teacher lose control can be scary. (College junior)

Students need to feel safe reporting this kind of problematic behavior to administrators of other teachers—or also to parents. In addition to bullying behavior or an inability to manage anger, students experience sexual harassment and victimization—not only at the hands of their peers but also, unfortunately, at the hands of adults assigned to protect them. Quite recently, there has been a spate of reports about teachers sexually victimizing their students. Student reports of teacher misconduct must be acted upon immediately and treated as very serious. An Associated Press survey found that over five years, across all kinds of schools and districts, twenty-five hundred incidents of sexual misconduct were formally punished. However, most experts agree that the number of incidents reported represents a mere fraction of the actual sexual-abuse cases in which students are the victims of their teachers. As written in the Associated Press report,

> Most of the abuse never gets reported. Those cases reported often end with no action. Cases investigated sometimes can't be proven, and many abusers have several victims. And no one—not the schools, not the courts, not the state or federal governments—has found a surefire way to keep molesting teachers out of classrooms. (Associated Press 2007, para. 3)

The following headlines were published in October 2007:

- 125 Wash. Teachers Punished for Sexual Misconduct over 5 Year
  By Donna Gordon Blankinship, The Associated Press, *The Seattle Post-Intelligencer*, October 20, 2007
- Sexual Misconduct Plagues U.S. Schools AP Finds 2,500 Teachers Punished in 5 Years
  By Martha Irvine and Robert Tanner, The Associated Press, *Seattle Post-Intelligencer*, October 20, 2007
  Associated Press, "Teacher Sexual Abuse on Rise," auburnpub.com, October 20, 2007
- Juliet Williams and Martha Irvine, Associated Press, "Sex Offenses by Teachers Stay Secret in Many Cases," *LA Daily News*, October 20, 2007
- Admitting Abuse but Free to Teach Oregon Education—Criminal Convictions for Admitted Sexual Misconduct Are Hit and Miss
  By Amy Hsuan, Melissa Navas, and Bill Graves, *The Oregonian*, October 21, 2007
- Patchwork Laws Fail to Stop Teacher Sexual Misconduct, Asbury Park Press on 10/28/07
  By Robert Tanner, The Associated Press

The AP found attempts to stop particular offenders, it also found a firm resistance towards identifying and preventing abuse. Fellow teachers often ignore the abuse or believe they cannot help. School administrators cut backdoor deals to sidestep lawsuits or bad press. In state governments and Congress, lawmakers are loath to impose harsher punishments or any national policy in fear of harming the teaching profession.

This astounding convoluted thinking leaves children to fend for themselves against cunning sex offenders.

New York State Education Department reports, the number of "moral misconduct" accusations against educators in New York has doubled in five years. In 2005, 134 cases of "moral misconduct" were reported involving teachers and other school employees, as compared to just 70 cases in 2001. According to an overview of the cases, almost 75 percent of the "moral conduct" cases involved sexual acts or an improper relationship. In all, 485 misconduct cases occurred over the five-year period in New York State. (Neddermeyer 2007, para. 3-7)

As adults caring for children, we must respond to any reports children make about adults abusing their power. Children also need to know that something is being done and that someone is advocating on their behalf, or they will be less likely to report in the future.

Fingerprinting and encouraging student reporting. The recent efforts to require all adults working in a school to submit fingerprint reports may help reduce instances of teachers victimizing students. The criminal background checks can only do so much. Many are concerned that because many cases are never resolved, teacher-predators are just shuffled from school to school, from district to district. Many of the curricular programs that encourage children to tell on adults who make them feel uncomfortable do not specifically address adults within the school.

Teachers and other adults in a school are in a position of authority over children, who are very reluctant to report problematic behavior (or don't feel that they are allowed to say anything bad about a teacher, staff, or administrator). We don't want to make children afraid either, so it is a challenging balance to let children know that they should report any adult behavior that makes them feel strange, without having them be fearful. Adults must take all accounts seriously.

All too often, "favorite teachers" are the ones who end up being found guilty of child molestation, so we need to take all cases very seriously.

Parents, teachers, and other school staff need to remain vigilant about potential predators and make sure that predators are prosecuted and lose their teaching certification (and get a criminal record that prevents them from being hired in a school) permanently.

Classroom violence. Some children suffer from anxiety from school phobia because of fear of being victimized in the classroom. See other chapters for more information on bullying, harassment, and anxiety for warning signs. Violence does happen in classrooms. For example, consider this story of a college junior:

> A fight broke out during tech education in middle school and one of the boys was pushed through the glass door. The glass shattered and the boy received cuts and was rushed to the hospital to get stitches.

Although this is an extreme case, teachers need to pay attention to conflicts as they arise in the classroom and have conflict-resolution strategies so they can respond appropriately.

Fires and bomb threats in school. Most schools are often best prepared to respond to fires. They are legally required to conduct fire drills. In an earlier study in a large urban district, I (KW) found that teachers and administrators alike rated responses to fire drills as the safety procedure that their schools consistently did best. This is partly because schools are required to practice responses to fires. We need to have students practice other evacuation procedures as well. Arson does happen on school property, as in this example:

> Someone started a fire in the school. (College junior)

The statistics on fires in schools shows that fires in schools are rare. The U.S. Fire Administration reported the following:

- Fatalities from school fires are rare.
- The three leading causes for school structure fires are incendiary or suspicious (32%), cooking (29%), and heating (9%).
- The leading area of fire origin for school structure fires is the lavatory.
- Kindergarten through high school fires increase at the beginning and end of the academic year (2007, 1).

Schools should have well-known evacuation plans that are practiced regularly. Also, school personnel should be sensitive to children's fears of fires. When my daughter (KW) was in kindergarten, she had nightmares following her first fire drill at school and asked, "Is the school going to catch on fire?" She was very frightened by the noise and movement and the fire trucks and sirens. Early elementary-aged children should have fire safety explained carefully to them. More on fire safety at home will be discussed in a later chapter.

Bomb threats should always be taken seriously. There are schools that experience a spate of bomb threats (especially when the weather gets nice), and students (and sometimes adults) seem to take these threats less seriously over time, as in this example of a college sophomore reflecting on her experiences:

> After the Columbine tragedy, my school was receiving bomb threats quite often for a while. They were pretty frightening at first, but then it happened so often that it became less scary.

Federal Bureau of Investigation (FBI) statistics estimated that roughly "5 percent of bombing incidents in the United States in 1999 (the most recent year for which FBI data are available) were targeted at schools. It is unknown what proportion of these incidents involved threats. For the period of 1990 to February 2002 the U.S. Bureau of Alcohol, Tobacco, Firearms and Explosives (ATF) recorded 1,055 incidents of bombs being placed on school premises. . . . For the most part, however it is probably reasonable to conclude that bomb incidents involving real bombs in school are relatively rare, though they have been with us for quite some time" (Newman 2005, 3).

A report by the Center for Problem-Oriented Policing describes that the more specific a bomb threat, the more credible. Newman (2005) suggests that the more clear the time and place of the bombing, the description of the bomb type to be used, the specific targets, and the reason for bombing, the more seriously the threat should be taken and investigated (although all threats should be taken seriously). Newman provides statistics from the Secret Service suggesting that 75 percent of bomb attacks are planned, they often occur when the attacker has told peers that something bad would happen, and attackers often devote a lot of attention (sometimes somewhat obsessively) to planning.

The U.S. Department of Justice offers a series for community-oriented police officers (COPS) and individuals interested in the COPS program at their website at www.cops.usdoj.gov.

In addition, the Federal Bureau of Investigation has designed a program for schools called Threat Assessment that involves examining the nature of a potential threat—including bombs, terrorist attacks, shootings (which will be discussed in a later chapter), and other violent concerns. More on this program is available at the FBI website at www.fbi.gov/pressrel/pressrel02/dojoig100102.htm.

BRING TOGETHER ALL ADVOCATES WHO CAN ASSIST IN MAKING CHILDREN SAFER IN THESE SITUATIONS

The following groups of people are important to involve in making schools safer:

- school board members to be sure that guidelines for criminal reporting and fingerprinting are being carefully followed
- all school personnel and school staff to be vigilant to report any danger of adults mistreating children in school and plans for responding to dangers
- parents and parent organizations (e.g., PTA or PTO)
- students, who need to be educated about acceptable adult behavior (e.g., schools could consider creating an adult and student code of conduct, or rights and responsibilities, or student/faculty contracts where the codes of behavior are clearly spelled out for both groups)

CONSIDER THE OPTIONS (PARTICULARLY ONES WITH DEMONSTRATED SUCCESS)

Giving children a voice in the development of school and classroom rules is a helpful way to get children invested in and caring about their classroom community. Providing clearly stated sanctions for misbehavior is also useful. There are many useful strategies for creating positive discipline strategies for children—both in the classroom and hopefully, for consistency's sake, in the home. There are programs that teach children their rights and responsibilities using the U.S. Constitution as a guide, such as Forrest Gathercoal's *Judicious Discipline*. There are other programs that use more of a behaviorist model, using positive reinforcement to encourage good behavior and negative reinforcement or punishment to prevent problematic behavior (e.g., classic behavior-modification programs). There are also programs where the punishment is perceived to be appropriate for the infraction (i.e., one draws on the desk, one must stay in at recess to clean up the mess). Needless to say, teachers, parents, and any adult working with a child need to be consistent in meting out discipline with children and have some identified strategy for dealing with behavior in the classroom and out.

Educators for Social Responsibility offer their "Five Steps to Guided Discipline and Student Support Program," which includes the following:

Know yourself, your students, and your school: This step focuses on your teaching stance, personal authority, boundaries, and responses to conflict; increasing awareness of developmental needs of diverse learners; and exploring the behavioral norms of your school culture and community.

Prevention and practice: Effective discipline is all about modeling, teaching, practicing, and assessing what you expect of students. How do you manage, organize, and structure your teaching time and the learning environment? How do you teach and practice routines and procedures that tell students, "This is how we do class here—this is how we treat each other—this is how we learn?" How do you prevent unwanted behaviors by teaching, practicing, and assessing the behaviors you want?

Invitations to cooperate, problem solve, and self-correct: When students are engaging in unwanted behaviors, effective discipline invites them to self-correct, refocus, and get back on track. How do you prevent confrontations and diffuse potential power struggles? How do you help students develop better problem solving and communication skills? This step emphasizes effective "teacher talk" and "student talk."

Interventions and consequences: Sometimes prevention and invitations are not enough. When unwanted behaviors and habits persist, what do you do? This step offers a graduated set of concrete interventions and consequences that support positive changes in students' behavior.

Support and maintenance of individual students and the group: Teachers need to balance the needs of individual students and the needs of the group. What do you do to provide the kinds of differentiated support that will help all of your students increase their internal motivation and develop greater personal efficacy? What do you do to maintain positive group cooperation and participation throughout the year? (Educators for Social Responsibility 2008, para. 4-8)

Discipline must be transparent to all parties in a school and at home with clear and consistent consequences for problematic behavior and encouragement for positive behavior.

Know the laws—teacher and administrator legal liability: According to the Supreme Court case of *Sheehan v. St. Peters Catholic Church* (1971), teachers can be found negligent if they fail to do what a "reasonable person" in the same situation would have done when a student is injured. So, for example, if a student is injured in the classroom when the teacher has left the class unsupervised to talk to a friend, he or she might be held liable.

Teachers are also required to report suspected cases of child abuse or neglect according to the Child Abuse Prevention and Treatment Act of 1974. However, according to *McDonald v. State of Oregon* (1985), teachers cannot be sued when they make a "good faith" effort to report suspected abuse or neglect.

If teachers inappropriately place children in special education classes, they can be found guilty of "malpractice" according to the U.S. Supreme Court case *B. M. Berger v. State of Montana* (1982). Teachers and parents alike need to be careful when making decisions about student placement in special programs or risk being sued for malpractice.

Conflict-resolution training should engage all adults and children in a school, and each school should have a plan for resolving conflicts before they escalate. Teachers and other adults in the school should be well trained to examine warning signs and assess potential threats using programs with demonstrated success, such as the FBI's Threat Assessment program.

DO WHAT YOU CAN

As an adult concerned with the well-being of children, you can do a number of things to protect children:

- Talk to children about their relationships with their teachers and other adults in the school.

- Create a home and school environment that is based on trust—where children feel that they can say anything and will be cared for and protected.
- As parents, observe your child's classes/teachers—keep communication lines with teachers open.
- Get to know other adults in the school and bus drivers, crossing guards, and so forth.
- As teachers, pay close attention to how other adults interact with children, and report anything suspicious.
- Encourage children to tell adults they trust any time another adult (including teachers or other adults in the school) makes them "feel funny."

Teachers, parents, and all other adult care providers should report any suspicious behavior of adults toward children as quickly as possible. All child reports should be taken seriously, and those who report should be protected from liability. As parents, involvement of pediatricians and child psychologists/psychiatrists when possible is important as well. As teachers, involving families of affected children is critical too.

EVALUATE YOUR SUCCESS

Evaluation of success is challenging, but surveys may be useful, that is, asking young people to report in anonymous and confidential surveys how safe they feel and how protected they feel. Asking children to specifically rate or describe their relationships with their teachers and other adults in the school can be useful as well.

FIND OUT MORE

Associated Press. 2007. Sexual misconduct plagues U.S. schools. MSNBC.com. October 20. www.msnbc.msn.com/id/21392345.

Educators for Social Responsibility (ESR). 2008. Middle school: Five steps to guided discipline and student support. ESR. www.esrnational.org/index.php?location=pages&l=mid&link=1000010.

Mack, M. G., J. J. Sacks, and D. Thompson. 2000. Testing the impact attenuation of loose fill playground surfaces. *Injury Prevention* 6: 141–44.

Neddermeyer, Dorothy M. 2007. Teacher sexual abuse of students increasing. SearchWarp.com. November 5. http://searchwarp.com/swa268212.htm.

Newman, G. 2005. Bomb threats in schools. *Problem-Oriented Guides for Police.* Problem-Specific Guides Series 32 (February), www.cops.usdoj.gov/files/ric/ Publications/e07063413.pdf (accessed March 7, 2008).

Phelan, K. J., J. Khoury, H. J. Kalkwarf, and B. P. Lanphear. 2001. Trends and patterns of playground injuries in United States children and adolescents. *Ambulatory Pediatrics*, 1(4): 227–33.

Suecoff, S. A., J. R. Avner, K. J. Chou, and E. F. Crain. 1999. A comparison of New York City playground hazards in high- and low-income areas. *Archives of Pediatrics & Adolescent Medicine*, 153, 363–66.

U.S. Fire Administration. 2007. School fires. *Topical Fire Research Series* 8, no. 1 (August), www.usfa.dhs.gov/downloads/pdf/tfrs/v8i1.pdf (accessed March 7, 2008).

Williams, Kimberly. 2003. *The PEACE approach to violence prevention: A handbook for teachers and administrators.* Lanham, MD: Scarecrow Education Press.

Chapter Three

Getting to and from School

Safety on Buses and When Walking

When I was in kindergarten, my bus drove off the snowy, icy road and into a large ditch—turning almost upside down. I remember that I was alone except for the driver and one other boy, who was my classmate. It was the first time we had to go out the emergency back door. I remember being scared, but unhurt.

—KW

I was in a bus accident in Virginia when on our school trip to Washington, D.C. Two of the buses collided with each other on the highway. This was very scary for everyone involved. This was the first time many of us had been away from home or been in an accident. The teachers and firefighters all handled the situation very well. The only problem was that the school called all the parents and told them their child was in an accident [and] there were injuries, but they didn't know who was injured.

—College junior

Every school-aged child must get to and from school every school day. Millions of schoolchildren ride school buses long distances to and from school. And millions of school-aged children walk, sometimes through dangerous places, to get to and from school. School personnel and parents/caregivers must work together to make sure that the journey to and from school is as safe as possible for our children.

> ASK: WHAT IS POTENTIALLY DANGEROUS OR
> PROBLEMATIC FOR CHILDREN? WHAT CAN I
> DO (OR WHAT CAN BE DONE) TO MAKE THIS
> CHILD (OR THESE CHILDREN) SAFER OR
> HEALTHIER OR MORE SUCCESSFUL IN
> THIS/THESE SITUATION/S (OR SIMILAR ONES)?

School buses are perhaps the safest form of transportation for children riding on them. However, buses still have some hidden risks associated with them. For example, injuries to children riding as passengers of other vehicles hit by buses happen with greatest frequency, followed by injuries to children hit by school buses while walking or riding bikes, and then by injuries to children riding as passengers on school buses. Children also are at risk of being bullied, harassed, or hurt in fights on buses because buses typically lack appropriate and adequate adult supervision. Also, children who walk to school are at risk of abduction or being hit by other vehicles. More information about each of these is elaborated below.

Statistics on Buses, Bus Safety, Bus Accidents, and Issues on Buses

School buses are the biggest type of mass transit in the United States, providing almost nine million student trips every year. In comparison, this is twice as many passenger trips than are provided by transit buses across the nation. Almost half a million school buses transport 24 million students to and from school, or school related activities, each school day. Since 1990, 407,000 fatal traffic accidents have occurred in the United States. School bus related accidents account for one third of one percent of these deaths. (www.onlinelawyersource.com/personal_injury/bus/statistics.html, accessed November 18, 2007)

We see from the above evidence that school buses are the most widely used type of mass transportation in this country, yet are involved in a very small fraction of fatal traffic accidents. They are among the safest modes of transportation in the United States. However, there are still some hidden dangers associated with transporting children to and from school. There are three ways children can be hurt that involve school buses:

1. riding as a passenger in a different vehicle hit by a school bus (67 percent)
2. walking or riding a bike (25 percent, more than half of whom are children between the ages of five and seven)
3. riding as a passenger on the bus (9 percent) (www.onlinelawyersource .com/personal_injury/bus/statistics.html, accessed November 18, 2007)

From a physical harm standpoint, buses are among the safest places for children (for example, not a single child was killed in a school bus crash in 2003). Those walking or riding bikes or riding in other vehicles are in more danger. Other concerns face children on the school bus, as illustrated in the example below:

> I remember vividly, being in sixth grade and being terrified of riding the school bus. I had never had an issue with it in elementary school, and I'm not sure if it was the change in schools or things that were going on in my personal life, but I developed an overwhelming fear of riding the bus. I used to call my mom from the payphone at school every day to make sure she would pick me up at school, and on the days she couldn't and I had to take the bus I would stress all day long. My family never knew why it bothered me so much, but there were older 8th grade boys who sat at the back of the bus who used to talk about things they wanted to do sexually to girls on the bus and at school so I was terrified to get off the bus with them and walk the 1/2 mile to my house. (Twenty-year-old female college student)

The same kinds of bullying, fighting, and harassment that happen in other school spaces also happen on buses and during walks to and from school. Because school buses are typically undersupervised (the only adult is concentrating on driving the bus), these spaces are fertile ground for cruel behavior. Like the above college student, I (KW) too remember daily sexual harassment—unwanted comments about my breasts and clothing or other sexually inappropriate comments—on the bus. These topics will be addressed in later chapters, but on the bus, adequate adult supervision needs to be available to protect children from these kinds of harassment, taunting, and violence.

BRING TOGETHER ALL ADVOCATES WHO CAN ASSIST IN MAKING CHILDREN SAFER IN THESE SITUATIONS

Who are all the possible advocates concerned with the transportation safety of children getting to and from school? In rallying support to improve bus and walker safety, one could consider appealing to the following groups:

- school transportation director/supervisor
- bus drivers
- local police department
- school district administration
- parent-teacher organizations
- department of transportation
- local school board
- local chapter of the American Federation of Teachers (AFT)

School board meetings and parent-teacher organizations should discuss bus and walker safety every year and collect information from students to see how safe they feel. Careful screening of bus drivers is also critical. Bus drivers should be included in plans and discussions about safety.

CONSIDER THE OPTIONS (PARTICULARLY ONES WITH DEMONSTRATED SUCCESS)

The American Federation of Teachers, for example, offered the following examples of strategies that have improved safety on buses:

How the AFT and our affiliates are working to improve bus safety

- School bus drivers in Hillsborough County, Fla., and in Oklahoma City are practicing what they learned during a weeklong course on managing student behavior. Developed by the AFT, the intensive course was offered through the union's Educational Research & Dissemination (ER&D) program.
- AFT affiliates in Florida and Washington have responded to growing concerns about assaults against bus drivers by gang members, students

and others. These local unions have lobbied to help pass laws that treat physical attacks on school bus drivers just as seriously as attacks on other school personnel.

• The AFT local in St. Tammany Parish, La., has ensured that school bus drivers have the same authority as other district employees to enforce the code of student conduct. Drivers can attempt to resolve relatively minor incidents themselves—first by talking with the student and then, if necessary, by contacting parents. If neither approach works, school officials are brought in to handle the matter.

• In Alachua County, Fla., St. Tammany Parish, La., and other districts, AFT locals have worked successfully to get bus drivers appointed to districtwide committees on student discipline.

• Bus drivers in Cazenovia and Wappingers Falls, N.Y., are required to attend in-service training each year. Drivers in Oswego County, N.Y., are eligible for a safe driving incentive every year.

What can parents and the community do?

• Support the passage of state laws that impose strict penalties for motorists who illegally pass school buses that are loading or unloading or who otherwise endanger students through unsafe driving. Communities also should support passage of laws that require passengers on school buses to be seated at all times.

• Find out whether your school system has a discipline code—and, if it does, whether it covers student behavior on buses. This code should identify unacceptable behavior and the specific consequences for that behavior. If there is no discipline code or if the code doesn't address bus behavior, raise the issue at a school board meeting.

• Ensure that your children understand basic safety rules and proper procedures. For example, children should know not to attempt to pick up books or other objects that are dropped near or under a school bus.

What can school boards and administrators do?

• Prepare and distribute a standard form—which students and their parents must sign at the start of the school year—that clearly outlines the rules and expectations for behavior on school buses. These rules and procedures should be included within your district's student discipline code.

• Hire bus monitors whose specific responsibility is to maintain order on board. School systems should make sure these monitors receive proper training and that they have the full support of administrators.

- Consider equipping more school buses with cameras to record the activities of students on board. This can help determine what really happened in the case of a serious incident on a bus.
- Repair or replace handrails that are prone to snag children's clothing, book bags and other belongings. In recent years, several students have been killed and others injured after their clothes or personal items became caught on the door or handrails as they were getting off of the bus.
- Ensure that drivers have the necessary equipment on board (cell phones or two-way radios) to communicate with a central facility in the event of an emergency.
- Provide drivers with training on discipline and good safety practices and incorporate bus safety training into school curricula.
- Participate in National School Bus Safety Week activities every October. (www.aft.org/psrp/pubs-reports/protectingpreciousresource.htm)

Use of seat belts. Recently (November 2007), Mary Peters, secretary of the U.S. Department of Transportation, announced new school bus safety measures, including the wearing of seat belts by children. However, the school bus seat belt controversy is unresolved to date. Some have provided evidence that seat belt wearing on buses does not improve safety, and some have provided counterevidence. In addition to the issue of providing seat belts on buses is that of enforcing children's wearing them.

> There was not one particular experience I could distinguish as negative; riding the school bus was overall a negative experience. In middle school we would be crammed three students to a seat, and guess what? Three middle schoolers do not fit in one bus seat. I always worried that if the bus was ever in an accident, I would get hurt because I was either already being squished into a seat, or I was barely sitting on one and I could go flying. (Twenty-one-year-old female college student)

The need for adult supervision. In addition to the rare, but tragic, deaths and injuries reported on buses, we must attend to the daily forms of violence children experience in these undersupervised spaces. First, bullying, fights, and harassment (to be discussed in a later chapter) are experienced on buses. All too often, the school bus driver is the only adult on a bus, leaving children riding on sometimes overcrowded buses unsupervised. The driver, responsible for driving and keeping children on and off the buses safe, cannot possibly be expected to be a disciplinarian in these settings.

I think that one of the things that I have noticed the most [about riding the bus] is teasing. There is no adult supervision and the bus driver is concentrated on driving more than the students. This leaves the perfect opportunity for kids to tease each other ruthlessly. (Twenty-year-old female college student)

Buses need to have caring, respected adults on board to help mediate problems that arise. However, when resources are limited, hiring an additional adult can be difficult to impossible. Some schools have enlisted adult volunteers. However, educating these adult supervisors is essential as adults need to pay attention to the subtle teasing that happens on buses too, as in this case:

One day when I was in elementary school I had kids picking on me because I was the youngest girl on the bus. Everyday they would call and hang up on me and tease me about what I was wearing. It got to the point where I didn't take the bus anymore, and I never took the bus. (Twenty-year-old female college student)

The best measure of success is the percentage of bus riders who actually take the bus. Conduct interviews or surveys with those students who do not take the bus. With today's rising gas prices, encouraging as many students as possible to make sure buses are full is economically and environmentally helpful.

DO WHAT YOU CAN

Consider the following recommendations:

- Place adult supervisors on buses (teacher or parent volunteers). Make sure that any volunteers have had criminal background checks.
- Train adult supervisors in conflict-resolution and mediation skills.
- Train children how to deal with conflicts.
- Encourage children to report bad behavior to adults.
- Have clearly defined sanctions for misbehavior on the bus. Discuss these (or even develop these) with children.
- For younger children, push for a bus-buddies or mentoring program, where responsible older children facilitate the bus-riding experience for

younger riders. Make sure these programs are carefully monitored by responsible adults.

- Have clearly posted, positively stated messages concerning what behavior is acceptable on the bus and what good bus behavior looks like specifically (e.g., sit in your seat with your seat belt fastened).
- Encourage adults to be present at bus stops to keep children safe as they walk home.
- Work with the police department to make sure that drivers are ticketed and fined if they fail to stop at flashing school bus lights or pass buses illegally (and make sure there are sufficient numbers of police officers around during the peak bus travel times to enforce driving laws).

Children who walk to school—the "Walking School Bus": Walking is a great activity for today's children, who get far too little physical exercise. Walking to school can be a great way to get much needed physical activity. However, children who walk to school face dangers. Children need to be protected from child predators, injury from cars or buses (as pedestrians), and bullying and harassment. One model that has been proposed to keep these children safe is the Walking School Bus program, where children are "picked up," just like on a school bus route, but led to school by an adult, who is paid or volunteers, to help keep children safe. In more dangerous neighborhoods, "safe harbor" homes have signs telling children where they can go. The adults in these homes should have criminal background checks just like any adult volunteer working with children in a school. The National Center for Missing and Exploited Children recommends the following precautions for children traveling to and from school:

1. Instruct your child to always take a friend when walking or riding his or her bike to and from school.
2. Even though there is safety in numbers, it is not safe for children to walk to and from school, especially if they must take isolated routes before or during daylight. Always provide supervision for young children to help ensure their safe arrival to and from school.
3. Your child should stay with a group while waiting at the bus stop. If anyone bothers your child while going to or from school, you should teach him or her to get away from that person and tell you or another trusted adult.

4. Visit the bus stop with your children and learn the bus number. This will avoid confusion for your children about knowing what bus to ride.
5. Instruct your children, if anyone they don't know or a person who confuses, scares, or makes them feel uncomfortable offers a ride, say NO. Children should never hitchhike. Also, children should never accept a ride from anyone unless you have told them it is okay to do so in each instance. (www.missingkids.com/missingkids/servlet/ResourcServlet?Language Country=en_US&PageId=893)

EVALUATE YOUR SUCCESS

Evaluating the success of a prevention program is a challenge, but even if informally, discuss with other parents, school board members, teachers, and so on, their sense of bus safety and awareness. Surveys are helpful too.

The best sign of success is children being unafraid to ride the bus. In the case with my own daughter (KW), I worked with the teachers, administration, and the bus driver to remedy the teasing and cruel behavior my then kindergartener experienced on the bus (teasing, not letting her sit down, not letting her get off the bus at her stop). We established "bus buddies," where the younger children were paired with slightly older children, who would help them negotiate the bus safely. When my daughter was older, she became a "bus buddy" herself and helped others.

This kind of informal program worked wonders for my child and cost no money. These kinds of creative options are needed at schools with limited funding. How did I know it was successful? My daughter no longer refused to ride the bus and stopped coming home crying. Sometimes informal evaluation is just that simple. However, we cannot assume that silence is a sign that all is well. Anonymous surveys can be very useful. For preliterate children, consider designing surveys with ☺ and ☹ and having the teacher read questions or having children respond to statements like "I am afraid to ride the bus."

Sometimes parents and children assume that cruel bus behavior is just a part of life. We need to send the message that bullying, taunting, and harassment are not acceptable anywhere—including on school buses. We need to make buses and walking to and from school as safe and anxiety free for children as possible. Adults in a community can work together to improve bus and walker safety.

FIND OUT MORE

American Federation of Teachers. Protecting our most precious resource: What we
should do to improve school bus safety. www.aft.org/psrp/pubs-reports/protecting
preciousresource.htm.
National Center for Missing and Exploited Children, www.missingkids.com.
School Bus Information Council, www.schoolbusinfo.org/index.html.
School Transportation News, www.stnonline.com/stn.
Walking School Bus Program, www.walkingschoolbus.org.

Chapter Four

Athletics

Injury, Hazing, and Bullying on Sports Teams

Rates of concussions and anterior cruciate ligament (ACL) injuries increased significantly during the [past] 16-year period—though the higher rates likely are due in part to improved identification of and reporting of the injuries. Still, head injuries are becoming more common in "noncontact" sports like basketball, and concussion rates overall have increased an average of 7 percent per year.

> —National Collegiate Athletic Association,
> downloaded March 13, 2008, from www.ncaa.org

An estimated 300,000 sports- and recreation-related head injuries of mild to moderate severity occur in the United States each year. Most can be classified as concussions.

> —Centers for Disease Control at www.cdc.gov

There was an inverse relationship between the number of [soccer] ball impacts [to the head] and verbal learning.

> —David Janda, Cynthia Bir, and Angela Cheney, "An
> Evaluation of the Cumulative Concussive Effect
> of Soccer Heading in the Youth Population,"
> *International Journal of Injury Control and
> Safety Promotion* 9, no. 1 (March 2002): abstract

Millions of schoolchildren participate in organized athletics. There are risks associated with participation, and some are more obvious than others. There are some hidden risks of which every parent and educator should be aware. This chapter discusses some of the common and grow-ing-in-popularity injuries associated with athletics that interfere with learning: concussions and traumatic brain injury, as well as bullying and hazing on athletic teams, are discussed.

ASK: WHAT IS POTENTIALLY DANGEROUS OR PROBLEMATIC FOR CHILDREN? WHAT CAN I DO (OR WHAT CAN BE DONE) TO MAKE THIS CHILD (OR THESE CHILDREN) SAFER OR HEALTHIER OR MORE SUCCESSFUL IN THIS/THESE SITUATION/S (OR SIMILAR ONES)?

A concussion, or mild traumatic brain injury (MTBI), is an injury to the brain and as such should always be taken seriously. Recognition of con-cussions when they first happen is critical to the prevention of additional brain injury or death. Children can experience concussions in any sport— including noncontact sports—by experiencing a blow to the head. Concus-sions among young participants are most common in the following sports: soccer, football, lacrosse, field hockey, ice hockey, baseball, softball, bas-ketball, skiing, and horseback riding. However, those sports in which there is a greater likelihood for collisions—especially at high speeds—have higher risk. In addition, activities like heading a soccer ball at young ages, while the brain is developing, can be problematic for brain development.

> I actually just got a concussion a couple weeks ago. I was riding my snow-mobile and lost control going around a corner at about sixty mph. I landed on the back of my head and fortunately was wearing a helmet. I had a pounding headache and felt nauseous for about 24 hours, but I never went to the hospital. (College junior)

Many concussions, like the one in the above example, go unreported, or medical attention is not sought because sometimes the symptoms are somewhat mild, like headache and dizziness. Once one has had a head in-jury like a concussion, he or she is at higher risk for another one. There are a couple of important hidden or lesser-known dangers associated with head injuries like concussions. Perhaps the most serious is that if one suffers another concussion before fully recovering from the first (typically within a short period of time), this experience, called *second-impact syndrome*, can lead to brain swelling, possibly even permanent brain damage or death.

> A repeat concussion that occurs before the brain recovers from the first—usually within a short period of time (hours, days, or weeks)—reportedly can result in brain swelling, permanent brain damage, and even death. This condition is called second impact syndrome. (Institute of Medicine 2002 and CDC.gov)

> I had two concussions [*sic*] from snowboarding during high school, and had to wear a neck brace after the bus accident. I was also diagnosed with transverse myleitis [*sic*] during the beginning of my 8th grade year. At first they thought I had a brain tumor, and thought I would need to have a nasty operation. I was picked on at school by some of my friends when I came back from the hospital. They were trying to make light of the situation but it really just hurt my feelings. As a result of that I have lost a lot of feeling in my right arm, and can't tell temperature differences in some fingers, and get bad migraines. But I am very lucky that's the only result. (College sophomore)

Many adults have become somewhat cavalier about concussions, but we need to take them all seriously and be even more vigilant if a young person receives a second concussion shortly after the first. Some very helpful guides and fact sheets have been developed for coaches, parents, teachers, and all interested adults. For example, The CDC developed the following fact sheet for parents and coaches that included the following "signs and symptoms" of a concussion, indicating that any one or more of these symptoms may indicate a concussion and to seek medical attention immediately if you suspect a child might have one:

Signs observed if a child has a concussion:

- Appears dazed or stunned
- Is confused
- Forgetful
- Unsure of parts of game (score, opponent)
- Clumsy
- Slow in talking and movement
- Loss of consciousness

- Behavior/personality change
- Unable to recall events before or after injury

Athlete symptoms reported include:

- Headache
- Nausea
- Dizzy/balance problems
- Double or fuzzy vision
- Sluggish, foggy, groggy
- Sensitive to light
- Memory problems/confusion (CDC's tools for coaches www.cdc.gov, p. 4)

Medical attention should be sought immediately if you suspect a young person has a concussion. Even more important, the youngster should stop immediately whatever activity caused the head injury in the first place to avoid second-impact syndrome.

Hidden dangers: Heading the soccer ball. A recent research study, "An Evaluation of the Cumulative Concussive Effect of Soccer Heading in the Youth Population," by David Janda, Cynthia Bir, and Angela Cheney (*International Journal of Injury Control and Safety Promotion* 9, no. 1 [March 2002]), examined the impact of heading the soccer ball on learning. They looked at fifty-seven young soccer players (average age 11.5) and found that there was an "inverse relationship between the number of ball impacts and verbal learning" (2002, 25) with many (nearly half) of the participants complaining of headaches following heading.

> Concussions have occurred more than once in my lifetime. The soccer field was always the scene, and the goal post was usually the culprit. (College junior)

Young children, even adolescents (and adults for that matter), should be discouraged from heading soccer balls, particularly as young brains are still developing (up to age twenty-five). Damage can be done to the brain later in life too. Clearly, in addition to heading soccer balls, dangers include collisions with other players and/or goalposts.

> I received a concussion when I was snowboarding. I was going down the mountain and took a huge fall. I laid there for a second and started crying but got back up and snowboarded down the remainder of the mountain. I felt

okay for about a half hour with only suffering a head ache. After the half hour I was completely delirious. I was with my brother who took me to a store, and he described to me how I was walking into clothing racks and completely out there, all of which I do not even remember. (College sophomore)

Kids are often asked to shake it off or keep going after a brain injury, often because well-intentioned adults underestimate the possible risk to a child's brain. We, as adults, must intervene to keep kids safe—and we need to be especially protective of children's developing brains.

Traumatic Brain Injury in Athletics

From a parent's and educator's perspective, we should be very concerned about any blow to the head as the long-term impact on a child's learning may not be immediately apparent but may manifest itself in ways we might not realize until adulthood, if ever. We must attend to these blows and do whatever possible to avoid them altogether.

Another significant problem resulting from a major blow to the head is traumatic brain injury (TBI). The Centers for Disease Control follow the prevalence of, and provide assistance and information about, TBI for caregivers. They define TBI as follows: "A traumatic brain injury (TBI) is caused by a blow or jolt to the head or a penetrating head injury that disrupts the normal function of the brain. Not all blows or jolts to the head result in a TBI. The severity of a TBI may range from 'mild,' i.e., a brief change in mental status or consciousness, to 'severe,' i.e., an extended period of unconsciousness or amnesia after the injury."

The CDC reports that of the 1.4 million people who experience a traumatic brain injury, 1.1 million are treated and released from emergency rooms, 235,000 are hospitalized, and 50,000 die. For children aged zero to fourteen, of the reported cases of TBI, the CDC reports the following statistics: 435,000 annual emergency room visits, 37,000 hospitalizations, and 2,685 deaths. Of course, these are only the reported brain injuries. Many health professionals believe that the number of TBIs is much higher as many brain injuries go unreported. According to the CDC's surveillance system, the number one cause of TBI is falls (28 percent of reported cases). Car accidents comprise 20 percent, followed by being struck by or against something (19 percent) and assaults (11 percent).

Traumatic brain injury can be insidious—many young people may be affected but unaware. It may affect learning in subtle ways and is perhaps responsible for some types of learning disabilities and difficulties. It is estimated that as many as one in fifty Americans has a TBI to the point that it impacts learning and ability to engage in basic functioning (e.g., long-term and short-term memory and retention of new ideas). The CDC reports that

> TBI can cause a wide range of functional changes affecting thinking, sensation, language, and/or emotions. It can also cause epilepsy and increase the risk for conditions such as Alzheimer's disease, Parkinson's disease, and other brain disorders that become more prevalent with age. (www.cdc.gov/ncipc/tbi/TBI.htm, para. 12)

Bullying and Hazing on Sports Teams

> My school had a huge hazing issue w/ the football team. One individual decided to speak out to prevent it in the future. He explained how he was held down while the senior football players stuck a banana up his rear end. He was also flipped around and "tea-bagged." The acting out players were only suspended one day and only had to sit out one game. The school decided to keep it within the school system, so not a lot was heard of it after that. Besides the school couldn't ensure his safety anymore, so he was forced to drop out of the school system. (College junior)

While bullying is addressed elsewhere in this book, there is concern about bullying on athletic teams in middle and high school. Also problematic, particularly on athletic teams, is hazing. Hazing includes initiation rituals or rites of passage or activities that group members are expected to engage in that humiliate or harm them emotionally or physically. Hazing happens to people at every developmental level who want to join a particular organization or group—and sometimes it can be subtle or very overt.

Most people believe hazing is just a part of adolescence, but it can be very harmful to one's psychological and/or physical health. Hazing is not just associated with fraternities and sororities but with athletics and other social groups, even in middle school. A government website for girls' health (www.girlshealth.gov) lists the following as common types of hazing:

- depriving rookies/new members of sleep and placing restrictions on their personal hygiene
- yelling at, swearing at, and insulting new members/rookies
- forcing them to wear embarrassing or humiliating clothing in public
- forcing them to eat vile substances or smear such on their skin
- branding them
- subjecting them to physical beatings
- demanding that they engage in binge drinking and play drinking games
- forcing sexual simulation and assaulting them sexually

No degree of hazing should be tolerated. Adults should intervene even in what may appear on the surface to be relatively "benign" hazing, such as in the following example:

All of the sports teams at my high school involved some sort of hazing. It was just something you went through. I played soccer, and I think many of the traditions were lost, but I do remember hearing my freshman year that they were going to make us jump into a manmade lake right on our school property that wasn't even fit for fish, bugs or birds let alone humans. That of course never happened to us, but freshman were mandated to carry all the soccer balls out to the field each day and the heavy jugs of water. We all did it so we all reinforced it on the younger grades once we were upper classman. Many jokes were made at the freshman's expense and nobody felt bad for them when they complained because of course we all felt that it was just a rite of passage. (College sophomore)

We need to pay attention and respond to all forms and reports of hazing, including examples like these, where younger players are treated differently than veteran players and are teased and harassed. Hazing can be very dangerous physically and emotionally, and adults must address and stop it. Because hazing tends to happen outside of adult awareness, little is written or known about the specific extent of the problem (e.g., statistics). More research needs to be conducted to determine the extent of hazing on sports teams and gather more specifics about the experience.

BRING TOGETHER ALL ADVOCATES WHO CAN ASSIST IN MAKING CHILDREN SAFER IN THESE SITUATIONS

Some of the adults who should be most keenly aware of the dangers of concussions from athletic injuries and hazing on sports teams are the following:

- coaches/assistant coaches/athletic directors/athletic trainers
- pediatricians and school nurses and team doctors
- parents
- children/students/athletic participants
- teachers and school staff and administrators
- referees

These interested stakeholders should be trained to look for signs of head injuries as well as hazing in sports, and they should work together to prevent and stop these problems from happening. Awareness of the above issues related to hazing and head injuries is a start, but schools and parents need to explore athletic policies and handbooks and encourage workshops to improve understanding of these issues.

CONSIDER THE OPTIONS (PARTICULARLY ONES WITH DEMONSTRATED SUCCESS)

For head injuries:

Take seriously all blows to the head.

Do not let players play after a head injury (to prevent second-impact syndrome).

Parents, coaches, teachers, and all adults working with children need to be educated about the signs and symptoms of head injuries like concussions—and work to prevent them.

The CDC's fact sheet for coaches outlines the following steps that should be taken to prevent concussions (or all major head injuries), as well as steps to create an action plan if a young athlete is injured:

Preseason

- Ensure that players are medically evaluated and are in good condition to participate.

- Establish an action plan for handling concussions that occur. Be sure that other appropriate school officials know about your action plan and have been trained in its use.
- Explain your concerns and expectations about concussion and safe play to athletes and school officials.
- Ask if players have had one or more concussions during the previous season.
- Remind athletes to tell coaching staff if they suspect that a teammate has a concussion.
- Determine whether your school would consider conducting preseason baseline testing of brain function (neuropsychological assessment) in athletes.

During Season, Practice, and Games

- Monitor sports equipment for safety, fit, and maintenance.
- Enlist other teachers to monitor any decrease in grades that could indicate a concussion.
- Be sure appropriate staff are available for injury assessment and referrals for further medical care.
- Continue emphasizing with players, staff, and parents your concerns and expectations about concussion and safe play.
- Report concussions that occurred during the school year to appropriate school staff. This will help in monitoring injured athletes as they move to the next season's sports.

Postseason

- Work with appropriate staff to review injuries and illnesses that occurred during the season.
- Discuss any need for improvements in your action plan with appropriate health care professionals and school staff.
- Discuss with other staff any needs for better sideline preparations.

Create an Action Plan

To ensure that concussions are managed correctly, have an action plan in place before the season starts.

- Identify a health care professional to manage injuries during practice and competition.
- Fill out the pocket card enclosed in this kit and keep it with you on the field of play so that information about signs, symptoms, and emergency contacts is readily available.

- Be sure that other appropriate athletic and school staff and health care professionals know about the plan and have been trained in its use.

When a Concussion Occurs

If you suspect that a player has a concussion, implement your action plan by taking the following steps:

1. Remove the athlete from play. Learn how to recognize the signs and symptoms of concussion in your players. Athletes who experience signs or symptoms of concussion should not be allowed to return to play. When in doubt, keep the player out of play.
2. Ensure that the athlete is evaluated by an appropriate health care professional. Do not try to judge the severity of the injury yourself. Health care professionals have a number of different methods that they can use to assess the severity of concussion.
3. Inform the athlete's parents or guardians about the known or possible concussion and give them the fact sheet on concussion. Make sure they know that the athlete should be seen by a health care professional.
4. Allow the athlete to return to play only with permission from an appropriate health care professional. Prevent second impact syndrome by delaying the athlete's return to the activity until the player receives appropriate medical evaluation and approval for return to play. (www.cdc.gov/ncipc/tbi/CGToolKit/Coaches_Guide.htm, para. 13-18)

Other chapters in this book will discuss the importance of driver safety to prevent motor vehicle accidents and the importance of wearing helmets, but in general these recommendations are useful for avoiding serious brain injuries like TBI:

- *Seat belts:* Make sure you always wear a seat belt every time you drive or ride in a motor vehicle and insist that your passengers wear them too. And never operate a vehicle under the influence of alcohol or other drugs.
- *Car seats and booster seats for children:* Make sure your child's car seat is properly installed and make sure the proper seat is used for your child's weight and height. Car seats should be rear facing until your child reaches twenty pounds; use booster seats after forty pounds and until your child is at least 4 ft. 9 in. tall. Buckle your child into the car using a child safety seat, booster seat, or seat belt (according to the child's height, weight, and age). Many police stations will assist parents

in installing car seats for infants and children. Check with your local police station for help.

• *Appropriate, well-fitting helmets:* Make sure your child wears a helmet when playing any contact sport; riding a bike or any motorized device; skateboarding, rollerblading, or skating; playing baseball or softball; horseback riding; or skiing, sledding, or snowboarding.

• *Safety-proofing:* Safety-proof your home for children, which should include putting safety gates on stairs, installing window guards so children cannot fall out, keeping railings around porches and decks up to code, and using mulch or sand on playgrounds for softer landings.

Schools can work to develop awareness about these issues by working with the National Safe Kids Campaign website and the National Program for Playground Safety website. These sites have plans for teachers and have student handouts about playground, motor vehicle, and sports and recreation safety.

Importance of helmets and new concussion-reducing technology. New helmets are coming onto the market that are designed to reduce the risk of concussions and other head injuries. For example, *Sports Business Daily* reported about a "new helmet [that] helps protect players from concussions." Recently, Harvard University quarterback Vin Ferrara designed one to be available in 2008. Also, the *Journal of Neurosurgery* reported that the Riddell's Revolution helmet "reduced concussions by 31 percent" (www.sportsbusinessdaily.com/index.cfm?fuseaction=sbd.main&ArticleID=116063&requesttimeout=500).

Preventing bullying and harassment on athletic teams. As parents and teachers or individuals working with children and adolescents, we must pay attention to any of these signs and speak with the young person right away. There tends to be a culture of secrecy associated with hazing, so it will be difficult to get young people to speak out against the cruelty they experience. Still, it is important to push.

Adult supervision in locker rooms and other undersupervised places will help, as will teaching children to recognize the signs of hazing and encouraging them to tell a caring, responsible adult. Of course, children fear retaliation for reporting such incidents and that their participation on sports teams will be compromised. Coaches and parents, as well as other school personnel, need to set very clear guidelines that make it known that hazing and bullying are unacceptable.

DO WHAT YOU CAN

Be sure that coaches, parents, and athletes have access to information about head injuries like concussions, traumatic brain injuries, and bullying and harassment on sports teams. Encourage schools to offer workshops on these topics for all the stakeholders.

EVALUATE YOUR SUCCESS

There are a few ways to evaluate your success for preventing or reducing head injuries. First would be to interview or survey coaches. A second would be to get statistics from local emergency rooms or care facilities to see if such injuries are reduced after coaches, parents, teachers, and others are trained to pay more careful attention to head injuries and prevention. Third would be to survey children themselves to reflect on head trauma experienced in the past twelve months and whether they wear seat belts, helmets, and so forth.

As far as determining success and reducing and/or preventing hazing on sports teams, the best measure is adult supervision in locker rooms and anywhere athletes go. The second best would be to administer anonymous surveys to all students asking questions about treatment on sports teams: for instance, do students get treated in mean ways if they are new to a sports team? The phrasing of the questions is important to elicit honest and appropriate feedback. Regular survey use can be very helpful to determine if problems are occurring.

FIND OUT MORE

Additional Resources

Brain Injury Association of America (www.biausa.org): This organization provides information and resources to improve the quality of life for individuals with brain injuries.

Centers for Disease Control and Prevention (www.cdc.gov/ncipc): This website has English and Spanish fact sheets and brochures on concussion and traumatic brain injury.

Statistics on Sports Injuries

Catastrophic Sports Injuries and Young People

- *NCAA comparisons and statistics:*
  - www1.ncaa.org/membership/ed_outreach/health-safety/iss/ Game_Comparison
  - www.nata.org/jat/readers/archives/42.2/i1062-6050-42-2-toc.pdf

- *National Center for Catastrophic Injury Research:* www.unc.edu/depts/ nccsi

There are a number of places for more information on bullying, hazing, and protecting your child in athletics:

- *U.S. Department of Health and Human Services (http://mentalhealth .samhsa.gov/15plus/parent):* This website provides tips for parents, grandparents, and caregivers, as well as for teachers and administrators.
- *GirlsHealth.gov (www.girlshealth.gov/bullying/index.htm):* This website has information for these groups on bullying, cyberbullying, and hazing.

The following groups were involved in the Centers for Disease Control's studies reported above:

- American Academy of Pediatrics
- American Association for Health Education
- American College of Sports Medicine
- American School Health Association
- Association of State and Territorial Health Officials
- Brain Injury Association of America
- Institute for Preventative Sports Medicine
- National Association for Sport and Physical Education
- National Athletic Trainers' Association
- National Federation of State High School Associations

- National Safety Council
- North American Brain Injury Society
- University of Pittsburgh Medical Center Sports Medicine Concussion Program
- U.S. Department of Education

The websites of these agencies would be useful for more information on these topics too.

References for CDC Fact Sheet Cited Above

Centers for Disease Control and Prevention (CDC). 1997. Sports-related recurrent brain injuries—United States. *Morbidity and Mortality Weekly Report* 46, no. 10: 224–227, www.cdc.gov/mmwr/preview/mmwrhtml/00046702.htm.

Guskiewicz, K. M., N. Weaver, D. A. Padua, and W. E. Garrett. 2000. Epidemiology of concussion in collegiate and high school football players. *American Journal of Sports Medicine* 28, (5): 643–50.

Harmon, K. G. 1999. Assessment and management of concussion in sports. *American Family Physician* 60, (3) (September 1): 887–92, 894.

Institute of Medicine. 2002. Is soccer bad for children's heads? Summary of the IOM workshop on neuropsychological consequences of head impact in youth soccer. Washington, DC: National Academy Press.

Kushner, D. S. 1998. Mild traumatic brain injury. *Archives of Internal Medicine* 158: 1617–24.

Lovell, M. R., M. W. Collins, G. L. Iverson, K. M. Johnston, and J. P. Bradley. 2004. Grade 1 or "ding" concussions in high school athletes. *American Journal of Sports Medicine* 32, (1): 47–54.

Powell, J. W. 2001. Cerebral concussion: Causes, effects, and risks in sports. *Journal of Athletic Training* 36, (3): 307–11.

Powell, J. W., and K. D. Barber-Foss. 1999. Traumatic brain injury in high school athletes. *Journal of the American Medical Association* 282: 958–63.

Sosin, D. M., J. E. Sniezek, and D. J. Thurman. 1996. Incidence of mild and moderate brain injury in the United States, 1991. *Brain Injury* 10: 47–54.

Zemper, E. D. 2003. Two-year prospective study of relative risk of a second cerebral concussion. *American Journal of Physical Medicine and Rehabilitation* 82 (September): 653–59.

Chapter Five

Promoting Safe and Healthy Developing Brains for Learning and Positive Behavior

Learning has always been a struggle for me, and I have always tried so hard. Sometimes the outcome is good, and other times I feel like giving up.

—College sophomore

Children in the United States spend a great many of their waking hours in some kind of structured education—most spend this time in schools. However, a child's learning is not limited to the school building. A child's brain is always learning, growing, developing, and maturing. Adult care providers and teachers alike should have a basic understanding about how the brain works to facilitate the best possible learning environment for young people—and to recognize signs if learning is problematic for a child.

Knowing how the brain learns will help parents and teachers alike in creating this best possible environment both at home and in schools. Success in school can provide resiliency for even the most at-risk child. Helping children become excited about learning and how their own brains learn can be a powerful strategy for promoting their emotional and physical well-being.

> ## ASK: WHAT IS POTENTIALLY DANGEROUS OR PROBLEMATIC FOR CHILDREN? WHAT CAN I DO (OR WHAT CAN BE DONE) TO MAKE THIS CHILD (OR THESE CHILDREN) SAFER OR HEALTHIER OR MORE SUCCESSFUL IN THIS/THESE SITUATION/S (OR SIMILAR ONES)?

General background on how the brain learns. With the advent of functional magnetic resonance imaging (fMRI) to examine the brain in action, research in cognitive neuroscience has provided wonderful new insight into how the brain learns. Substantial work still needs to be done in this area to be able to make sweeping proposals for change in schools and learning at home, but there are some major ideas and themes that parents, teachers, and others working with children can use to improve learning for all children.

- *Understand that new learning is connected to prior knowledge.* We all build new learning on what we already know. As a parent, teacher, or other person working with children, it is critical that you try to connect new material with what a child already knows.
- *Encourage the use of visual tools.* Visual tools, such as Thinking Maps (developed by David Hyerle; see www.thinkingmaps.com or www.thinking foundation.org for more information), are useful to help with the cognitive strategies that children need in and out of the classroom.
- *Provide opportunities for rehearsal/practice/feedback.* Children need opportunities to practice skills and concepts that they have learned, and they need to do this with adults who can give them thoughtful, useful, and immediate feedback on their understanding and performance. Real learning is transferred from the classroom to a child's world outside. Families and schools working together have the best chance of learning success if they work to facilitate this kind of transfer of learning from the classroom to the world outside.
- *Understand that emotions are critical to learning and memory.* We remember best what we care most about or have strong emotional associations with. We also remember traumatic events vividly because of the strong emotional connection. Teachers, parents, and others concerned with children's learning need to connect what they want to teach with positive emotions. Long-term stress and trauma can inhibit classroom

learning. But positive emotional associations can facilitate learning. As teachers and parents (acting as a child's at-home teacher), we must pay attention to a learning child's emotional state.

- *Value social/emotional intelligence.* As parents, caregivers, and teachers, we must be concerned with the social and emotional development of children and their brains. We need to cultivate ethical/moral development in our children to build respectful, caring citizens who know how to interact in caring ways with each other.
- *Teach kids that intelligence is multifaceted and dynamic.* Researchers have found that children who believe that intelligence can be changed perform better academically than those children who believe that intelligence is fixed. Intelligence can increase with environmental and academic inputs that are conducive. Also, Howard Gardner proposes in his book *Frames of Mind* (2006) that there is not a single "intelligence" but rather "multiple intelligences," which include

  - *Linguistic intelligence:* A person who has linguistic intelligence is said to be very skilled with language and its usage. Poets and other writers or linguists have high linguistic intelligence.
  - *Logical-mathematical intelligence:* A person with logical-mathematical intelligence has high ability in mathematics or with number systems and other complex logical systems.
  - *Musical intelligence:* A person who is high in musical intelligence thinks in music or musically. He or she has the ability to understand and create music. Skilled musicians, composers, and dancers show a heightened musical intelligence.
  - *Spatial intelligence:* People spatial intelligence have the ability to recognize patterns and spatial relationships in the visual world. Artists, designers, and those who are able to think spatially are said to have high spatial intelligence.
  - *Bodily-kinesthetic intelligence:* This entails the ability to use one's body well. Dancers and athletes are thought to have high bodily-kinesthetic intelligence.
  - *Interpersonal intelligence:* People who are empathetic with others and can read and perceive other individuals' moods, desires, and motivations have high interpersonal intelligence.
  - *Intrapersonal intelligence:* This entails having an understanding of one's own self.

- Later Gardner added an eighth intelligence, the *naturalist intelligence*, which entails the ability to work within nature and the natural world. Charles Darwin, he argues, possessed this form of intelligence.

Building on his work with multiple-intelligence theory, Gardner proposes the most essential kinds of "minds" we need to cultivate in ourselves and our young people in his book *Five Minds for the Future* (2007). The minds Gardner proposes are important for success not just in school but in adulthood in our ever-changing, technological and global society. He proposes focusing on helping children (and adults) with developing the following:

- *The disciplined mind:* Young people need exposure to a variety of disciplines and a solid grounding in at least one discipline to be able to become very knowledgeable or even "expert" in their adulthood.
- *The synthesizing mind:* Children need to learn strategies for taking ideas and putting them together in ways that make sense for themselves and possibly improve understanding for others.
- *The creative mind:* We need to cultivate creativity in young people—to encourage children to think of unique ways of solving problems, to write their own songs, and to engage in the creation of new ideas and strategies. In Benjamin Bloom's revised taxonomy, the highest form of learning is believed to be creating new ideas or things.
- *The respectful mind:* As adults in our society, we must help children learn the skills of working and playing well with others. We need to teach children to respect, honor, and appreciate differences and provide opportunities for children to interact with others from diverse backgrounds.
- *The ethical mind:* Children learn a lot from watching adults. We need to model ethical behavior, especially in challenging situations. Discuss ethical dilemmas with children and talk about options for behavior in these complex situations. Talk with children about what it means to be a good citizen, a good worker, and a good person.

As adult caregivers and teachers, we need to think about the kinds of brains/minds we want to cultivate in our next generation—particularly to equip them with skills that will serve them well in the global marketplace of ideas and things. Gardner's framework provides us with some important points to consider when working with young people and their developing brains.

Developing essential cognitive skills. Author David Hyerle, creator of the Thinking Maps program, has had demonstrated success with all kinds of learners—struggling, typically developing, and gifted. The research on his successes is carefully documented on the Thinking Foundation website (www.thinkingfoundation.org). The website offers examples and video clips of the successful implementation of Thinking Maps within schools around the world—from Japan to England to several U.S. states. In addition, specific evidence and suggestions for implementation and links for more information are available. Hyerle offers the following eight essential, universal cognitive skills that children (and adults) use in schools, at work, and at play:

1. describing attributes (e.g., describing a character in a story or the characteristics of a science experiment or mathematical formula)
2. comparing and contrasting (e.g., comparing similarities and differences between subplots in a story or two different characters, different properties of matter, or different mathematical calculations)
3. understanding cause and effect (e.g., understanding what caused the Civil War and what some of the effects were or what causes different responses in behavior or science experiments)
4. sequencing (e.g., examining the order of ideas, plots, historical events, recipes)
5. defining in context (e.g., making sense of new ideas by exploring what we already know about them)
6. examining part to whole (e.g., examining parts of the body, parts of a car engine, or parts of a story or equation)
7. making analogies (e.g., understanding the relationships of similar ideas—that is, what common elements make two ideas analogous)
8. classifying (e.g., organizing things into categories—rocks, toys, parts of the brain, chemical elements)

Parents and teachers alike can work with children to build these eight essential cognitive skills, thereby improving children's learning. Sharing these skills with children so that they become aware of their own thinking is also useful for developing young learners. In addition, Hyerle's Thinking Maps provide visual tools representing these essential cognitive skills, which have had demonstrated success in improving learning for all types of learners around the world.

BRING TOGETHER ALL ADVOCATES WHO CAN ASSIST IN MAKING CHILDREN SAFER IN THESE SITUATIONS

Presumably every human being in our society is concerned with the education and welfare of our next generation of leaders. In working to improve the formal education of young people, there are groups of people who should always work together: school boards, school leaders, teachers, families, taxpayers, and policy makers.

We all need to work together to improve the learning for all children in our society and ultimately around the world. Bringing in experts on the above topics (i.e., Thinking Maps, multiple intelligences, five minds for the future, and, as will be discussed later, the neurodevelopmental approach of Mel Levine) who can conduct regular training and feedback sessions with adults can improve learning for all children.

CONSIDER THE OPTIONS (PARTICULARLY ONES WITH DEMONSTRATED SUCCESS)

What about children who have trouble with their brains and learning? Consider the following all-too-familiar example:

> Learning has always been a struggle for me and I have always tried so hard. Sometimes the outcome is good and other times I feel like giving up. (College sophomore)

Mel Levine's work on children with learning differences focuses attention on neurodevelopmental profiles to which teachers and parents alike should be attuned in the growth and development of their children. Parents and teachers are closest to a child's development in these areas, and when any one developmental system (or more) appears to be having difficulty, these adult caregivers should be the first to sound an alarm to get help for the child. Levine is resistant to giving children labels like "ADD" and "autistic"; rather, he discusses each child's unique "neurodevelopmental profile," which might be perfectly suited for school or perhaps something else. He believes understanding the uniqueness of each individual child's mind is healthier than the traditional labels we have come to use in our society with children and disabilities. He offers the following framework in which, as a teacher or parent, you can pay attention to an individual child's strengths and weaknesses. For example, consider this young woman reflecting on her brother:

> My younger brother has a hard time learning sometimes. He is only in the sixth grade, and is brighter than me (as much as I hate to admit it). He reads novels I can barely understand, and helps me with my homework. Yet, with his ADHD he often struggles, as he is not challenged enough in the classroom. (College junior)

Attention is a complex matter—as Mel Levine suggests, it is too complex to be lumped into a single "diagnosis" like attention deficit hyperactivity disorder (ADHD), especially when you consider that so many children with attention issues are gifted in other areas, like this young woman's brother, who is very bright linguistically and in other areas of school. Levine suggests that there are several components to attention. For example, a few he describes are

- mental energy controls (e.g., ability to control the level of energy the brain expends on a given task)
- alertness control (e.g., controlling one's level of energy or how awake one is during a learning task)
- sleep arousal control (e.g., ability to control wake-sleep cycles—falling asleep and waking up)
- intake controls (e.g., ability to control information that the brain attends to and takes in)

Levine describes these in greater detail in his book *A Mind at a Time* (2002). As a teacher or parent or other adult concerned about a child's learning, it is important to be aware of the complexities of attention so that you can get more information and pay attention to the complexities.

Memory is another complex system according to Levine. True learning (retention and application of information) requires a good short-term, active working, and long-term memory. Levine analyzes the components of memory and describes the ways that learning can break down in each of these places:

- short-term memory (e.g., ability to remember ideas for a short time, like when cramming for a test)
- active working memory (e.g., keeping between five and nine ideas active in one's brain for a short time—such as a telephone number or list of items)
- long-term memory (e.g., ideas that are actually retained and result in a change in the brain); however, one may remember something in long-term memory but have difficulty with the following:
- recalling information from long-term memory
- recognizing an idea or thing that you know in your memory

As adults concerned with a child's learning, we also need to pay attention to memory systems and refer for help when a memory system seems to be breaking down. Memory problems may be masked by other academic deficiencies, so they can be difficult to diagnose. Adults who are knowledgeable about the insidious ways that memory problems can show themselves can be helpful in identifying children with such difficulties.

Many children have difficulty with their language system, which makes it even more difficult or nearly impossible to learn a second language, as is the case with this college student's sister:

My sister has had trouble with spelling, and reading. She was in resource classes during elementary and middle school and was evaluated for special education but did not need the services. She is now in High School, in "fundamental" classes. The ranking in our high school is "AP, Enriched, General, Fundamental." Because my sister needed to attend resource classes for reading in middle school, she was not able to take a language. She is now experiencing extreme difficulty in her Spanish class this year.

Levine breaks down the language system as follows:

- automatic-literate (what we use everyday without thinking about it)
- concrete versus abstract
- basic versus higher
- receptive (language we hear or read) versus expressive (language we use ourselves in reading and writing)
- thinking about language (metalinguistics)
- language in big chunks (discourse, or the way we speak, write, or communicate with language)
- words put into sentences (or words in context with correct syntax)
- word meanings (semantics, or what individual words mean)
- word bits (morphemes, or chunks or syllables of words)
- sounds (phonemes, or the sounds of letters)

Language in the form of reading, speaking, and interpreting can be challenging for some children and adolescents. Consider this statement from a preservice teacher candidate in her junior year reflecting on her difficulty reading:

> It would always take me forever to get my reading done. This would cause me to fall behind in class and I wouldn't be able to participate.

Mathematics and spatial ordering is another area in which children struggle with learning. Consider this statement from a college junior:

> I was never good in math and was taken out of the classroom in elementary school for extra help. When I moved up to high school I still had trouble and my teachers instead of helping me made me feel as though I should know the information being taught to me and I was stupid for not knowing it.

Levine examines the complexities of our "spatial ordering system" as well as the "sequential ordering system," both of which encompass mathematical learning as follows:

- spatial ordering system (understanding spatial relations and objects in space, geometry, and so on)

- sequential ordering system (understanding sequences of numbers, order of operations, and so on)

Clearly, children can struggle in one area of mathematics (e.g., computation) but do relatively well in a different area (e.g., geometry) because these skills seem to be handled differently by the brain. Recognizing these as different can be useful in identifying children with mathematical struggles.

Some students struggle with their gross motor skills (e.g., running, jumping, hitting a volleyball) and some with their fine motor skills (e.g., writing, cutting with scissors). Levine differentiates also our speaking motor system and our musical motor system (used to play an instrument). Children may struggle in one or more of these areas:

- gross motor (using large muscle groups)
- fine motor (using smaller muscle groups)
- graphomotor (writing)
- oromotor (speaking)
- musical motor (playing an instrument)

Some children struggle with higher forms of learning. Levine outlines the components of the "higher-order thinking system" that encompasses a variety of strategies often used in school and out:

- understanding concepts
- problem solving
- knowing that a problem is a problem
- previewing the outcome
- assessing feasibility
- mobilizing resources
- thinking logically
- considering different strategies and picking the best one
- starting and pacing
- self-monitoring
- dealing with impasses
- arriving at a solution (and checking one's answer)

- critical thinking

  - enumerating the facts
  - uncovering the author's or creator's point of view

- establishing what one thinks
- searching for errors and exaggerations
- getting outside help
- weighing the evidence
- communicating
- following rules

- creativity

  - risk taking
  - integrating technical skill with originality
  - maintaining autonomy from peer pressures and standards
  - suspending self-evaluation
  - discovering and pursuing the right medium
  - achieving stylistic distinctiveness

Finally, and arguably most important, is our social thinking system. How we interact with others can make the difference between success and failure. As Daniel Goleman discusses in his books *Emotional Intelligence* and *Social Intelligence*, one's emotional intelligence may be a better predictor of success in life than IQ. Many children struggle with social-relationship building. Adults should help facilitate those relationships and provide tools to children who are struggling. Children with autism or Asperger's syndrome in particular might struggle to read nonverbal/facial cues and need to learn strategies for interpreting the emotions of others. Levine breaks down what he calls the "social thinking system" for places where problems may occur:

- accomplishing the big three social missions:

  1. friendship mission
  2. political mission (e.g., understanding political relationships in school and out, such as who tends to make decisions in groups, who causes trouble, and so forth)
  3. popularity mission

- social functions and dysfunctions

  - expressing accurate feelings
  - interpreting the feelings of others accurately

- code switching (e.g., using behavior appropriate in a given setting)
- regulating humor
- developing requesting skills
- mood-matching
- complimenting
- developing lingo fluency

- understanding social behaviors

  - resolving conflict
  - monitoring one's own behavior and that of others
  - self-marketing and image development
  - collaborating
  - reading and acting on social information (Levine 2002, pp. 60–64 based on Levine's neurodevelopmental model described in depth in his book *A Mind at a Time*)

Learning and learning problems are complex, and we as adults need to examine each child and consider his or her unique learning profile. A child may appear to have "attention problems," but this may be a result of a problem with "mental energy control" or "intake controls." The bottom line is that we should avoid "lumping" children with learning difficulties into one single category without exploring the complexities of the problem first.

Turn off the television; open a book. Consider the following examples:

When I was younger, I had some trouble reading, but got into a reading group before school began and came to love reading. I am 29 and I still love to read books whenever I get a chance to. (Graduate student)

We grew up in front of the television. To this day, I am a television junkie. It is very difficult for me to choose to read when the television is on. (College junior)

Recently, *Scientific American Mind* published an article titled "Television Is No Mere Metaphor," outlining the ways that television has been found to affect the brain. The authors begin this article with the statement, "Perhaps the most ironic aspect of the struggle for survival is how easily organisms can be harmed by that which they desire" (Kubey and Csikszentmihalyi

2002, 74). There are numerous issues that parents and teachers alike should attend to when it comes to children and adolescents' television viewing:

- *Addictiveness:* Television itself can be addictive in that the brain cannot help but attune to it. The *Scientific American Mind* article reports, "As one might expect, people who were watching TV when we beeped them reported feeling relaxed and passive. The EEG studies similarly show less mental stimulation, as measured by alpha brain-wave production, during viewing than during reading" (Kubey and Csikszentmihalyi 2002). Also, the brain's "orienting response," which makes us pay attention to something sudden or new, is activated almost constantly during television viewing. Some research has shown that the "orienting response" can be activated as often as once per second—for instance, in the case of music videos. In other experiments where participating families were asked to stop viewing television for a week or a month, many fought more often verbally and physically and dropped out of the studies because they couldn't go that long without watching.
- *Computer screens as replacements for televisions.* Some children spend as much time, if not more, in front of the computer. Many of the same concerns expressed above apply to children's playing computer games and viewing certain websites.
- *Inactivity.* Children who sit in front of their computers and televisions for hours a day are not as physically active as those who do not. The brain needs physical activity to produce oxygenated blood cells for healthy functioning.

The authors of the *Scientific American Mind* article make the following recommendations:

Kicking the Habit
Individuals or families that want to achieve better control of their TV viewing can try the following strategies:

Raising awareness. As with other dependencies, a first critical step is to become aware of how entrenched the viewing habit has become, how much time it absorbs and how limited the rewards of viewing actually are. One way to do this is to keep a diary for a few days of all programs viewed. The diary entries might rate the quality of the experience, denoting how much the viewer enjoyed or learned from various programs.

Promoting alternative activities. As soon as they finish dinner, many families rush to the television. To supplant viewing with other activities, it may prove helpful to make a list of alternatives and put it on the fridge. Instead of reflexively plopping down in front of the tube, those interested in reducing their viewing can refer to the list.

Exercising willpower. Viewers often know that a particular program or movie-of-the-week is not very good within the first few minutes, but instead of switching off the set, they stick with it for the full two hours. It is natural to keep watching to find out what happens next. But once the set is off and people have turned their attention to other things, they rarely care anymore.

Enforcing limits. A kitchen timer can come in handy when setting time limits, especially with video games. When it rings, the kids know to stop. Some parents find that this works much better than announcing the deadline themselves. The kids take the bell more seriously.

Blocking channels/v-chip. Television sets now come equipped with microchips that can be used to prevent viewing of violent shows. In addition, electronic add-on devices can count how many hours each family member has viewed and block access beyond a particular quota.

Viewing selectively. Rather than channel-surf, people can use the television listings ahead of time to choose which programs to watch.

Using the VCR. Instead of watching a program, record it for later viewing. Many people never return to much of the material they have taped.

Going cold turkey. Many families have succeeded in reducing viewing by limiting the household to one set and placing it in a remote room of the house or in a closet. Others end their cable subscriptions or jettison the set altogether.

Supporting media education. Schools in Canada and Australia, as well as in an increasing number of states in the U.S., now require students to take classes in media education. These sharpen children's ability to analyze what they see and hear and to make more mindful use of TV and other media. (Kubey and Csikszentmihalyi 2002, 80)

Why Read?

Reading is a skill essential to functioning in our society, but it is perhaps one of the most challenging tasks we ask the young brain to learn to do (Sousa 2006). We are bombarded by print images, and perhaps the most essential skill to functioning well in school is the ability to read. Parents are children's first teachers and need to be vigilant about their child's early literacy development. Teachers pick up the literary "baton" in this relay and help children build their literacy skills. The University of Michigan's Health System synthesized the research on early development of literacy skills as follows:

Research has identified five early reading skills that are all essential. They are:

- Phonemic awareness—Being able to hear, identify, and play with individual sounds (phonemes) in spoken words.
- Phonics—Being able to connect the letters of written language with the sounds of spoken language.
- Vocabulary—The words kids need to know to communicate effectively.
- Reading comprehension—Being able to understand and get meaning from what has been read.
- Fluency (oral reading)—Being able to read text accurately and quickly.

How can we make reading part of our family's lifestyle?

Parents play a critical role in helping their children develop not only the ability to read, but also an enjoyment of reading.

- Turn off the tube. Start by limiting your family's viewing time.
- Teach by example. If you have books, newspapers and magazines around your house, and your child sees you reading, then your child will learn that you value reading. You can't over-estimate the value of modeling.
- Read together. Reading with your child is a great activity. It not only teaches your child that reading is important to you, but it also offers a chance to talk about the book, and often other issues will come up. Books can really open the lines of communication between parent and child.
- Hit the library. Try finding library books about current issues or interests in your family's or child's life, and then reading them together. For example, read a book about going to the dentist prior to your child's next dental exam, or get some books about seashore life after a trip to the coast. If your child is obsessed with dragons, ask your librarian to recommend a good dragon novel for your child.

There are many ways to include reading in your child's life, starting in babyhood, and continuing through the teen years. Focus on literacy activities that your child enjoys, so that reading is a treat, not a chore.

(Boyse 2008, para. 3-7)

Encourage play. Play has been found to improve such essential brain functions as self-regulation. As children are spending more and more hours in front of televisions and video games, they have fewer opportunities to practice self-regulation and other imagination-building activities during free play. Also, during free play children are able to practice an important skill called "private speech." We need to encourage children to talk to themselves. In so doing, they learn how to regulate their own language.

DO WHAT YOU CAN

Based on the information presented in this chapter, parents and teachers can do the following to improve learning for children and identify when a child is having difficulty learning:

- Help your child pay attention to what he or she is learning in school by connecting the information to areas outside of school. Provide feedback about a child's understanding of concepts.
- Learn about visual tools like Thinking Maps yourself and teach them to your children. These maps have been shown to improve learning for both adults and children.
- Pay attention to neurodevelopmental profiles. Is a child struggling in one or more of these areas? Consult with a pediatrician or other medical professional if necessary.
- Set limits on television and computer game usage, and pay attention to what children are watching.
- Read to and with your child. Encourage reading and build reading skills. If a child is having early reading problems, work with a reading professional and/or pediatrician as early as possible.
- Encourage children to play particularly imaginative games, games with rules and structure, games like Simon Says and Red Light/Green Light that promote self-control, and play involving self-talk.

EVALUATE YOUR SUCCESS

Traditional methods of examining student learning (e.g., school report cards and standardized tests) may be inadequate for truly assessing what a child can or cannot do well. Teachers and parents need to be partners in the learning success of children. There are many ways to determine what children know and can do. The first is to ask children to perform tasks so that you can determine what they can and cannot do or what they do and do not know. One such task is to have children create Thinking Maps so you can determine what they do and do not understand. Observation of children and multiple assessment strategies, such as classroom quizzes, tests, projects, and portfolios, used together can give helpful insight into a child's learning and/or learning struggles.

FIND OUT MORE

Boyse, Kyla. 2008. Reading and your child. University of Michigan Health System. www.med.umich.edu/1libr/yourchild/reading.htm (accessed August 30, 2008).

Gardner, H. 2006. *Multiple intelligences: New horizons in theory and practice.* New York: Basic Books.

———. 2007. *Five minds for the future.* Cambridge, MA: Harvard Business School Press.

Golman, D. 1995. *Emotional intelligence.* New York: Bantam Books.

———. 2007. *Social intelligence: The new science of human relationships.* New York: Bantam Books.

Hyerle, D. 2004. *Student successes with thinking maps: School-based research, results, and models for achievement using visual tools.* Thousand Oaks, CA: Corwin Press.

Kubey, Robert, and Mihaly Csikszentmihalyi. 2002. Television addiction is no mere metaphor. *Scientific American Mind,* February. www.sciam.com/article.cfm?id=television-addiction-is-n-2002-02 (accessed August 30, 2008).

Levine, M. D. 2002. *A mind at a time.* New York: Simon & Schuster.

Sousa, D. 2006. *How the brain learns.* Thousand Oaks, CA: Corwin Press.

Spiegel, A. 2008. Old-fashioned play builds serious skills. NPR. February 21. www.npr.org/templates/story/story.php?storyId=19212514 (accessed February 21, 2008).

Chapter Six

Learning Disabilities and Attention Deficit Hyperactivity Disorder

LEARNING DISABILITIES

Children come to school to learn and be successful. Schools are institutions and are mandated by law to teach all students, but not all schools are able to meet the unique learning needs or styles of all students. Not all institutions are equal. Not all teachers are excellent, and not all schools meet the needs of all children. According to annual data collected, anywhere from 2.8 to 3 million children between the ages of six and twenty-one have learning disabilities (U.S. Department of Education 2006). This number represents about 4.3 to 5 percent of the entire school population.

The term *learning disability* is a broad one encompassing possible deficits in the areas of reading, language, mathematics, spelling, problem solving, processing, and attention-behavioral problems. Learning disabilities have been defined according to federal law, Public Law 101-476 (Individuals with Disabilities Education Act). The rights of children with learning disabilities are protected.

Students with documented learning disabilities have access to individual education plans to guide their instruction. Children begin school with an enthusiasm for learning. More often than not, reading, writing, and communication problems manifest themselves early on, causing children to feel disconnected and disheartened and to lose any positive sense of self. Such children experience failure in many of the tasks required at that particular level.

All they see is that they are falling further and further behind their peers. It is crucial that parents and teachers monitor progress or lack of progress on the part of each child. Early identification and intervention is essential to remediation.

There are several risk factors for learning disabilities:

- physiological

  - brain injury
  - heredity
  - chemical imbalance

- curricular and environmental

  - home environment
  - poor nutrition
  - extended periods spent in a highly adverse emotional climate
  - toxins in the environment
  - lead poisoning
  - too little stimulation
  - poverty
  - poor medical care
  - low parental education level (Skiba 2002)

> **ASK: WHAT IS POTENTIALLY DANGEROUS OR PROBLEMATIC FOR CHILDREN? WHAT CAN I DO (OR WHAT CAN BE DONE) TO MAKE THIS CHILD (OR THESE CHILDREN) SAFER OR HEALTHIER OR MORE SUCCESSFUL IN THIS/THESE SITUATION/S (OR SIMILAR ONES)?**

Several red flags can be identified at the school level. The first is dyslexia. Many people have become familiar with this term due to the fact that many famous people—Tom Cruise, Cher, Beethoven, George Washington etc.—have been identified as dyslexic. Dyslexia is well researched and well understood. The core problem is in phonological processing. There are a total of forty-four phonemes, or basic sounds, in the English language.

Children with dyslexia have problems understanding when phonemes are put together in word combinations. Reading becomes a huge task for kids because it is difficult to identify the sound units that make up words.

For dyslexic children, identifying the number of syllables and decoding are insurmountable tasks. Children with dyslexia usually speak well but have struggles with interpreting what they hear.

Children are often seen as having lots of potential but may be labeled bad listeners or as inattentive, unmotivated, noncompliant, and at times behaviorally challenged because of noncompliance or failure to complete tasks. One of the major issues in the past was the lack of effective diagnosis or recognition of the disorder. Children may go for years before they are identified as learning disabled. Children often learn to become great chameleons and will try to go undetected in many different classrooms.

Specific signs may indicate that a reading disorder is present. This list is not exhaustive and absolutely should not be used to diagnose; rather, it should serve as a starting point for a conversation between educators and parents. When investigating the possibility of a reading disorder, look for the following red flags, which are usually present, and consider whether they have stood the test of time (they have been evidenced more than once and have been present for at least three to four months):

- difficulty learning colors or letter names
- problems remembering basic math facts
- lack of age-appropriate number of sight words
- difficulty with decoding
- inability to understand what is read aloud
- frequent substitution of words that are visually similar
- slow reading rate
- reliance on finger pointing and lip moving to say every word
- letter reversals while writing
- limited vocabulary
- trouble remembering verbal sequences
- behavior refusal around reading

These are but a few of the signs that may warrant a discussion with school officials, especially reading and literacy teachers.

Communication involves both receptive and expressive language skills. Children with learning disabilities in either area will have problems with receiving or producing information. Some dyslexic children may appear as if they are listening and comprehending the message given orally; however, more often than not, they have been unable to string the words together to make a concrete thought or understand the sequence of steps required for task completion.

At times children will almost appear as if they are being instructed in a foreign language, even though all the instruction is in English. They are unable to make sense of the content, syntax, and formation of these words strung together in sentences. Frequently children learn to depend on visual cues or peer assistance to get the message of what is required to complete the task.

Some children choose not to speak publicly and are often labeled as shy, when in reality they have either receptive issues (they don't understand what is truly going on and do not want anyone to know) or expressive issues (they do not possess the vocabulary or do not recall specific words to explain the task or show competence), so they choose to be quiet and hope that no one pays them too much attention.

Learning disorders may also be strongly related to emotional and behavior disorders. Learning disorders have a subset of issues that develop because of the inability to be successful in a school setting. When a child is unsuccessful in a setting in which he or she is placed for seven hours every day, learning begins to be affected by social and emotional developmental issues. A child who has difficulty communicating will not be very good at problem solving, mediation, communicating their needs and wants, or using their words when frustrated or angry. Instead, acting-out behaviors are usually manifested. We see an increase in children manifesting depressive symptoms, such as

- sadness
- apathy
- social withdrawal
- irritability
- negative self-view
- passivity
- fatigue
- sleepiness
- poor or excessive appetite
- poor concentration
- reluctance to go to school
- suicidal thoughts

We often see an increase in anxiety symptoms:

• excessive distress and stress
• worry
• restlessness
• irritability
• tendency to become easily fatigued
• hypervigilance

Some children will decide not to internalize their frustration and anger and instead will begin externalizing it in the following ways:

• initiation of fighting
• disobedience
• defiance
• destruction of property
• bullying
• argumentiveness
• verbal hostility
• conflict with authorities
• rebelliousness
• antisocial behavior
• truancy (American Psychiatric Association 2000)

Educators and parents long ago figured out that a child will do whatever is necessary to survive in any environment he or she is put into for any period of time.

BRING TOGETHER ALL ADVOCATES WHO CAN ASSIST IN MAKING CHILDREN SAFER IN THESE SITUATIONS

The advocates for children with learning disabilities are professionally trained special education and reading-and-writing specialists. These individuals can provide specific interventions leading to the acquisition of specific study and learning strategies that will empower the student to process information more efficiently. Specialized computer programs monitored and taught by highly trained education personnel can decrease the likelihood of failure and frustration on the part of learning-disabled children and youths.

CONSIDER THE OPTIONS (PARTICULARLY ONES WITH DEMONSTRATED SUCCESS)

A method with demonstrated success for effectively working with children with learning disabilities is direct instruction. Direct instruction is a comprehensive approach based on decades of research that emphasizes maximizing not only the quantity of instruction students receive but also the quality (National Institute for Direct Instruction 2006). The point to remember about direct instruction is that the information must be presented in small segments, practice must be adult guided, and immediate feedback must be provided to the child about the work.

DO WHAT YOU CAN

Whether you are a teacher, coach, parent, or other person in charge of delivering a concept to a learning-disabled child, you must remember these guiding principles as highlighted by Martin Henley, Roberta Ramsey, Robert Algozzine (2001), and Marilyn Friend (2008):

- Present the information in a well-organized, sequenced manner.
- Begin with a review to find out what the child remembers from other contexts or prior experience.
- Provide clear, concise explanations and illustrations of what is to be learned.
- Present material in small steps with lots of practice and demonstration at each step. Provide initial guidance through practice.
- Provide the child with frequent opportunities to practice and generalize skills.
- Ask questions to check the child's understanding and obtain responses that match what is suppose to be demonstrated.
- Help the child develop independence.
- Give the child strategies for planning and remembering information.
- Present information as a series of steps and explain how each step leads to another step till completion.
- As parents, redefine your image of your child's ability to learn and how he or she learns.

- As parents, partner with the school to achieve the best outcomes for the child. Develop appropriate and effective teams, consult with special education educators, access resources, and provide both emotional and academic support.

EVALUATE YOUR SUCCESS

Success will be measured by a child who is successful academically within a school environment. The child will enjoy school, feel able to keep up with the curriculum, do well on tests, and be able to perform at grade level or above.

FIND OUT MORE

Resources for More Information

The Council for Learning Disabilities website (www.cldinternational.org) is for professionals interested in current issues regarding learning disabilities.

The Davis Dyslexia Association International website (www.dyslexia.com) discusses all aspects of dyslexia and resources available.

The Division for Learning Disabilities (www.teachingld.org) is part of the Council for Exceptional Children. At this website, you can communicate with professionals working with students with learning disabilities, find answers to questions, explore tips for teaching students, and read current news affecting the field.

The LD Online (www.ldonline.org) website is one of the best-known sites for teachers and parents of children with learning disabilities. It offers expert advice, contains recent news on learning disabilities, and has a section for children to share experiences.

The LD Resources website (www.ldresources.com) contains published resources and materials for learning disabilities.

The Learning Disabilities Association of America website (www.ldanatl.org) contains numerous links and resources for individuals with disabilities and their families, including information about rights and recent legislation regarding learning disabilities.

The Matrix Parent Network and Resource Center website (www.matrixparents .org) includes a discussion board where parents of learning-disabled children can exchange ideas.

References

American Psychiatric Association (APA). 2000. *Diagnostic and statistical manual of mental disorders*. 4th ed., text rev. Washington, DC: APA.

Friend, M. 2008. *Special education*. 2nd ed. Boston: Allyn & Bacon.

Gorman, J. C. 2001. *Emotional disorders and learning disabilities in the elementary classroom, interactions and interventions*. Thousand Oaks, CA: Corwin Press.

Henley, M., R. S. Ramsay, and R. F. Algozinne. 2001. *Characteristics of and strategies for teaching students with mild disabilities*. Boston: Allyn & Bacon.

National Institute for Direct Instruction (NIDI). 2006. Research base for the effectiveness of direct instruction. www.nifid.org/pdfs/research_Bse.pdf (accessed December 2, 2007).

Skiba, R. J. 2002. Special education and school discipline: A precarious balance. *Behavioral Disorders* 27: 81–97.

U.S. Department of Education. 2006. Annual report to Congress on the implementation of the Individuals with Disabilities Education Act. Washington, DC: U.S. Department of Education.

ATTENTION DEFICIT DISORDER

Children with attention deficit disorder (ADD) have received extensive consideration in our schools, media, communities, and society as a whole. Within this category, there are two types of attention issues: attention deficit hyperactivity disorder (ADHD) and attention deficit disorder. They are two distinct disorders. ADD is a syndrome usually characterized by serious and persistent difficulties with attention span and impulse control. ADHD has three components: predominantly inattentive type, combined type, and hyperactive type.

> I have several students who have been diagnosed with AD problems. Many struggle to pass their classes and experience social problems. Most who are on medication say it helps with school however they don't like the way it makes them feel. (Elementary school teacher)

Currently, ADHD is one of the most commonly diagnosed childhood psychiatric disorders. Most professionals estimate that 3 to 5 percent of the population has ADHD (National Institute of Mental Health 2005). Research has indicated that boys are nine times more likely than girls to have this disorder (Neuman 2005). Although girls may have the same symptoms of ADHD as boys, research suggests they may display lower levels of these symptoms (Barkley 2006). ADD and ADHD are usually diagnosed by using the American Psychiatric Association's *Diagnostic and Statistical Manual of Mental Disorders* (DSM IV).

> My cousin has ADD. He is only 5, perhaps 6 and already is on medication for ADD. He is very hyper, cannot control himself at times, loud and doesn't know his own strength. His brother now is developing ADD too, at least according to his parents. I feel that my cousin is much to young for such medication. (College student)

There has been some controversy as to whether ADD and ADHD truly exist and whether they should be considered disorders or maladjustment issues. Although a few professionals and parents contend that ADHD is not a real disorder, nearly one hundred years of research has demonstrated that ADHD is chronic and pervasive, affecting every aspect of an individual's life (Centers for Disease Control and Prevention 2004). Evidence appears to indicate that ADD is a permanent condition, but some children may outgrow the hyperactive portion.

> Well I have never been tested for it, but I have many problems trying to concentrate on certain things. Its very hard for me to just sit and listen to people talk, its very hard to understand them after a while because all I want to do is count how many words are on the paper they handed out, or I draw a lot on the side lines of papers. And sometimes I just play with my hair continuously or move my body. Its really hard to concentrate. (College student)

ASK: WHAT IS POTENTIALLY DANGEROUS OR PROBLEMATIC FOR CHILDREN? WHAT CAN I DO (OR WHAT CAN BE DONE) TO MAKE THIS CHILD (OR THESE CHILDREN) SAFER OR HEALTHIER OR MORE SUCCESSFUL IN THIS/THESE SITUATION/S (OR SIMILAR ONES)?

According to the DSM IV, the following criteria must be present and have persisted for at least six months to a degree that is maladaptive and inconsistent with developmental level.

A child with attention deficit disorder without hyperactivity

- is easily distracted by extraneous stimuli
- has difficulty listening and following directions
- has difficulty focusing and sustaining attention
- has difficulty concentrating and attending to tasks
- performs inconsistently in school work
- tunes out, may appear spacey
- is disorganized, loses belongings
- has poor study skills
- has difficulty working independently

A child with attention deficit disorder with hyperactivity

- has a high activity level
- appears to be in constant motion
- often fidgets with hands or feet
- plays with objects
- roams freely around the classroom
- is impulsive
- lacks self-control
- blurts out verbally
- cannot wait for his or her turn
- often interrupts or intrudes on others
- talks excessively
- acts before thinking
- engages in risk-taking activities
- has difficulty with transitions
- displays aggressive behaviors and is easily overstimulated
- is socially immature
- has low self-esteem
- experiences high frustration

Note that not all symptoms apply to each child and they will vary in degree. Each child is unique and will show differences in behaviors, strengths, interests, skills, and deficits. One should also be cautioned that many of these behaviors can be considered normal at certain developmental stages of a child's life. The concern occurs when there is a higher level of frequency compared to children of that developmental level.

Risk Factors for ADD/ADHD

Researchers have identified some possible causes of this disorder:

- heredity (25 percent of relatives of individuals with ADHD also have ADHD)
- biology-neurology (some scientists describe ADHD as neurological inefficiency in the area of the brain that controls impulses and aids in screening sensory input and focusing attention, possibly due to imbalances of the chemical dopamine, which transmits neurosensory messages)
- complications or trauma during pregnancy or birth
- lead poisoning
- diet or food allergies
- prenatal alcohol and drug exposure
- brain damage
- poverty and lack of structure in home environment
- less electrical activity in brain function
- brain metabolizing glucose at a lower level
- lower levels of blood flow in the brain region
- differently functioning brain frontal region, basal ganglia, and cerebellum (Friend 2008)

ADHD may occur simultaneously with other disorders, such as

- learning disabilities
- emotional disabilities
- autism
- traumatic brain injury
- psychiatric disorders
- sleep disorders
- substance abuse problems (Friend 2008)

Myths and Misconceptions about ADHD/ADD

- Medication stunts growth. The medication may cause an initial and mild slowing down of growth, but over time the growth-suppression effect is minimal, if nonexistent, in most cases.
- ADD/ADHD children who take medication attribute their success only to medication. When self-esteem is encouraged, a child taking medication attributes his success not only to the medication but to himself as well.
- Medication should be stopped when a child reaches his or her teen years. For those teens who meet the criteria for a diagnosis of ADD, there is a benefit to continuing to take their medication.
- Children build up a tolerance to medication. Although the dose of medication may need adjustment from time to time, there is no conclusive evidence that a tolerance is built up.
- All children with ADHD are hyperactive. Psychiatric classification of ADHD includes inattentive type, hyperactive-impulsive type, and combined type. Some children show no hyperactivity at all.
- ADHD is a fad, a trendy diagnosis of recent times with little research to support its existence. Reports of cases of ADHD go back to the mid-nineteenth and early twentieth centuries. There is a gamut of research proving ADHD's existence.
- ADHD is primarily the result of minimal brain injury. In most cases of ADHD, there is no evidence of actual damage to the brain. ADHD is the result of neurological dysfunction, which is often linked to hereditary factors.
- The social problems of students with ADHD are due to their not knowing how to interact socially. Most people with ADHD know how to interact, but their problems with behavioral inhibition make it difficult to implement socially appropriate behaviors.
- Using psychostimulants, such as Ritalin, can easily turn children into abusers of other substances, such as cocaine and marijuana. There is no evidence that using psychostimulants directly leads to drug abuse.
- ADHD largely disappears in adulthood. The majority of children diagnosed with ADHD in childhood will continue to have the condition as adults.

| BRING TOGETHER ALL ADVOCATES WHO CAN ASSIST |
| CHILDREN WITH ADD/ADHD |

The major advocates for children with ADD/ADHD are the parents, classroom teacher, and school personnel, such as a school counselor who can provide social skills instructions, group-communication skills, and some anger-management training if applicable.

| CONSIDER THE OPTIONS (PARTICULARLY |
| ONES WITH DEMONSTRATED SUCCESS) |

Many strategies have shown some success in working effectively with children with this disorder. I will focus on recommendations for teachers and parents:

Educators

- Be flexible, committed, and willing to work on a personal level. These children need constant attention, energy, and support, as well as extra time and accommodation for class work. Above all, they need you not to be reactive to small things and events.
- Seek training and acquire knowledge about this disorder. Look for strategies and professional workshops.
- Have an excellent communication plan between home and school.
- Provide clarity and structure in the classroom and at school. These children need to have academic tasks broken down into manageable chunks, as well as direct instruction, clear directions, organized work spaces with all materials ready and at hand, and effective transitions.
- Prepare creative, engaging, and interactive teaching strategies. Use technology, multisensory teaching strategies, cooperative learning, and reciprocal teaching. Understand learning styles and multiple intelligences, and use strategies that match these styles and intelligences.
- Encourage teamwork both on the part of regular education and special education teachers. Help all members of the academic and behavioral teams be consistent and supportive. Become a collaborative team with the parents.

- Seek administrative support. Incorporate the principal in the plans for the effective management of a child with this disorder so that consistent messages can be given by all who work with the child.
- Respect student privacy and confidentiality around academic work, test results, and medication usage.
- Modify assignments and workloads. As a teacher, be realistic about what an ADD/ADHD child can realistically do in a certain time. Reasonable amounts of work are more likely to be completed.
- Limit the amount of homework; prioritize and modify.
- Give additional time for assignments, assessments, and tests, or give tests in an alternative format.
- Assist with organization. Have a plan. Offer specific note-taking and study skills, notebooks, and materials.
- Make environmental modifications. Is your environment welcoming and affirming for these children? Can they be successful in your grade for that year? What kinds of behavioral changes do you as a teacher need to make to help this child have a wonderful, enriched school year?

Parents

Having spoken to many parents of ADD/ADHD children, I know that raising this type of child can be very challenging. Fundamentally, parents must understand that much time and effort must be invested in raising these children. They require additional support and training to be successful. The following strategies will not work with all children. Some children will learn the skills more quickly than others, and some will continue to be defiant and noncompliant.

- *Transitioning:* These children have a tough time with changes. Warning children of upcoming changes (e.g., we will be leaving in ten minutes) can lessen their impact.
- *Rules, rewards, and consequences:* It is important to have clear, realistic expectations that can be measured, observed, and recorded. Once the child is able to recognize the rules, he or she is rewarded appropriately. The child should not be punished for not meeting an

expectation but taught how to achieve it with regular practice and repetition.

- *Time outs:* If you are going to use this method, then a specific process must occur after the time out to help the child know what he did wrong and what he could do differently the next time and to teach him to make better choices.

- *Removal of privileges:* This is often used but rarely changes behavior. An ADD/ADHD child will work better if he works at maintaining what he already has rather than constantly losing privileges.

- *Physical violence:* This will not change behavior. It will only make the child more afraid and aggressive, and he may seek revenge or act out violently. This is not a viable strategy.

- *Structure and consistency:* These children do very well in a highly structured and consistent home. Chaos seems to accelerate ADHD's symptoms.

- *Redirection:* This helps these children to refocus, redirect, and channel their energy in a more useful way and seems to lead to more productivity.

- *Advocacy education:* The parents must become advocates on behalf of their child. They must teach all who come into contact with their child how to deal and interact effectively with him or her.

- *Praise:* This is a simple but effective method of highlighting things that a child does well. It builds self-esteem and confidence.

- *Medication:* Make sure to monitor whether this is effective as an intervention or not.

EVALUATE YOUR SUCCESS

As a parent you will experience and notice success when there is a child or youth in front of you who is more able to be organized, on time, and in control and who seems to be effectively managing the daily routines of and expectations for his or her age level. Educators can notice success by seeing an increased motivation to do well in school, higher test scores, better performance on projects, and completion of assignments. The individual will appear to be on top of his or her game and will be better at following directions and completing required expectations with little to no frustration or acting-out behavior.

FIND OUT MORE

Resources

Websites

The Children and Adults with Attention Deficit Disorder website (www.chadd .org) includes fact sheets, general information about ADD in both children and adults, and a summary of the legal rights of children with ADD/ADHD.

The National Institute of Mental Health has published booklets on ADHD (www.nimh.nih.gov/publicat/adhd.cfm).

The National Resource Center (www.help4adhd.org) is a clearinghouse for all kinds of materials and resources on ADHD.

The ProTeacher Directory (www.proteacher.com) includes many links and specific strategies for teachers.

Books

Bain, Lisa J. 1991. *A parent's guide to attention deficit disorders*. New York: Dell.

Beugin, Mary Ellen. 1990. *Coping with ADD*. Calgary, Alberta: Detselig Enterprises.

Detselig, Moghadam.1988. *ADHD revisited: A concise source of information for parents*. Calgary, Alberta: Detselig Enterprises.

Garber, S., Maryanne Garber, and Robyn Freedman Spizman. 1995. *Is your child hyperactive, inattentive, impulsive and distractible*. New York: Villard.

Goldstein, P. D., and B. Ingersoll. 1993. *Controversial treatments for children with ADHD*. New York: Doubleday.

Hallowell, Edward, and John J. Ratey. 1995. *Driven to distraction*. New York: Simon & Schuster.

Kelley, Kate, and Peggy Ramundo. 1993. *You mean I'm not lazy, stupid or crazy?* New York: Scribner.

Moss, Robert. 1990. *Why Jonnie can't concentrate: Coping with attention deficit problems*. New York: Bantam Books.

Rief, Sandra. 2005. *How to reach and teach ADD-ADHD children*. New York: Wiley & Sons.

References

American Psychiatric Association (APA). 2000. *Diagnostic and statistical manual of mental disorders*. 4th ed., text rev. Washington, DC: APA.

Barkley, R. A. 2006. ADHD in adults: Developmental course and outcomes of children with ADHD, and ADHD in clinic referred adults. In *Attention-deficit hyperactivity disorder: A handbook for diagnosis and treatment*, ed. R. A. Barkley, 248–96. New York: Guilford Press.

Centers for Disease Control and Prevention (CDC). 2004. Attention deficit hyperactivity disorder. A public health research agenda. www.cdc.gov/ncbdd/adhd/dadphra.htm (accessed December 3, 2007).

Friend, M. 2008. *Special education*. 2nd ed. Boston: Allyn & Bacon.

National Institute of Mental Health (NIMH). 2005. Mental illness exacts heavy toll, beginning in youth. www.nimh.nih.gov/press/mentalhealthstats.cfm (accessed December 3, 2007).

Neuman, R. J., N. Sitdhiraksa, and S. Reich. 2005. Estimation of prevalence of DSM-IV and latent class defined ADHD subtypes in a population based sample of child and adolescent twins. *Twin Research and Human Genetics* 8: 392–401.

Part II

KEEPING KIDS
SAFE IN CYBERSPACE

Chapter Seven

Cyberbullying

Meanness Goes Online!

Bullying has reformatted itself to keep up with the times. In addition to the more classic bullies on the playground or in the neighborhood, harassing kids on the playing field or when they are walking home from school, bullying has become technological. Tech-savvy students are turning to cyberspace to harass their peers. Consider the following example from our Internet survey of college students and graduate students (many of whom are parents):

> When my daughter was in high school a boy was harassing her. People were using other's screen names to harass her. He said hurtful things i.e.: "she was a slut." She had dated him once and did not want to go out with him again. It was after this that the harassment started. It stopped as quickly as it started and we didn't take any action against him. I had wanted to contact the school my daughter was strongly opposed to this and since it stopped I didn't report it. (Graduate student/parent)

In a U.K. report, one in four children, some as young as eleven years old, are bullied in Britain. A Canadian study reported that 13 percent of students are bullied monthly. A U.S. study says that one in seventeen youngsters between the ages of ten and seventeen has been threatened or harassed online (Phi Delta Kappa 2007). Another respondent to our survey wrote,

> I was actually harassed via instant messenger back in early high school. It was obviously a classmate I knew (but not well) who brought up my personal life and made threats. I had to go to the police. (College sophomore)

Despite this example, where this young woman went to the police, many people do not know what to do, so they end up doing nothing, as is the case in this example:

> My boyfriend's sister (eighth grade) was harassed by her ex-boyfriend on-line. He would swear at her, degrade her, and call her every horrible name I have heard about. She didn't do anything about it because I don't think she knew what to do. (College sophomore)

There are strategies that adults can use to prevent and intervene in cases of Internet harassment, as this chapter will discuss.

ASK: WHAT IS POTENTIALLY DANGEROUS OR PROBLEMATIC FOR CHILDREN? WHAT CAN I DO (OR WHAT CAN BE DONE) TO MAKE THIS CHILD (OR THESE CHILDREN) SAFER OR HEALTHIER OR MORE SUCCESSFUL IN THIS/THESE SITUATION/S (OR SIMILAR ONES)?

Cyberbulling is defined as willful and repeated harm inflicted through the medium of electronic text (Patchin and Hinduja 2006). Traditional bullying involves threatening, pushing, fighting, and violence. Traditional bullying is associated with malicious intent, intimidation, and a power differential between aggressor and victim. Cyberbullies exist because they can use a medium that creates fear by taping a keyboard key.

One can assume that cyberbullies are malicious aggressors seeking some sort of power, control, or revenge. Somehow they are receiving pleasure in the form of watching the chaos and mental anguish that is being caused, or for some reason, they may profit from their efforts. Cyberbulling involves harmful behaviors that are repetitive in nature and can become addictive to some personality types. The power gained from destroying lives can be intoxicating.

The nature of this type of bullying entails some perceived or actual power over victims. Bullies are often cowards and manipulative as well as fearful, so what better way to intimidate or take control than to navigate the electronic world in such a way that they continue to exert power. Many have discovered that when you are physically present and you are violent, other people see your actions and you are more likely to be caught. On the

World Wide Web, you only get caught if you are not technologically aware or make a stupid mistake.

Cyberbullies harass via the Internet (e.g., in chat rooms and e-mails or on bulletin boards, websites, MySpace, and other personal Web pages) and via cellular phones mainly through text and voice messages. One thing is for sure and that is that it's very difficult to apprehend cyberbullies. They can be virtually anonymous. Many offenders develop temporary e-mail accounts, pseudonyms, and instant messaging programs and can hide in plain sight. There are many tricks.

It is interesting to note that once a bullying strategy has been discovered, there is a new way around it. Technology in all its glory and its need to be progressive makes it more difficult to catch perpetrators. Because it is harder to catch them on the Internet, bullies become emboldened because it takes less energy to type accusations and threats than it does to use one's voice.

Another key element to cyberbullying is that there are very few monitors for these chat rooms and websites. The freedom-of-expression laws have allowed people to post and say whatever they wish. Adolescents do not have the ability to self-monitor and self-regulate with any level of consistency and accuracy.

The fact that this generation is more proficient than the adults in their lives allows them to circumvent any adult or parental interventions due to the limited knowledge of those same adults. Parents are often unaware of their child's activity, whether the child is a bully or a victim. Cell phones have now become an appendage in many people's lives. This unfortunately puts all who possess a cell phone at risk of becoming a victim, never free of the potential dangers of being victimized.

The sad part is that groups of adolescents can coordinate a bullying attack with ease. Since the bullies do not have to be present, coordination can happen anywhere in the world. The results can be devastating for the victims. Attacks from all aspects of the person's life can be overwhelming and lead to self-destruction or acting-out behaviors. Bullies often send text messages involving sex, sexual orientation, or racial comments.

Boys seem to be victims of homophobic harassment, racial slurs, and threats of violence. Girls are often victims of unwelcome sexual comments and threats of sexual abuse. Here are two such examples: A girl broke up with her boyfriend only to find out that her ex had superimposed her face on a pornographic Internet picture and distributed it to the whole school. An overweight male student had his picture taken while changing in the locker room, and it was sent throughout the school as well, causing him humiliation and grief. The consequences can be very serious in that victims suffer in terms of their schoolwork and self-esteem; many drop out of school because of the attacks, and some even commit suicide.

Statistics. In a study conducted in 2005 by Justin Patchin and Sameer Hinduja, fifteen hundred Internet-using adolescents reported their experiences with cyberbullying: 80 percent reported online bullying; 32 percent males and 36 percent females reported being bullied; 40 percent were disrespected; 12 percent were threatened; 5 percent were scared for their safety; 56 percent were bullied in chat rooms; 49 percent were bullied in computer text messages; 28 percent were bullied via e-mail; and 40 percent told no one of the bullying (source www .cyberbullying.us (Patchin and Hinduja 2006).

Other studies have indicated the following: 18 percent of students in grades six to eight said they had been cyberbullied at least once in the last couple of months, and 6 percent said it had happened to them two or more times (Kowalski et al. 2005); 11 percent of students in grades six to eight said they had cyberbullied another person at least once in the last couple of months, and 2 percent said they had done it two or more times (Kowalski et al., 2005); 19 percent of regular Internet users between the ages of ten and seventeen reported being involved in online aggression, and of these, 15 percent had been aggressors, and 7 percent had been targets (3 percent were both aggressors and targets) (Ybarra and Mitchell 2004).

According to Fight Crime: Invest in Kids (Opinion Research Corporation 2006), 17 percent of six- to eleven-year-olds and 36 percent of twelve- to seventeen-year-olds reported that someone had said threatening or embarrassing things about them through e-mail, instant messages, websites, chat rooms, or text messages. Cyberbullying has increased in recent years. In nationally representative surveys of ten- to seventeen-year-olds, twice as many children and youth indicated that they had been victims and perpetrators of online harassment in 2005 compared to 1999/2000 (Wolak, Mitchell, and Finkelhor 2006).

Several indicators exist for parents and educators to know if a child is being bullied or bullying others. This list is not exhaustive and only serves as a beginning to identifying the issue.

- Victims of bullying

  - child stops using the computer
  - child appears nervous or jumpy when an instant message or e-mail appears
  - child appears uneasy about going to school or outside in general
  - child appears to be angry, depressed, or frustrated after using the computer
  - child avoids discussions about what he or she is doing on the computer
  - child becomes abnormally withdrawn from usual friends and family members
  - child withdraws from usual activities
  - child's academic performance drops
  - child is a target of traditional bullying at school
  - child appears depressed or sad (Kowalski et al. 2007; Willard 2006)

- Cyberbullies

  - child quickly switches screens or closes programs when you walk by
  - child uses computer at all hours of the night
  - child gets unusually upset if he or she cannot use the computer
  - child laughs excessively while using the computer
  - child avoids discussions about what he or she is doing on the computer
  - child uses multiple online accounts or an account that is not his or her own (Patchin and Hinduja 2006)

BRING TOGETHER ALL ADVOCATES WHO CAN ASSIST IN MAKING CHILDREN SAFER IN THESE SITUATIONS

The main protectors of bullying victims are informed adults both at home and at school. Teachers need to be advocates for putting an end to bullying of any type. Parents need to be better able to monitor their children and the use of technology. Parents must become as technologically savvy as their children. Police officers, lawyers, and judges must not treat offenders leniently. Maximum adult monitoring is an absolute necessity to prevent this phenomenon. Administrators of social-networking sites must also be vigilant in monitoring what is occurring on their websites. Telephone companies must become better at tracing calls and preventing violence perpetrated through the phone networks.

CONSIDER THE OPTIONS (PARTICULARLY ONES WITH DEMONSTRATED SUCCESS)

At times, parents may feel helpless in discovering what is wrong with their adolescent. Adolescents in general may be moody, reactive, hyper, withdrawn, and emotional. So how do parents know that their child is being bullied, and what can they do about it? The list below includes some suggestions for parents dealing with an adolescent who may be a target of electronic bullying. This list is not exhaustive but contains recommendations for starting points or interventions that may lead to the ceasing of the bullying.

- *Communicate:* Keep everyone talking about what is happening on the computer and cell phones. Internet filters do not protect against cyberbullies, but make sure that the affected student has strategies to talk about it and do some problem solving. Peer support can be key as the other youths can help with the problem-solving options and solutions. Community and parental involvement can minimize the online bullying occurring in some neighborhoods.
- *Encourage openness:* Bullies function in secrecy. They do their best work of intimidation and humiliation when no one is watching. They hope that their victim will keep quiet and isolated. Openness is one key because telling parents, teachers, and supportive adults can make the bullying stop or at least reduce the impact of the verbal harassment. Talk regularly with your child about his or her online activities. Talk specifically about cyberbullying and encourage your child to tell you immediately if he or she is the victim of cyberbullying, cyberstalking, or other illegal or troublesome online behavior. Encourage your child to tell you if he or she is aware of others who may be the victims of such behavior. Explain that cyberbullying is harmful and unacceptable behavior. Outline your expectations for responsible online behavior and make it clear that there will be consequences for inappropriate behavior.

- *Engage the bully:* This is very difficult for many youths. The function of the bully's behavior is to get attention and a reaction from the victim. Not responding to or ignoring the behavior may help to extinguish the harassment. However, one needs to be careful in this area, as some bullies will escalate their behavior till they get a response. If this occurs, then a phone call to the local police authorities may be necessary.
- *Monitor e-mail, Internet, and cell phone use.* Parents need to be aware of their child's electronic activity. They need to decide when the youth is mature enough to handle electronic devices. Adults need to monitor online chat room visits consistently, track instant messaging discussion records, and help their child to be responsible and accountable for what they say and write on these electronic tools.
- *Hold bullies responsible.* Electronic bullying is a punishable offense. When bullies are caught, the victims must press criminal charges regardless of the age of the aggressor. Cyberbullies must be held accountable for all of their actions. Schools must become more vigilant and enforce their antibullying policies.
- *Monitor the computer:* Keep your home computer(s) in easily viewable places, such as a family room or kitchen.
- *Put safety before privacy:* Although adults must respect the privacy of children and youth, concerns for your child's safety may sometimes override these privacy concerns. Tell your child that you may review his or her online communications if you think there is reason for concern.
- *Keep evidence:* Do not erase messages or pictures. Save these as evidence.
- *Identify the bully:* Try to identify the individual doing the cyberbullying. Even if the cyberbully is anonymous, if the cyberbullying is coming through e-mail or a cell phone, it may be possible to block future contact from the cyberbully.
- *Notify the school:* Contact your school if the cyberbullying is occurring through your school district's Internet system.
- *Notify the parents:* Consider contacting the cyberbully's parents if the bully is known and proceed cautiously. If you decide to contact a cyberbully's parents, communicate with them in writing—not face-to-face. Present proof of the cyberbullying (e.g., copies of an e-mail message) and ask them to make sure the cyberbullying stops.

- *Contact a lawyer:* Consider contacting an attorney in cases of serious cyberbullying. In some circumstances, civil law permits victims to sue a bully or his or her parents in order to recover damages.
- *Contact the police:* Contact the police if cyberbullying involves threats of violence, extortion, obscene or harassing phone calls or text messages, harassment, stalking, hate crimes, or child pornography, and the like. If you are uncertain if cyberbullying violates your jurisdiction's criminal laws, contact your local police, who will advise you (Kowalski 2005).
- *Save information:* What kind of information should be saved? To report cyberbullying, it is really important to save as much info as you can. The more you have saved, the easier it will be to track down the people bothering you.

  - *Save the following from e-mail:*

    - e-mail address
    - date and time received
    - copies of any relevant e-mails with full e-mail headers

  - *Save the following from groups or communities:*

    - URL of offending MSN group site
    - nickname of offending person
    - e-mail address of offending person
    - date you saw it happen

  - *Save the following from profiles you see on the Web:*

    - URL of profile
    - nickname of offending person
    - e-mail address of offending person
    - date you viewed this profile

  - *Save the following from chat rooms:*

    - date and time of chat
    - name and URL of chat room you were in
    - nickname of offending person
    - e-mail address of offending person
    - screenshot of chat room (cyberbullying.us/)

DO WHAT YOU CAN

Suggestions for educators. The place where youths spend the most time is at school. This is where cyberbulling finds its roots and develops. It is due to social conflicts at school that students become targets. The upheaval of adolescence creates little monsters who will become mean due to several factors. Educators must be aware of nuances and changes in behavior on the part of their students as both perpetrators and victims. Teachers need to be very conscious of these small changes in behavior. It is important that teachers have an excellent handle on what is going on in the classroom. Being able to pay attention and listen for clues may save many hours of anguish on the part of the victim. Responsible adults must be present to monitor and supervise consistently. Here are several recommendations for schools and educators:

- Educate your students, teachers, and other staff members about cyberbullying, its dangers, and what to do if someone is cyberbullied.
- Make sure that your school's antibullying rules and policies address cyberbullying.
- Closely monitor students' use of computers at school. Use filtering and tracking software on all computers, but don't rely solely on this software to screen out cyberbullying and other problematic online behavior.
- Investigate reports of cyberbullying immediately. If cyberbullying occurs through the school district's Internet system, you are obligated to take action. If the cyberbullying occurs off campus, consider what actions you might take to help address the bullying. When cyberbullying is either known or suspected, notify parents of both the victims and the perpetrators.
- Notify the police if the known or suspected cyberbullying involves a threat. Closely monitor the behavior of the affected students at school for possible bullying.
- Talk with all students about the harms caused by cyberbullying. Remember, cyberbullying that occurs off campus can travel like wildfire among your students and can affect how they behave and relate to each other at school.
- Investigate to see if the victim(s) of cyberbullying could use some support from a school counselor or school-based mental health professional (Kowalski et al. 2005).

- Hold classroom discussions in morning meetings about the effects of bullying.
- Do role plays and problem-solving exercises around bullying.
- Teach students to be active reporters of bullying. Help them understand that being a bystander is a crime of omission. They need to be involved in helping the victims by speaking up.

EVALUATE YOUR SUCCESS

Success can be measured by an overall reduction in threats, harassments, and violent acts against teenagers and youth. Once youths have been prosecuted and held responsible for their actions, cyberbullying will be decreased and hopefully eliminated totally. At present, due to the lack of consistent monitoring, youths will continue violating the rights of others through technology. Parents, educators, and law-enforcement officials are on the front line to effect the most change in the shortest time. We need to begin our effort toward control and accountability immediately.

FIND OUT MORE

Resources

Adina's Deck: Developed, directed, and produced by Debbie Heimowitz for her master's thesis at Stanford University, this is a thirty-minute, interactive, "choose your own adventure" television pilot series geared toward girls aged nine to fourteen. It concerns four tech-savvy characters with experiences in cyberbullying who now help their friends on the Internet.

Bewebaware.ca: This is "a national, bilingual public education program on Internet safety. The objective of everyone involved in this project is to ensure young Canadians benefit from the Internet, while being safe and responsible in their online activities."

Bully Online: This is "the world's leading website on workplace bullying and related issues which validates the experience of workplace bullying and provides confirmation, reassurance and re-empowerment."

Bullying Online: This is a website "run by a UK-based charity that provides practical advice to parents and students on all aspects of school bullying—including high-tech issues such as text message bullying, abusive websites, and happy slapping."

Connect with Kids: This is an organization focused on improving the lives of children and, along the way, helping parents to become better parents. Connect with Kids works with hundreds of communities, school districts, and schools nationwide and has produced award-winning documentaries dealing with kids' issues.

Cyberbully.org: This site is run by the Center for Safe and Responsible Internet Use and provides a number of helpful resources for educators and parents.

Cyberbullying.ca: This is a very comprehensive site created by Bill Belsey. Useful facts and prevention strategies are detailed throughout. A large list of relevant external links is also provided.

Cyberbullying—What Parents Can Do: The website http://uacoe.arizona.edu/wren/about.html (regional network), created by the West Regional Equity Network, provides helpful background information on the phenomenon, as well as links to practical resources that adults can utilize in accomplishing their goal to safeguard children and teenagers.

Documatica Legal Forms: The site www.documatica-forms.com/bullying/ offers a free, customizable "notice of harassment" kit, which can help victims record incidences of bullying (including cyberbullying) and notify their teachers or the bully's parents that the events are occurring.

Internet Safety Consulting: Rick Anderson is a twenty-five-year law-enforcement veteran who speaks to schools and organizations regarding the sexual exploitation of children and other issues related to online safety.

Internet Safety—Keeping Our Children Safer Online: This is an informative blog and resource archive created by Jace Shoemaker-Galloway, who contributes to her school, district, and region in educating youth about Internet safety issues (www.enterprisenews.com/lifestyle/columnists/x1050980586/Jace-Shoemaker-Galloway-Web-cast-to-address-online-safety).

i-Safe.org: This is "the worldwide leader in the Internet safety education. Founded in 1998 and endorsed by the U.S. Congress, i-SAFE is a non-profit foundation dedicated to protecting the online experiences of youth everywhere. i-SAFE incorporates classroom curriculum with dynamic community outreach to empower students, teachers, parents, law enforcement, and concerned adults to make the Internet a safer place."

Katiesplace.org: This is "a special program of WiredSafety.org, designed by and for young victims of Internet sexual exploitation. But Katiesplace.org is not only for victims, it is also for those who love and care about them, such as their family members, friends and loved ones. With the gentle support and guidance they find at Katiesplace.org, many victims can share what happened to them and start their healing process."

LearningPeace.com: Conflict-resolution expert Naomi Drew's professional website provides numerous resources for parents, teachers, employees, and children who desire peaceful and productive relationships with others.

MindOH!: This is "a company that creates character-based, interactive computer modules that teach students problem-solving techniques and communication skills, reinforcing universally held virtues such as respect and responsibility."

Netsmartz.org: Created by the National Center for Missing and Exploited Children (NCMEC) and the Boys and Girls Clubs of America (BGCA), this site provides an "interactive, educational safety workshop for children aged 5 to 17, parents, guardians, educators, and law enforcement that uses age-appropriate, 3-D activities to teach children how to stay safer on the Internet."

Report Bullying: The site www.jimjordan.ca/ was created by professional motivational speaker Jim Jordan, whose efforts involve examining the roots of bullying, both in the school setting and the corporate workplace. His team provides relevant programming and information through school assemblies and various other presentations.

SafetyZone.org: This is a "clearinghouse for information and material related to school safety."

Stop Bullying Now: Created by the Health Resources and Services Administration, the site www.hrsa.gov/ focuses on traditional bullying, and a wealth of information is provided in a visual format that appeals to kids.

StopCyberbullying.org: This site provides a broad overview of the phenomenon. It also provides prevention tips and proactive measures that can be taken.

References

Cyberbullying, www.cyberbullying.us.

Kowalski, R., et al. 2005. Electronic bullying among school-aged children and youth. Poster presented at the annual meeting of the American Psychological Association. Washington, DC, August 18–21.

Kowalski, R., S. Limber, and P. Agatston. 2007. *Cyberbullying: Bullying in the digital age.* Malden, MA: Blackwell Publishers.

Opinion Research Corporation. 2006. Cyberbully preteen. Fight Crime: Invest in Kids. www.fightcrime.org/cyberbullying/cyberbullyingpreteen.pdf.

Patchin, J. W., and S. Hinduja. 2006. Bullies move beyond the schoolyard: A preliminary look at cyberbullying. *Youth Violence and Juvenile Justice* 4, (2): 148–69.

Phi Delta Kappa. 2007. Electronic Bullying. Classroom Tips. www.pdkintl.org/

Willard, N. 2006. A parent' s guide to cyberbullying and cyberthreats. Center for Safe and Responsible Internet Use. www.csriu.org/cyberbully/docs/cbctparents.pdf.

Wolak, J., K. Mitchell, and D. Finkelhor. 2006. Online victimization of youth: Five years later. National Center for Missing and Exploited Children. www.missingkids.com/missingkids/servlet/ResourceServlet?LanguageCountry=en_US&PageId=2530.

Ybarra, M. L., and K. J. Mitchell. 2004. Youth engaging in online harassment: Associations with caregiver-child relationships, Internet use, and personal characteristics. *Journal of Adolescence* 27: 319–36.

Chapter Eight

Cyberspace

Online Dangers and Predators

While advances in technology have made all of our lives easier, they have also created a series of new issues and problems. The Internet was a tool developed to increase the flow of information, share resources, and simplify some of our more mundane clerical tasks. The Internet sprouted a new way for dysfunctional people to have access to children and youth who seem to be most at risk. It is this population that has become the target of online predators.

The following statistics confirm that the issue has become very problematic. Currently there are over 600,000 registered sex offenders in the United States, but an estimated 150,000 have been lost in the system (National Center for Missing and Exploited Children 2006). The predominant sex-crime scenario doesn't involve violence or strangers posing online as children; only 5 percent of offenders conceal the fact that they are adults from their victims.

Almost 80 percent of offenders are explicit about their intentions with youth. In 73 percent of crimes, youth go to meet the offender on multiple occasions for multiple sexual encounters (National Juvenile Online Survey 2007). Teens are willing to meet strangers: 16 percent of teens have considered meeting someone they've only talked to online, and 8 percent have actually met someone they only knew online (Wolak, Mitchell, and Finkelhor 2006). Of all youth Internet users, 4 percent received aggressive sexual solicitations, which threatened to spill over into real life. These solicitors asked to meet the youth in person, called them on the telephone, or sent offline mail, money, or gifts.

Also, 4 percent of youth Internet users have had distressing sexual solicitations that left them feeling upset or extremely afraid (Wolak, Mitchell, and Finkelhor 2006). Worldwide pornography revenue in 2006 was $97.06 billion. Of that, approximately $13 billion was in the United States (Internet Filter Review 2006). Of all websites, 12 percent are pornographic websites. There are 4.2 million pornographic websites, 420 million pornographic Web pages, and 68 million daily pornographic search engine requests, or 255 of total search engine requests (Internet Filter Review 2006).

Seventy-nine percent of unwanted youth exposure to pornography occurs in the home (Wolak, Mitchell, and Finkelhor 2006). The largest group of viewers of Internet porn is children between the ages of twelve and seventeen (Family Safe Media 2005). As you can surmise from the statistics just presented, we have a national crisis on our hands.

> ### ASK: WHAT IS POTENTIALLY DANGEROUS OR PROBLEMATIC FOR CHILDREN? WHAT CAN I DO (OR WHAT CAN BE DONE) TO MAKE THIS CHILD (OR THESE CHILDREN) SAFER OR HEALTHIER OR MORE SUCCESSFUL IN THIS/THESE SITUATION/S (OR SIMILAR ONES)?

Online predators lurk on the information superhighway and initiate contact via chat rooms, instant messaging, e-mail, or discussion boards. How does the predator do it? There is a common pattern of behavior. They try to gradually seduce through attention, affection, kindness, and even gifts. It is not a case of grab and run.

They often invest a large amount of time, money, and energy in their hunt for and recruitment of vulnerable prey. Part of the profile of online predators is that they are great judges of kids' issues. They are able to become very empathic and offer active listening to these vulnerable youths who may be struggling with a myriad of personal issues and emotional problems. They are able to discuss in a very calm way solutions to these many problems, and in so doing they build trust and relationships.

They lose their inhibitions once they feel the youth trust them, and at that point they start to introduce sexual content in conversations, and eventually sexually explicit material finds its way into e-mails and text messages or gets posted on discussion boards. Once they gauge the response to the material, they may continue contact, which may lead to a face-to-face meeting. If the youth is not receptive to the material, they may stalk or harass the youth or just show up in the youth's life or home community.

Young adolescents are the most vulnerable group and are most likely to be approached by predators. It is also true that this group is the most often online. Adolescents are experiencing all kinds of developmental and personality changes, and they are often looking to assert their independence by venturing out on their own. They are also more likely to take risks online. The youth who become targets are more likely to have the following characteristics:

- new to online activity
- actively seeking attention or affection
- rebellious
- isolated or lonely
- curious
- confused regarding sexual identity
- easily tricked by adults
- attracted to subcultures apart from their parent's world

It is also common to see as victims youths who are naïve and very trusting of adults once they think they know that person well.

How can you tell if your child is being targeted? There are several indicators to identify or to look for. The following are just some of the more common indicators:

- Your child spends a great deal of time online, especially in chat rooms.
- You find pornography on the family computer. Online predators often use pornography to normalize adult-child sexual relationships. Make sure that the youth does not hide files.
- The child receives phone calls from unknown people.
- The child makes long-distance calls to unknown numbers. Make sure to check out any 800 numbers and collect calls or ask the youth to whom he has given out his number.
- The child or teen gets mail, gifts, or packages from unknown people. Make sure that airline tickets have not been sent to entice the youth to visit.

- The child or teen withdraws from family and friends.
- The child or teen quickly turns off the computer monitor or changes the screen when you walk in.
- The child or teen is using someone else's online account.

One needs to be concerned about the increase of the Internet as a venue for social interaction, a place where youths can share creations, tell stories, and interact with others. The Pew Internet & American Life Project has found that 64 percent of online teens aged twelve to seventeen have participated in one or more of a wide range of content-creating activities on the Internet, up from 57 percent in a 2004 survey. Their study showed that 39 percent of online teens share their artistic creations online, such as artwork, photos, stories, or videos, up from 33 percent in 2004.

As many as 33 percent create or work on Web pages or blogs for others, including those for groups they belong to, friends, or school assignments. A full 28 percent have created their own online journal or blog, 26 percent remix content they find online into their own creations, and 27 percent have private Web pages. Girls continue to lead the charge as the teen blogosphere grows. The growth in blogs tracks with the growth in teen use of social-networking sites, but they do not completely overlap.

Online boys are avid users of video-sharing websites such as YouTube, and boys are more likely than girls to upload. Digital images, both still and video, play a big role in teen life. Posting them often starts a virtual conversation. Most teens receive some feedback on the content they post online. Most teens restrict access to their posted photos and videos at least some of the time. In the midst of the digital media mix, the landline is still a lifeline for teen social life. E-mail continues to lose its luster among teens as texting, instant messaging, and social-networking sites facilitate frequent contact with friends (Lenhart et al. 2007).

BRING TOGETHER ALL ADVOCATES WHO CAN ASSIST IN MAKING CHILDREN SAFER IN THESE SITUATIONS

The Media Awareness Network can provide valuable information about pornography, online predators, cyberbullying, violent or hateful content, safety tips, gambling, and Internet addiction. They can be found at www.bewebaware.ca.

Enough Is Enough: Making the Internet Safer for Children and Families has provided a series of age-based guidelines that can be used to help monitor your children by identifying the behaviors that can be indicators of possible involvement in an online relationship. Consult www.enough.org for more information. This organization also provides rules and tools for guidelines for Internet safety. They give very specific strategies to implement both safety rules and software tools to protect children online. These strategies focus on the positives of Internet use while teaching children about the dangers and how to make wiser choices online.

Microsoft Corporation has been in the forefront of developing tools to help parents protect their children by using some of their Internet parental control protection software. It would be wise to check out their website for e-mail filters and safety tools that you can download onto your computer.

Schools can offer curricula and protocols in their computer classes to help children protect themselves from online predators. Open discussion can be had about unsafe behaviors and ways that predators trap and connect with children. Knowledge and awareness is the first step to safety. Safety prevention can be taught as it has been successful in helping protect children from unwanted adult advances or abusive behaviors.

It is essential that the parent monitor and establish certain guidelines and establish boundaries as to what will be posted on these personal websites.

If by chance a sexual offender does enter your community, it is important that local police, school officials, and government leaders inform community members about protocols for safety.

CONSIDER THE OPTIONS (PARTICULARLY ONES WITH DEMONSTRATED SUCCESS)

When it comes to options for protecting children, several key factors must be put into place. First and most importantly, do you know what your child is doing, where your child is, and with whom? There are no better options than parental supervision and involvement in a child's life.

An important point to understand about teens is that they require a social network. The use of social media from blogging to online social networking to creation of all kinds of digital material is central to many teenagers' lives. This network is also an opening for online predators. Older teens, particularly girls, are more likely to use social-networking sites. For girls, social-networking sites are places to reinforce existing friendships, while for boys, the networks provide opportunities to flirt and make new friends.

As a parent, are you aware of what social networks your child or teen is part of? How often does he or she access it, and how often is your child involved with the people in that network? Social-networking sites can be very useful and supportive for a teen. Teens can create a profile and build a personal network that connects him or her to others. The sites www.myspace.com and www.facebook.com are prime examples of this type of social network. The explosive growth in the popularity of these sites has generated concerns among parents, school officials, and government leaders about the risks posed when personal information is made available in such public settings.

DO WHAT YOU CAN

Some recommendations. As technology continues to evolve, it is easy for parents to feel left behind. Follow these nontechnical measures to help you become a cybersavvy, virtual parent. As you educate yourself about the benefits and risks of the Internet and become more involved in your child's online behaviors, your actions and beliefs will set the tone for your child's interactions online. Helping kids differentiate between right and wrong is essential both in real life and online.

Nontechnical Measures

Parents can minimize the risk of a child's becoming a victim by doing the following:

- getting involved and talking to kids about online predators
- not allowing young children to use chat rooms

- choosing monitored chat rooms
- asking who the youth is talking to in the chat room and monitoring conversations
- instructing the youth never to go to private chats and to stay in the public chat room
- keeping the computer in common areas in the home and never in a child's bedroom
- e-mail addresses are easily accessible to parents
- instructing the youth never to respond to e-mail or texts from strangers
- making sure the child is using safe, monitored computers outside the home
- establishing rules for meeting Internet friends and making sure a parent goes along for a new meeting
- contacting the local police if your child receives any type of sexually explicit material
- checking your computer frequently for pornographic files, or any IM discussions that have sexual communication

Don't blame kids if they get caught by a predator. Go into action immediately to make sure that the predator is caught or identified to the authorities.

Tools: Technical measures. An effective method for safeguarding your child's use of the Internet is to install parental control software that helps to censor questionable content and prevent dangerous people from getting to your child online. Microsoft Vista and AOL provide free Internet packages for parental controls. These parental controls should include customizable filters, monitoring software, time-managing controls, and instant messaging and chat controls.

You can also take the following precautions:

- Set age-appropriate filters.
- Utilize monitoring software.
- Limit and monitor the amount of time that your child spends on the Internet, especially at night, and use time-limiting software tools.
- Consider disallowing access to chat rooms, unless preapproved by you.
- Limit your child's instant messaging to a parent-approved buddy list.
- Use access control if available, as this prevents the child from bypassing existing parental controls by using other Web-based access software.

- Use safe search engines.
- Check the history to see what sites your kids are visiting.
- Delete peer-to-peer file-sharing programs.
- Set up the family's Internet service accounts, set up firewalls, and maintain up-to-date antispyware and antivirus software.

Social networks. Social networks like MySpace and Facebook are used most frequently, but Xanga, Yahoo!, Piczo, Gaiaonline, and Tagged.com are also sites on which teens post profiles available to many. There are some subtle differences between MySpace and Facebook. MySpace is open to anyone and has loose age restrictions; users can create whatever type of profile they choose. Facebook users are encouraged and often required to register using their real names, effectively connecting the user with his or her offline identity. Facebook is organized around colleges and high schools and is more closed than MySpace.

Teens and parents need to be aware of several factors and ask several questions when using this type of social network:

- How often does the teen visit social-networking sites and post information?
- Does the teen limit access to his or her profile pages?
- Is this the main way that the teen is managing or developing friendships?
- If the network provides public and private communication tools, which does the teen use most frequently and with whom?
- If the teen has pictures online, he or she is more likely to be contacted online by unknown people. Limiting access to photos is essential.
- Girls are more likely than boys to have unwanted encounters online. Monitoring of both genders is essential. Gender is the primary predictor of contact that is scary or uncomfortable.
- The presence of Internet-monitoring software on the computer a teen uses at home is associated with a somewhat lower likelihood of stranger contact once other factors are controlled for. There is no similar effect for Internet filters that block certain websites.
- The sameness of gadgets in the home helps to alleviate parent naïveté about what the teens are using.
- Communication about the profile and friends network is important for parents to monitor and talk openly about what is posted.

- Parents have to become less concerned about media content than the amount of time their kids spend with media devices.
- Parents need to have media rules for both content and time.

Parents are responsible for setting boundaries with their children. It is suggested older teens be involved in the development of these guidelines and rules. Here are some possible rules or guidelines that could begin the discussion in the home:

- It is not okay to give out personal information like phone number, address, or school over the Web.
- The child is not allowed to buy things over the Internet without your supervision. Internet thieves can collect and steal the child's identity if safety procedures are not followed.
- The child may not post personal photographs on the Web without prior approval from the parent. This is easier for younger children; with older teens, negotiation must occur about what is posted.
- The child should tell you immediately if contacted online.
- The child should inform you of any material that makes him or her uncomfortable.
- There is to be no face-to-face meeting without a parent present.
- There are to be no face-to-face meetings in private settings, only in public settings and with another person present to meet the new friend from the Internet.
- The child must keep personal passwords private from strangers or friends online.
- The child must ask permission before revealing any personal information over the Web.
- The child must log in to chat rooms in invisible mode.
- The child is to discuss his or her interests and where he or she goes to find websites about those interests.
- The child is to be made aware of the various kinds of crimes that can occur online.
- Open communication of trust is to be fostered so that if anything happens, the child can come to you, the parent, immediately.

The Internet is a wonderful mode of communication if used appropriately. It is important that all who use it know the power it holds.

EVALUATE YOUR SUCCESS

How will you know that your child is safe? Unfortunately, you know this through the absence of crises or problems in your child's life. It is essential to be preventative to keep your child safe. Parental awareness is key to the safety of teen online activities. Parents' knowing what their child is doing, whom they are speaking to, whom they interact with, and whom they meet is paramount to keeping them safe. The responsibility for communicating is the parents'.

Many teens are now reporting that their parents talk to them often about Internet safety. The teens are stating that their parents are talking specifically about the potential dangers of posting personal information. The level of parental involvement is higher for younger teens and girls, although it has increased across all age groups and both genders. It is true that parents who talk to their kids about online predators have teens who are more concerned about posting personal information and are less likely to meet face to face with strangers whom they have met on the Internet.

Due to increased monitoring of computer use and where children go on the Internet, more situations have been prevented. Having become more aware of the chat lingo, parents have been able to decipher what their children are saying and thus to intervene earlier. Parents have introduced more rules around computer usage and have therefore been better able to protect children from their own curiosity.

Using education and technology, parents can help mitigate the chances of their own child being a victim. Youth are spending more time online, and that does not seem to be changing anytime soon. Parents have to become diligent in their efforts to monitor what their child or teen is doing at all times. The focus of this chapter has been on prevention as a strategy rather than on intervention after the victimization has occurred. That process will involve mental health practitioners, law and enforcement officials, and finally family resources and support networks. It is our beliefs that an ounce of prevention leads to safer kids and communities.

FIND OUT MORE

The Blog Safety: Keeping Up with Your Child's Online Social Life (http://new.vawnet.org/category/Documents.php?docid=507&category_

id=93) resource guide can be used to set limits for what goes on blogs and provides a list of possible resources.

Just the Facts about Online Youth Victimization Researchers (www .media-awareness.ca/blog/index.cfm?commentID=63) presents the facts and debunks myths.

The National Center for Missing and Exploited Children (www.missing kids.com) offers a wealth of information and guidelines to keeping your child safe.

The Online Predator website (www.onlinepredator.com) helps parents control what their children see on the Internet.

As a parent it is important that you visit and understand the content and the purpose of the following websites:

Blogger.com: Teens and children can develop a profile and post any information they want. Blogs are gateways for online predators to learn about the teen or child they are targeting. From a blog, they can learn about your child's habits, beliefs, needs, and interests. Wordpress.com is another blog site that is being used by teens and children alike.

Freeopendiary.com: This is another online diary site. This will give you an opportunity to see a list of about one hundred or more free sites your child may have access to on the Web by just typing online diary.

Livejournal.com: This is another online journal or blog site. It is important to know that predators are often looking for the isolated, alone, disturbed, young, and innocent.

Softforyou.com: This site enables you to download CyberSieve, which allows parents to monitor from remote sites. This program can help the parent know exactly what the child is doing on the Internet and where.

References

Enough Is Enough: Making the Internet Safer for Children and Families, www.enough.org (accessed February 10, 2008).

Family Safe Media. 2005. Family Safe Media in the news. Family Safe Media. www.familysafemedia.com/in_the_news.html (accessed February 5, 2008).

Internet Filter Review. 2006. http://internet-filter-review.toptenreviews.com/ internet-pornography-statistics.html (accessed February 3, 2008).

Lenhart, A., M. Madden, A. Rankin Macgill, and A. Smith. 2007. *Teens and social media: The use of social media gains a greater foothold in teen life as e-mail continues to lose its luster.* Washington DC: Pew Internet & American Life Project.

Media Awareness Network. 2007. Online predators. Be Web Aware. www.be
webaware.ca (accessed February 4, 2007).

National Juvenile Online Survey. 2007. www.unh.edu/ccrc/pdf/N-JOVmeth.pdf
(accessed February 6, 2008).

Wolak, Janis, Kimberly Mitchell, and David Finkelhor. 2006. Online victimization of youth: Five years later. National Center for Missing and Exploited Children. www.missingkids.com/missingkids/servlet/ResourceServlet?Language-
Country=en_US&PageId=2530 (accessed February 12, 2008).

Part III

KEEPING KIDS SAFE
IN ALL SPACES

Chapter Nine

Intrapersonal Violence

Suicide

This chapter investigates the dangers and factors that lead to a child's hurting him- or herself in self-destructive ways. Children seek help in a variety of ways. They are sometimes very subtle in their verbal and non-verbal communication. We need to be vigilant to recognize the signs.

ASK: WHAT IS POTENTIALLY DANGEROUS OR PROBLEMATIC FOR CHILDREN? WHAT CAN I DO (OR WHAT CAN BE DONE) TO MAKE THIS CHILD (OR THESE CHILDREN) SAFER OR HEALTHIER OR MORE SUCCESSFUL IN THIS/THESE SITUATION/S (OR SIMILAR ONES)?

Suicide in children usually can be prevented if someone realizes that the child is in danger and ensures that professional help is arranged. By adult standards, the problems of children can seem insignificant. They are not. They can be just as damaging to a child as adult problems can be to an adult. Help can mean the difference between life and death. Children with depression are at an increased risk of suicide due to multiple factors that may be present in their troubled lives. Several of the students in our survey were affected personally by suicide of friends and loved ones. Consider the following tragic examples:

> One of my classmates committed suicide when we were in 8th grade. He hung himself at the local playground with a belt. (College student)

A friend of mine who could be described as self-less, smart, funny, helpful and always happy one day did not come into work. We found out within a few hours that he had committed suicide the night before. He was a guy who had everything going for him and had a great future planned for himself but when the relationship between himself and his girlfriend fell apart he became desperate. Knowing that him and his girlfriend continually were on and off again it came to no surprise that they had once again broken up. Only this time he called her one afternoon explaining that he couldn't live without her and was thinking of committing suicide. While she thought it was a desperate attempt to get her attention she hung up the phone not realizing it was his first of many calls he would make that night reaching out to friends and family for help. He called many people explaining that he was having thoughts of suicide and was searching for people to talk him out of it but most people thought nothing of it and told him to just get some rest or do something to take his mind off his problems. After being met with no real help from anyone he wrote a letter, laid out the suit he wanted to be buried in, tied a noose and hung himself. It wasn't until after his funeral that they found he was recently prescribed anti-depressants and since he was put on the prescription his behaviors were described by people closest to him as erratic and abnormal. (College student)

When I was in 10th grade, a good friend committed suicide by hanging himself in his dorm room. His roommate found the body a few hours later. I knew he was struggling with his grades in school, but I had no idea that he was so depressed. I remember thinking that it was such a waste, to kill yourself over grades, but I also knew that he must have been dealing with issues far worse than what we all saw. For weeks afterward, the entire school seemed on the edge of a breakdown. (This was in the late 80s, and I actually wondered if our school would have a wave of suicides, like the film "Heathers." That didn't happen, but the intensity of emotions was there.) (College student)

The following indicators may be warning signs for elementary schoolchildren who may be at risk for suicide.

- Many suicidal children have difficulties in school and in their relationships with other children.
- Some feel rejected by their parents and their teachers, while others feel children are hostile toward them.

- Depression, particularly when accompanied by withdrawal and isolation, is a possible signal.
- Many have temper tantrums and become rebellious.
- Some run away from home.
- Children who are accident-prone may be at risk.
- Suicidal threats or a preoccupation with talk about being dead are common in children who end their lives.

Suicide is a leading cause of death in teenagers, with car accidents being first. There is some speculation that many car accidents are really disguised suicides. Some teenagers are prone to accidents. The suicidal teenager may take unnecessary risks, indulge in self-abusive behavior, or become self-recriminating and neglectful. Almost everyone who seriously intends to suicide leaves clues to the imminent action. The warning signs are more typical of adolescents. Suicidal threats or other statements indicating a desire to die are key indicators.

It is commonly believed that people who talk about suicide do not do it. This is not true. Before committing suicide, people often make direct statements about their intention to end their lives, or less direct statements about how they may as well be dead or that their friends and family would be better off without them. Threats of this nature, whether direct or indirect, should always be taken seriously.

The second indicator is a previous suicide attempt. Four out of five persons who commit suicide have made a least one previous attempt. Often the attempt(s) did not seem very serious. Preoccupation with final arrangements is another indicator. This may take the form of preparing a will or giving away treasured possessions.

Severe or prolonged depression may be expressed by

- sleep disturbances
- changes in eating habits
- nervousness
- anxiety
- difficulty concentrating
- a tendency to be uncommunicative
- lethargy
- crying

- a lack of emotional response
- gloom
- a decline in school grades or dropping out
- loss of interest in friends and activities
- a pervasive sense of hopelessness
- avoidance of friends (American Psychiatric Association 2000)

Depression often dulls the ability to act. As the depression lifts, the ability to act returns, and earlier suicide plans can be carried out.

Changes in personality or behavior are telling as well. When accompanied by a loss or other major change in a person's life, differences in personality and behavior are strong signals. The teenager may appear to have taken on a whole new personality. It is extremely important to remember that there is no single suicidal type. The shy person may become a thrill seeker. The outgoing person may become withdrawn, unfriendly, and disinterested.

Family structure and dysfunction play a role in a teenager's life. A disorganized home life or breakdown in the family structure will increase the likelihood of a teenager's becoming suicidal. Due to parental loss from death, divorce, or rejection, the suicidal teenager may feel lonely and isolated or that he or she is unloved or even responsible for the death or divorce. Studies of teenagers who committed suicide reveal a pattern of parents overtly striving for themselves and their children to be successful.

While this is hardly abnormal in itself, these parents tend to compensate for their own feelings of failure, inadequacy, and insecurity. They see their children as extensions of their own fantasized successes and are likely to block out other kinds of communication from their children, especially those implying failure. These children learn early that only by being a perfect projection of their parents' fantasies will they win approval.

The suicidal adolescent may come from an emotionally deprived family where there is a breakdown in communication. Teenagers often imitate the coping mechanisms employed by their parents: drugs, alcohol, frequent arguments, fights, and threats of leaving and of self-destruction. If these are the methods of dealing with stress that the parents employ, teenagers will fall into some variation of the same pattern. Facing a world of increased tension, competitiveness, pressure, and demands from parents, teachers, and peers is for some teenagers too much to cope with, and self-destructive behavior is a direct result.

A predisposing factor for suicidal feelings among many adolescents is poor self-esteem. For youth, a poor self-image contributes substantially to a lack of confidence in being able to cope with problems. Youth with poor self-esteem and poor coping skills are particularly vulnerable to suicidal feelings when confronting a problem for the first time. They do not know how to resolve it or even if they can (U.S. Department of Health and Human Services 1999).

BRING TOGETHER ALL ADVOCATES WHO CAN ASSIST IN MAKING CHILDREN SAFER IN THESE SITUATIONS

All personnel who work with teenagers and children are mandated to act when they suspect that a teen may attempt suicide. Teachers, school counselors, administrators, nurses, school psychologists, and social workers can all play a role within the school environment. Mental health practitioners in the local community are also valuable resources.

CONSIDER THE OPTIONS (PARTICULARLY ONES WITH DEMONSTRATED SUCCESS)

The following suggestions are by no means exhaustive. They are documented strategies that have been used successfully. In any type of strategy, use common sense. The specifics of the situation are paramount in the application and success of that particular intervention.

- Be observant.
- Know and recognize possible warning signs.
- Pay attention to your suspicions.
- Trust your judgment.
- Take any suicidal ideation seriously. (Belchuk, J. et al. 2005)

How you choose to intervene may vary depending on the situation, but any talk of suicide should, nonetheless, be taken seriously. It is important not to discount or rationalize (e.g., offer platitudes, ignore, and so forth), thereby missing the cry for help and possibly fostering an aggressive reaction.

DO WHAT YOU CAN

If you suspect someone may be suicidal, follow up. Inquire about less noticeable signs. Ask others about what they have noticed (if possible). Do not rationalize or discount the suspicion in your own mind. If you are unsure about what to do, at least get some direction from your principal, supervisor, colleague, or someone else who can help. Give yourself the freedom to be direct in dealing with the situation-intent.

Approach the suicidal person, and let him or her know that you are concerned. Here is a possible list of actions that you may take. This list is not exhaustive and is very much influenced by the individual situation.

- Hear what he or she is saying.
- If he or she denies that anything is wrong, point out some of the things you have been noticing.
- Try to be stable, positive, and calm. The other person is not in control so you need to be in control. It is helpful to present yourself as stable and positive in order to help bring stabilization and control to the person.
- Take the risk of being personal.
- Do not lose patience or be shocked by what the person is saying.
- Realize that others may back off from this child or adolescent.
- Do not discount, challenge, criticize, or moralize, as this may spur the adolescent to destructive activity. For some, this is their last means of trying to communicate their desperation and pain.
- In the conversation, ask the adolescent or child if he or she has thought of, or is thinking of, suicide. Be candid. Mentioning suicide will not give them the idea. In fact, your verbalization of it may be a relief to them.
- Normalize the child's or adolescent's feelings without discounting them. The child is not abnormal, alone, or crazy.
- If the child or adolescent does admit to thinking of suicide, explore his or her plan and means. The more detailed these are, the more the possibility of suicide exists.
- Ask about previous attempts and ideations.
- Do not discuss whether suicide is right or wrong. If a suicide plan is in process, try to reverse it or buy time until help arrives.

- Explore what led to these feelings of suicide. Normalize the child's or adolescent's feelings. Help establish the clarity of the problems as concretely as possible.
- Ask direct questions. Get to specific problems.
- Explore the person's own resources, assets, and strengths. How has he or she handled things in the past?
- Offer support and realistic hope. Identify other supports, such as parents, friends, family, crises lines, and so forth.
- Explore alternatives and options. This will reduce the apparent hopelessness, alienation, and aloneness and create adaptive change.
- Try to contract with the suicidal child or adolescent. Arrange to do something tangible, and meet with him or her soon after. If there is imminent danger of suicide, do not leave the child or adolescent alone.
- Call the police or drive the child or adolescent to the emergency room at your local hospital. If there is no imminent danger, write up a contract not to commit suicide. Align yourself with the child's or adolescent's desire to live.
- Clarify that you cannot be with the child or adolescent twenty-four hours a day and the person is responsible for the choices he or she makes. You can let the person know that with or without the threat of suicide, you will be there for him or her. The child or adolescent does not need to use threats of suicide to get attention. It is understood you are available to him or her.
- Do not get sworn to secrecy. If you do, break your promise. If a child or adolescent tells you that he or she is considering suicide, consult with supervisors, principals, partners, other adults and even call 911. Do not, under any circumstances, deal with this on your own. Suicidal children and adolescents have high potential for turning others away from themselves merely by what they are planning or talking about doing. They have intense feelings of anger, depression, and hopelessness. They may display various acting-out behaviors as a way of pushing you away. These children have limited communication abilities, and the threat or attempting of suicide is their last and possibly only mode of communication.
- Stay present and open to communication, and ensure the child or adolescent that you are seriously invested in helping him or her resolve the situation, that you will not abandon the child or adolescent in his or her

time of crisis. Sometimes this belief in getting help is enough to save the child or prevent him or her from acting out in a self-destructive way (Fausty 2005).

EVALUATE YOUR SUCCESS

Suicide is the ending of a young life! Society stills sees this act as one of shame and desperation. It highlights the fact that people are weak and could not make it. This attitude denigrates individuals who do not have the proper coping skills to stick it out. Parents and teachers must examine their practices of dealing with their children or students. Are you, the adult, creating so much helplessness and hopelessness that a child will want to take her life as the only solution to solving the situation that you are putting her in or inflicting upon her? The solution to preventing suicide in the young is to change the adult behaviors and teach our children and adolescents that no matter what the situation or crisis, there will always be an adult, an answer, or a way to deal with the problem. Nothing is worth ending a life for.

FIND OUT MORE

Resources

2-1-1 Big Bend, www.211bigbend.org
Psych Central Suicide Helpline, www.psychcentral.com/helpme.htm
Suicide Prevention Resources Center, www.sprc.org
Survivors of Suicide, www.survivorofsuicide.com/resources_links.shtml

Books

Alexander, Victoria. 1998. *In the wake of suicide: Stories of the people left behind.* San Francisco: Jossey-Bass.

Bolton, Iris, and Curtis Mitchell. 1983. *My son . . . my son: A guide to healing after a suicide in the family.* Roswell, GA: Bolton Press.

Cobain, Beverly, and Jean Larch. 2006. *Dying to be free: A healing guide for families after a suicide.* Center City, MN: Hazelton Foundation.

Collins, Judy. 2003. *Sanity and grace: A journey of suicide, survival and strength.* New York: Penquin.

Emswiler, Mary Ann. 2000. *Guiding your child through grief.* New York: Bantam Books.

Fine, Carla. 1997. *No time to say goodbye: Surviving the suicide of a loved one.* New York: Doubleday.

Kletter, Judy Raphael. 2001. *Trying to remember, forced to forget (my father's suicide).* Philadelphia: Xlibris Corp.

Linn-Gust, Michelle. 2001. *Do they have bad days in heaven? Surviving the suicide loss of a sibling.* Roswell, GA: Bolton Press.

Miller, Sara Swan. 2000. *An empty chair: Living in the wake of a sibling's suicide.* Bloomington, IN: Writers Club Press.

Minois, George. 1999. *History of suicide: Voluntary death in western culture.* Baltimore, MD: The Johns Hopkins University Press.

Rubel, Barbara. 1999. *But I didn't say goodbye: For parents and professionals helping child suicide survivors.* Kendall Park, NJ: Griefwork Center.

Scholz, Barb. 2002. *Our forever angel: Surviving the loss of a loved one to suicide.* Bloomington, IN: Author House.

Stimming, Mary, and Maureen Stimming. 1999. *Before their time: Adult children's experiences of parental suicide.* Philadelphia: Temple University Press.

References

American Psychiatric Association (APA). 2000. *Diagnostic and statistical manual of mental disorders.* 4th ed., text rev. Washington, DC: APA.

Belchuk, J., W. Dikel, J. Fawcett, F. K. Goodwin, K. Jamison, J. Kashtan, C. B. Nemeroff, D. Schaffer, and C. Schulz MD. 2005. Symptoms and danger signs of suicide: Suicide awareness voices of education. SAVE. www.save.org/depressed/symptoms.html (accessed December 3, 2007).

Fausty, C. 2005. *Depression and suicide in adolescents.* Bard College. http://inside.bard.edu/academic/specialproj/darling/adprob.htm (accessed December 3, 2007).

U.S. Department of Health and Human Services. 1999. Depression and suicide in children and adolescents. *Mental health: A report of the surgeon general report.* Office of the Surgeon General. www.surgeongeneral.gov/library/mental-health/chapter3/sec5.html (accessed December 3, 2007).

Chapter Ten

Intrapersonal Violence

Self-Mutilation

So what would possess a child to hurt him- or herself? What factors come into play to influence children to seek methods to hurt their bodies? Stereotypic self-mutilation involves repetitive, sometimes rhythmic acts, the most common form being head banging. Other forms include orifice digging, hitting, throat and eye gouging (though usually not eye enucleation, which is considered major self-mutilation), hair pulling, and self-biting. Stereotypic self-mutilation can sometimes result in tooth extraction or joint dislocation (Alexander 2002). Consider the following example from our survey of college and graduate students:

I struggled with the demons of self-injury throughout most of high school and the beginning years of college. I felt an enormous amount of pressure to be the bubbly, optimistic girl that everyone saw me to be, and on top of that pressure, I never felt happy. I never felt thin enough, pretty enough, smart enough, funny enough, and I had constant anxiety. On top of all of that, I was brought up to believe that crying was a form of weakness, and I would refuse to let myself do it. Cutting was my escape from my negative world. It was as if by physically opening up part of my body, I was letting all of the pressures and negative feelings flow out of me. (College sophomore)

> ASK: WHAT IS POTENTIALLY DANGEROUS OR
> PROBLEMATIC FOR CHILDREN? WHAT CAN I
> DO (OR WHAT CAN BE DONE) TO MAKE THIS
> CHILD (OR THESE CHILDREN) SAFER OR
> HEALTHIER OR MORE SUCCESSFUL IN
> THIS/THESE SITUATION/S (OR SIMILAR ONES)?

Major self-mutilation refers to acts that severely damage a significant amount of body tissue. These are usually injuries that can only be inflicted once, such as eye enucleation, facial skinning, and amputation of the limbs, breasts, or genitals. Major self-mutilation is usually inflicted upon the self when in a hallucinatory or zombielike state (Favazza 1998).

There are several explanations for this type of behavior. Some scientists believe that it is biological, social, psychological, or cultural.

Biological

The child will self-mutilate because

- the neurotransmitter dopamine influences the behavior.
- the pain of self-mutilation produces endorphins that reduce dysphoria; thus, people harm themselves to feel better.
- people hurt themselves for sensory stimulation (Favazza 1993).

Social

There is evidence that self-mutilation is influenced by social settings. Oftentimes, groups will self-mutilate as a way of dealing with emotional behaviors or to get out of certain responsibilities, and individuals are often influenced by peers and social group.

Psychological

There are several psychological and behavioral explanations:

- It is a purposeful act.
- It is an attempt to differentiate between ego boundaries (id, ego, superego).

- It reflects rage against self.
- It is a mechanism for dealing with sexual conflict.
- It is maintained by positive social reinforcement.
- It is an avoidance of more aversive stimuli (Alexander 2002).

Cultural Considerations

Sanctioned mutilative practices are often associated with healing, spirituality, or social status. Many culturally sanctioned, mutilative rituals are associated with establishing group identity, control over sexuality, or rites of passage (Alexander 2002).

For most self-injurers, the process of self-mutilation is a way of releasing stress, tension, and bad feelings. Self-harm can be used to take away a feeling of numbness, to express feelings that cannot be expressed otherwise, or as a form of punishment. Sometimes self-injury is used to make psychic pain more tangible.

According to some reports, self-injury has taken on the epidemic-like status of anorexia and bulimia. Studies show that approximately one out of every two hundred girls between the ages of thirteen and nineteen practices self-mutilation regularly. Girls tend to be more prone to self-injurious behaviors, but an estimated eleven thousand American boys are also affected each year. While only 1 percent of the general American population uses self-injurious practices to cope with extreme emotions, that number increases drastically among adolescents and females.

Nearly 50 percent of self-injurers have been sexually or physically abused at some point. A large portion of self-mutilating women have also struggled with eating disorders—anorexia, bulimia, or both. Most self-injurers do not harm themselves with the intention of committing suicide. Conversely, they see self-mutilation as a way of keeping themselves alive. Self-harm, for those who do it, is often a method of coping with emotional stress.

Though self-injury is characterized as an attention-seeking behavior, this is a falsehood. Most self-injurers take great pains to hide their scars and rarely seek medical attention. People who self-injure often avoid situations in which they are expected to wear revealing clothing (e.g., pool parties), and they may have frequent stories about accidentally hurting themselves (see www.gurl.com, 2007).

A common form of self-injury involves making cuts in the skin, with the arms, legs, abdomen, and inner thigh being the most frequent locations for self-injurious behaviors. This is referred to as "cutting," and the person doing it is the "cutter." How and when the cutter cuts is only limited by an individual's creativity. The locations are easily hidden and concealed from the detection of others.

Examples of self-injury other than cutting may include

- punching, hitting, and scratching
- choking or constricting of the airway
- self-biting of hands, limbs, tongue, lips, or arms
- picking at or reopening wounds
- hair pulling
- burning, including cigarette burns, self-incendiarism, eraser burns, and chemical burns (salt and ice)
- stabbing with wire, pins, needles, nails, staples, pens, and hair accessories
- pinching or clamping, as with clothes pins or paper clips
- ingesting corrosive chemicals, batteries, pins, or other nonfood items
- self-poisoning, overdosing on medication or alcohol without suicidal intent
- head banging or punching hard surfaces. (Wikipedia 2007)

A number of college students (and graduate students working as teachers) in our survey had experienced self-injurious behavior either first- or second-hand such as in these scenarios:

I was working in a group home with disturbed adolescents, a few of them would burn their wrists with curling irons. (Middle school teacher)

In middle school several of my friends cut themselves. I never really understood why they did. By the time 10th grade came they stopped or at least got better at hiding it. (College student)

A friend was taking anti-depressants but they were not helping her. She felt that she needed help and talked often that her medication was no longer working. It wasn't until she was removed from her daily routine and friends that she felt herself becoming isolated and further tapped into a world of depression. She described herself as having out of body experiences and doing anything to reconnect herself to reality including cutting herself. She explained that she wouldn't remember how she got the knife or what put the idea in her head to cut herself but suddenly realizing that she was performing the act of cutting and thinking to herself it wasn't right and she had to stop herself but she couldn't. She felt as though she had no control over her body's actions and this was the only way to have control. (College student)

BRING TOGETHER ALL ADVOCATES WHO CAN ASSIST IN MAKING CHILDREN SAFER IN THESE SITUATIONS

The advocates for these children are very intuitive and aware parents who monitor their children consistently and regularly. School personnel need to be on the lookout for some of the behavioral changes; however, many of these self-destructive behaviors do not usually occur in the school setting. Teachers may be the first people to receive messages about such behavior and must respond as soon and as carefully as possible. Consider the following example from an English teacher whose student let her know in an essay about her behavior:

I am a teacher, and one of my high school students cut her arms and admitted it to me in a class assignment.

CONSIDER THE OPTIONS (PARTICULARLY ONES WITH DEMONSTRATED SUCCESS)

The only intervention techniques with some success are mental health treatment followed by intensive follow-up and monitoring of self-destructive behaviors. For some of these children and youth, a medication regimen is imposed as a way of controlling the self-destructive thoughts. Cognitive behavioral therapy has had some success in long-term therapy or in a residential program. Persons who mutilate themselves should seek treatment from a therapist with some specialized training and experience with this behavior. Most self-mutilators are treated as outpatients, although there are some inpatient programs, such as SAFE, for adolescent females. A number of different treatment approaches are used with self-mutilators, including psychodynamic psychotherapy, group therapy, journaling, and behavioral therapy. Although there are no medications specifically for self-mutilation, antidepressants are often given, particularly if the patient meets the diagnostic criteria for a depressive disorder.

DO WHAT YOU CAN

As a parent, teacher, or other caregiver, you can support your child in an emotional and nurturing way. You can provide him or her with an outlet to verbalize fears, anxieties, and concerns. It is essential that the lines of communication be open at all times. It is imperative that the child or teen have an extensive network of support so that when the need or desire to self-mutilate arises, the individual can make a better choice than hurting him- or herself.

EVALUATE YOUR SUCCESS

You will only know that you have been successful through the absence of the self-destructive behavior. It is essential that mental health workers, parents, and the individual self-mutilating create an open and honest relationship that is based on communication and problem solving. The mental health worker will need to make sure that the individual in therapy is receiving and using the skills necessary to be a functional and happy individual within the context of day-to-day life.

FIND OUT MORE

Books

American Psychiatric Association (APA). *Diagnostic and statistical manual of mental disorders*, 4th ed., text rev. Washington, DC: APA, 1994.

Eisendrath, Stuart J., and Jonathan E. Lichtmacher. "Psychiatric Disorders." In *Current medical diagnosis & treatment 2001*, edited by L. M. Tierney Jr. MD et al. 40th ed. New York: Lange Medical Books/McGraw-Hill, 2001.

Pipher, Mary. *Reviving Ophelia: Saving the selves of adolescent girls*. New York: Ballantine Books, 1994.

Organizations

American Psychiatric Association
1400 K St. NW
Washington, DC 20005
Phone: (202) 682-6220
Website: www.psych.org

Focus Adolescent Services
Phone: (877) 362-8727
Website: www.focusas.com

National Institute of Mental Health
5600 Fishers Ln.
Rockville, MD 20857
Phone: (301) 443-4513
Fax: (301) 443-4513
Website: www.nimh.nih.gov

References

Alexander, V., V. Timofeyev, Katie Sharff, Nora Burns, and Rachal Outterson. Self-mutilitation. Retrieved October 22, 2008 from http://wso.williams.edu/atimofey/self_mutilitation.

Favazza, A. R. 1998. The coming of age of self-mutilitation. *Journal of Nervous and Mental Disease* 186, (5): 259–68.

———. 1996. *Bodies undersiege.* 2nd ed. Baltimore, MD: Johns Hopkins University Press.

Favazza, A. R., and R. J. Rosenthal. 1993. Diagnostic issues in self-mutilitation. *Hospital and Community Psychiatry* 44, (2): 134–40.

Favazza, A. R., and K. Conterio. 1988. The plight of chronic self-mutilators. *Community Mental Health Journal* 24: 22–30.

Favazza, A. R., L. De Rosear, and K. Conterio. 1989. Self-mutilation and eating disorders. *Suicide and Life-Threatening Behavior* 19, (4): 352–61.

Lieberman, R., and J. Davis. 2002. Suicide intervention. In *Best practices in school crisis prevention and intervention*, ed. S. E. Brock, P. J. Lazarus, and S. R. Jimerson. Bethesda, MD: National Association of School Psychologists.

Lukomski, J., and T. Folmer. Self-mutilation: Information and guidance for school personnel. In *Helping children at home and school II: Handouts for families and educators*, ed. A. Canter, L. Paige, M. Roth, I. Romero, and S. A. Carroll. Bethesda, MD: National Association of School Psychologists.

Suyemoto, K., and **X.** Kountz. 2000. Self-mutilation. *Prevention Researcher 7*, (4): 1–2.

U.S. Department of Health and Human Services (HHS). 2001. *National strategy for suicide prevention: Goals and objectives for action.* Rockville, MD: HHS.

Wikipedia. 2007. Self-injury. http://en.wikipedia.org/wiki/Self_mutilation (accessed December 3, 2007).

Chapter Eleven

Intrapersonal Violence

Choking

Choking is a thrill game kids usually play in secret, and the Internet has driven much of the current interest in the near-death experience. There is a game that is common knowledge to many of our youth—it is known as the "pass-out game," the "fainting game," the "tingling game," or the "something dreaming game," among other names.

Some medical experts estimate more than a dozen children have died nationwide in the past ten months while seeking the "high" that accompanies the loss of consciousness, though others put the number of fatalities much higher. Choking thrills are as old as civilization and perhaps most strikingly used in autoerotic asphyxiation. Sometimes belts or ropes are used to induce unconsciousness by pinching off the blood flow to the brain with pressure on the carotid arteries, which are on each side of the neck. Children get an out-of-body experience, but it just takes one mishap, and the child is dead.

> ASK: WHAT IS POTENTIALLY DANGEROUS OR
> PROBLEMATIC FOR CHILDREN? WHAT CAN I
> DO (OR WHAT CAN BE DONE) TO MAKE THIS
> CHILD (OR THESE CHILDREN) SAFER OR
> HEALTHIER OR MORE SUCCESSFUL IN
> THIS/THESE SITUATION/S (OR SIMILAR ONES)?

Signals to parents that their children may be engaging in the choking game include hoarseness, sore throat, marks around the throat, neck soreness, bloodshot eyes, and small red spots on the face (McConnell 2005). Unfortunately, this is a danger that cannot be dealt with effectively till it comes to light through an attempt. The best strategy to date is to talk openly with the child about the hazards of using choking as a game. Many children do not have the capacity to understand the long-lasting effects of using this thrill-seeking activity. Death is a concept that some children cannot fully fathom.

BRING TOGETHER ALL ADVOCATES WHO CAN ASSIST IN MAKING CHILDREN SAFER IN THESE SITUATIONS

The best advocates are parents and school personnel who can teach about the dangers of this type of activity. It can be spoken about in school guidance programs. Children can be made aware of the dangers and how to protect themselves and their friends.

CONSIDER THE OPTIONS (PARTICULARLY ONES WITH DEMONSTRATED SUCCESS)

Strategies for self-harm behaviors. The first area when working with children and youths with self-harm behaviors is to teach them emotion regulation. Individuals with self-harm and suicidal behaviors are frequently emotionally intense. They can be angry, intensely frustrated, depressed, or anxious. This suggests that these youths might benefit from help in learning to regulate their emotions. Dialectical behavioral therapy skills for emotion regulation include:

- *identifying and labeling emotions.* The child learns to use his or her words to identify emotions.
- *identifying obstacles to changing emotions.* The child recognizes challenges and can brainstorm ways to make changes.
- *reducing emotional vulnerability.* This helps the child to understand what makes her or him vulnerable and how that influences emotions.
- *increasing positive emotional events.* This focuses the child to look for more opportunities to find events that will continue to build self-confidence and self-esteem.

- *increasing mindfulness to current emotions.* This entails helping the child to have an accurate barometer of the scale and range of emotions.
- *taking opposite actions.* Instead of giving in to dysfunctional thinking, the child takes the opposite viewpoint, perspective, or action from the one he or she would normally take.
- *applying distress-tolerance techniques.* The child uses a variety of techniques to self-calm, self-monitor, problem solve, mediate, and become more able to apply stress-management techniques (Stone 1987).

DO WHAT YOU CAN

A second program that has demonstrated success with these children is cognitive behavioral therapy. This therapy is done within a counseling relationship and addresses the cognitive distortions that the child has and teaches the individual how to question his or her beliefs with evidence. This program is directed by a licensed professional. Many of the strategies highlighted for depression will also work with this group. Please see the depression section in this book.

EVALUATE YOUR SUCCESS

Success will be evidenced when there are very few children and youths experimenting with this activity. The lack of statistics and death will be proof that education has prevented this type of behavior.

FIND OUT MORE

Resources and References

Favazza, A. R. 1998. The coming of age of self-mutilation. *Journal of Nervous and Mental Disease* 186, (5): 259–68.

Favazza, A. R., and R. J. Rosenthal. 1993. Diagnostic issues in self-mutilation. *Hospital and Community Psychiatry* 44, (2): 134–40.

McConnell, M. 2005. Parents warned of dangerous choking game. *Daily Tribune*, November 11, 2005. http://staging.dailytribune.com/archives/index.shtml.

Stone, M. H. 1987. The course of borderline personality disorder. In *American psychiatric press review of psychiatry*, ed. A. Tasman, R. E. Hales, and A. J. Frances. Washington, DC: American Psychiatric Press, 8, 103–22.

Timofeyev, Alexander V., Katie Sharff, Nora Burns, and Rachel Outterson. 2002. Self-mutilation. Williams Students Online. http://wso.williams.edu/~atimofey/self_mutilation/Motivation/index.html (accessed December 3, 2007).

Wikipedia. 2007. Self-injury. Wikipedia. http://wikipedia.org/wiki/Self_harm (accessed December 3, 2007).

Articles

Colthup, Neil. Prison initiative reduces juvenile custody numbers. *Community Care* 1115 (April 11–17, 1996): 14. This is a letter from the delinquency-management coordinator for Humberside SSD regarding methods adopted to prevent self-harm in juvenile remand centers.

Downey, Rachel. Young and alone. *Community Care* 1111 (March 14–20, 1996): 23. The author goes behind the walls of Hull Prison to assess a radical new method of preventing self-harm and suicide among juveniles on remand.

Francis, Joy. Hurting only myself. *Community Care* 1053 (February 2–8, 1995): 10. Disturbing evidence suggests that practitioners are not equipped to meet the growing challenge of adolescent self-harm. Report on a Hackney initiative to address the needs in this small and underresearched area is needed to enhance the information on this topic.

Harrison, Diane. Scarred by pain. *Community Care* 1135 (August 29–September 4, 1996): 17. A young woman inflicts pain on herself because she feels it is the only part of her life over which she has any control. For that young woman and others like her, self-harm is a way of expressing the unspeakable.

Hartman, David. Cutting among young people in adolescent units. *Therapeutic Communities* 17, no. 1 (spring 1996): 5–17. This article discusses deliberate nonsuicidal cutting by adolescents in psychiatric units. *Professional Social Work* 2 (September 1996). A study of admissions at the Warneford Hospital in Oxford has found that teenage girls are more likely to inflict harm on themselves than boys and that self-harm is rare under the age of twelve.

Thompson, Audrey, and Humerah Miah. Wounds that never heal. *Community Care* (1999): 18–20. Most of us recoil from the idea of self-harm and those who inflict it on themselves. Unfortunately, many health and care professionals have the same reaction. This report describes how it feels to be so desperate that you harm yourself.

Wrate, R. M. Suicidal tendencies. *Scottish Child* (November/December 1995): 8–11. This article analyzes the reasons behind the increase in suicide and attempted suicide among children and adolescents. Teenage girls are more likely to harm themselves.

Books

Hanh, Thich Nhat. 1987. *The miracle of mindfulness*. Boston: Beacon Press.
Linehan, Marsha M. 1993. *Skills training manual for treating borderline personality disorder*. New York: Guilford Press.
——. 1993. *Cognitive behavioral treatment of borderline personality disorder*. New York: Guilford Press.
Yudovsky, Stuart C. 2005. *Fatal flaws: An introduction to disorder of personality and character*. Arlington, VA: American Psychiatric Press.

Internet

A number of helpful resources are listed at these websites:

Self-injury Abuse Trauma Directory, www.self-injury-abuse-trauma-directory.info.
Self-injury and Related Issues, www.siari.co.uk.
Teen suicide: "We Have to Talk about This," The International Child and Youth Care Network, www.cyc-net.org/features/ft-suicide2.html.

People

A well-known practitioner in the field is Tracy Alderman, PhD (licensed clinical psychologist), author of *The Scarred Soul: Understanding and Ending Self-inflicted Violence*, a very wise and useful self-help book for people who self-harm.

San Diego, CA 92102
Phone: (619) 855-3293
E-mail: DrTracyA@aol.com.

Newsletters

Cutting Edge
PO Box 20819
Cleveland, OH 44120
A self-injury newsletter

SHOUT (Self-harm Overcome by Understanding and Tolerance)
PO Box 654
Bristol BS99 1XH
United Kingdom

A bimonthly newsletter that aims to break down isolation and provide support. It includes articles, pen pals/contacts, letters, poems, cartoons, and book reviews, plus details about help lines, groups, and resources. The mailing list is confidential, and copies will be sent in a plain envelope. To subscribe, contact SHOUT at the above address.

Internet Support

Samaritans e-mail: jo@samaritans.org
Anonymous e-mail: samaritans@anon.twwells.com

The Samaritans are a nonreligious charity that has been offering emotional support to the suicidal and despairing for over forty years through phone calls, visits, and letters. Callers are guaranteed absolute confidentiality and retain the right to make their own decisions, including the decision to end their lives. The service is now available via e-mail, run from Cheltenham, England, and can be reached from anywhere with Internet access. Trained volunteers read and reply to mail once a day, every day of the year.

Organizations

SAFE Alternatives
7115 W. North Ave., Ste. 319
Oak Park, IL 60302
24-hour information line: (800) DONT CUT or (708) 783-0167.

New book: *Bodily Harm: The Breakthrough Healing Program for Self-injurers*
SAFE in Canada
306-241 Simcoe St.
London, Ontario N6B 3L4
Canada

This organization provides therapy and support for self-injurers in Canada, teen programs, professional education, workshops (including one for family and friends), and literature. It follows a cognitive-behavioral community-based model.

Chapter Twelve

Interpersonal Violence

Bullying

Bullying is defined as the act of intentionally causing harm to others through verbal harassment, physical assault, or other, more subtle methods of coercion, such as manipulation. Bullying is an act of repeated, aggressive behavior in order to intentionally hurt another person. Bullying is about power. Bullying can take many forms, such as name calling, verbal or written abuse, exclusion from activities and social situations, physical abuse, and coercion.

Bullying has made its way into the newspaper headlines; therefore, school officials need to address the problem. For years students have been bullied in silence. The victims were quiet due to intense fear of repercussions, while the bully was able to continue with very few consequences. In fact, it is the victim's silence that has fostered the bully's belief that his or her behavior is acceptable and one just needs to live with it.

ASK: WHAT IS POTENTIALLY DANGEROUS OR PROBLEMATIC FOR CHILDREN? WHAT CAN I DO (OR WHAT CAN BE DONE) TO MAKE THIS CHILD (OR THESE CHILDREN) SAFER OR HEALTHIER OR MORE SUCCESSFUL IN THIS/THESE SITUATION/S (OR SIMILAR ONES)?

Major findings presented in the research on bullying behavior include the following:

- American schools harbor approximately 2.1 million bullies and 2.7 million victims.

- It is estimated that nearly 160,000 students miss school each day due to fear of attack or intimidation.
- Bullied students are apt to tell a family member or friend about the abuse but rarely a teacher or an administrator.
- Young bullies carry a one-in-four chance of having a criminal record by the age of thirty.
- Bullying can be reduced as much as 50 percent with the implementation of an effective bullying-prevention program.
- Effective bullying-prevention programs include a needs assessment, student, staff, and community components, as well as an effective communications plan.
- Antibullying interventions are unlikely to work unless they are part of a comprehensive school-based or school-district-based program.
- Consistent use of consequences is a necessary component of effective prevention.
- Ongoing education is most effective after a system of consequences is firmly in place. A program should be aimed at the silent student majority (the 85 percent who are neither victims nor bullies).
- Structured counseling and education for bullies that stresses acknowledging actions and restitution is likely to be effective if it follows negative consequences for bullying behavior (Center for Professional Development 2007).

Bullying occurs when a person willfully subjects another person (the victim), whoever he or she may be, to an intentional, unwanted, and unprovoked, hurtful verbal and/or physical action that results in the victim's feeling oppressed (stress, injury, discomfort) or threatened at any school site, on any school bus, or at any school-board-sponsored activity or event. Bullying is a form of aggression.

Examples or types of bullying may include, but are not limited to,

- *physical bullying*, which includes punching, shoving, poking, strangling, hair pulling, beating, biting, excessive tickling, tripping, and pinching
- *verbal bullying*, which includes such acts as hurtful name calling, racial slurs, threats, taunts, insults, teasing, and gossip
- *emotional (psychological) bullying*, which includes rejecting, terrorizing, extorting, defaming, humiliating, blackmailing, rate/ranking of per-

sonal characteristics (such as race, disability, ethnicity, or perceived sexual orientation), manipulating friendships, isolating, ostracizing, and applying peer pressure
- *sexual bullying*, which includes many of the actions listed above as well as exhibitionism, voyeurism, sexual propositioning, sexual harassment, and abuse involving actual physical contact and sexual assault (in many cases, gender and cross-gender sexual harassment may also qualify as bullying)
- *cyberbullying*, which includes tormenting, threatening, taunting, ranking, degrading a target, harassing, humiliating, or otherwise targeting a student or staff member using the Internet, interactive and digital technologies, or mobile phones or inviting others to join in these acts (given the growth of this specific type of bullying, we address it in a section of this book on cyberbullying)

There are three essential components to any bullying situation. There must be a bully, a victim, and a location in which the bullying occurs. The fourth component is bystanders, who can play a role by encouraging the bully or protecting the victim. Bullying can be indirect or direct. Direct bullying is usually in your face, and the victim is physically harmed in some way.

In indirect bullying, the victim is attacked through gossip, rumors, writing, and instant messages, and his or her reputation is tarnished in some way. Regarding gender, boys are more likely to engage in direct bullying and girls in indirect bullying. The bully usually will possess levels of self-esteem that are as positive as their nonbully peers. Some bullies do not have empathy as part of their repertoire of skills and may actually enjoy hurting others.

There is no single descriptive profile of a child who is at risk for being bullied. Children who are socially isolated are easier targets because they lack a social network of friends to protect them. There are two subgroups of bully victims: the passive victims and the provocative victims. Passive victims are weaker physically, avoid confrontations, and are generally more anxious. Provocative victims are anxious and aggressive. They are more confrontational and tend to irritate or alienate their classmates. These children often explode quickly and are easy targets. Bullying is a covert activity, and adults rarely see it happening. Bullying is usually a hidden problem. Single teachers alone in a classroom are rarely able to pick up on the bullying occurring within that environment.

Locations are essential to the action of bullying. Bullies are opportunistic, preying on weaker students when there is no adult supervision. The far corner of a classroom, a deserted hallway, the bathrooms, or any area that is poorly supervised makes for a great zone for bullying behaviors.

Bystanders, those who observe the bullying, are more likely to encourage the bully than to attempt to help the victim. They do not remain neutral. They will often applaud the bully or be thankful that it is not them being bullied. This behavior is common in our society; the good Samaritan is no longer the right thing to be in American society. It is easier and safer to walk away. This is sad, but it is a twenty-first century reality!

BRING TOGETHER ALL ADVOCATES WHO CAN ASSIST IN MAKING CHILDREN SAFER IN THESE SITUATIONS

The advocates are teachers, administrators, parents, and other school personnel. Law-enforcement officials can also be used to control and prevent bullying. These adult caregivers must respond to all levels of bullying, paying attention even to lower, less dangerous forms of bullying to prevent the more aggressive and dangerous kinds. If adult caregivers fail to respond, they send the message that adults will no longer protect children in these situations. Teachers, parents, and other school and community personnel need to send consistent messages that renounce bullying.

CONSIDER THE OPTIONS (PARTICULARLY ONES WITH DEMONSTRATED SUCCESS)

- Adopt policies that address bullying behavior focused on assisting students to increase self-control and take positive responsibility for their actions.
- Build a school climate that instills trust and support by demonstrating respect for all.

- Conduct an annual survey to assist school staff, students, and parents in identifying and informing them about antibullying strategies to be implemented at the school site.
- Discuss the problem of bullying openly with students and gather their input on the seriousness of the problem and possible solutions.
- Provide staff training on how to identify and respond to bullying behavior.
- Increase staff supervision in areas where bullying behavior is likely to occur.
- Organize a bank of resources that can assist with bullying problems and offer practical solutions. Identify national and local experts who can speak on the topic in a compelling way.
- Recognize, celebrate, and acknowledge students and other groups who are making a positive difference in the school in reducing bullying behavior.
- Find out if there is a staff education system in place to assist in the identification of bullying behavior and a monitoring system to make sure that consequences and education are effective.
- Find out if there is a system in place to ensure that students know how to identify and respond to bullying behavior.
- Find out if parent and community organizations support school efforts to reduce bullying behavior.
- Compile a menu of appropriate consequences for bullying behaviors.
- Establish a policy for contacting parents of children who engage in bullying.
- Monitor the school's prevention efforts on an ongoing basis.

Teachers must also do the following:

- assess the extent of the bullying problem in their classroom
- ensure that the class understands what bullying is and why it is wrong
- confront any student engaged in bullying in a firm but fair manner
- provide appropriate and consistent consequences for bullying
- drop by unexpectedly to observe their classes in less structure environments
- watch for patterns of bullying among individuals or groups of students

- be on the lookout for prolonged teasing, name calling, or any verbal harassment
- interact with other school staff to communicate concerns about either the victims or the bullies
- define and have a common understanding with their students about what bullying entails
- address the problem of bullying immediately. This should be done in private—rarely should this be done publicly—in a brief and businesslike manner

Teachers can also do the following:

- hold class meetings and come up with appropriate rules and expectations
- find mentors for bullies that may help in changing behaviors and address some of the core issues around the reasons a child maybe bullying
- develop a reward chart to shape the bully's behavior in a more positive direction

Strategies to help the victim. Children who are bullied are often unhappy in school, suffer from low self-esteem, and are isolated from their peers. They are often rejected socially, which in turn affects their sense of self and academic performance. Victims can be helped if a school has a bully-prevention program schoolwide.

The following are some suggestions to help the victims of bullying:

- Take steps to ensure the victim's safety.
- Have the child fill out an anonymous questionnaire that asks where and when the bullying has occurred and who perpetrated it.
- Increase supervision in areas known for attacks.
- Create a safe room staffed with adults (study hall, counselor's office, resource room).
- Examine the victim's daily schedule; look for blind spots and unsupervised places and times the child may be alone.
- Help the child have at least one friend with him or her at all times.
- Help build the social standing of the child within the class group, school group, and community.

- Train socially inept children in basic social skills.
- Train the child how to ask to be included in games or social situations.
- Pair students for random interactive learning and leisure activities.
- Change the seating chart in a classroom periodically to foster friendships.
- Make sure the child is involved in class free-time activities.
- Have a mentor for the child so the child can speak openly to that person.
- Teach assertiveness skills.
- Teach the child to maintain his composure, stand firm, and continue to behave appropriately even when provoked.
- Teach the child to respond to taunts and teasing with bland responses.
- Teach the child to leave the situation if he or she is starting to get angry or fearful.
- Teach the child how to say no loudly.
- Teach the child how to posture assertiveness and confidence through role plays.
- Teach the child how to deal with peer pressure.
- Teach the child to report incidences immediately to an adult.

DO WHAT YOU CAN

Locations: Strategies for transforming schools into safe havens. Bullying takes place in a variety of environments. The bully must have a setting or location that is adult free so that he can exploit or intimidate his victim. Bullying occurs in deserted or unsupervised areas.

The following is a list of recommended strategies to prevent bullying in some locations:

- Teachers are a physical presence in the school.
- The school has uncovered the hot spots in the school and community where the bullying is occurring regularly.
- Teachers go on a school tour with their students. Students identify safe and unsafe areas.
- Students identify times of day these areas are safe and unsafe.
- Students are given community maps of the surrounding neighborhoods and asked to identify unsafe and safe places.

- The above information is shared with a local police or resource officer.
- Adult supervision in stairwells and hallways and on playgrounds is increased.
- Student peer monitors walk in these areas regularly.
- Adults learn student names so that there can be a personal connection.
- Older and younger students are separated when they are in less supervised areas.
- Noninstructional staff are trained to intervene when they see bullying behaviors.
- The natural surveillance of areas in the school is increased.
- Classroom layouts are changed or seating is rearranged to eliminate blind spots.
- Teachers circulate frequently.
- Antibullying posters are put up in the hallways and stairways.
- Personal spaces are created for students.

Action steps for children. Classroom discussions may help students develop a variety of appropriate actions that they can take when they encounter bullying. Students should be encouraged to

- seek immediate help from adults
- report bullying or victimization to school personnel
- speak up and/or support the victim when they see him or her being bullied
- privately support those being hurt with words of kindness
- express disapproval of bullying behavior by not joining in the laughter, teasing, or spreading of rumors and gossip
- attempt to defuse problem situations either single-handedly or in a group

Action steps for parents. When children are involved in bullying situations, it is crucial that the parents take notice and become aware of what is happening. It is important that parents have open lines of communication with their children. Children must be able to approach their parents with their concerns so that parents can then address appropriately the bullying behaviors experienced by their child at school. Parents should do the following:

- Make sure the child does not believe that he or she is to blame for the bullying and understands that the bully's behavior is the source of the problem.

- Call the school. Work collaboratively with the school personnel.
- Keep records of incidents so that you can be specific in your discussions with the school personnel.
- Arrange meetings with the school counselor, principal, or class teacher. Are they aware of the issues? Do they have first-hand knowledge of the situation?
- Do not speak directly to the bullying child.
- If speaking with the parents of the bully, be careful of the approach; this may turn violent as many parents of bullies are bullies themselves.
- Do not encourage your child to become aggressive and strike back.
- Teach your child to be assertive; use humor if appropriate.
- Be patient; conflict between children is rarely solved overnight.
- Spend time with your child to process the emotions and situations.
- Help your child develop new interests or strengthen existing talents and skills that help develop and improve self-esteem.
- If the problem persists or worsens, consult an attorney, contact local police, and press charges.

EVALUATE YOUR SUCCESS

Putting it all together. We are all hoping for a school and world without bullying. It is a dream that can become a reality, whether it is on a school playground or in the world of politics. Bullying is everyone's problem. Bullies at school become bullies in the work place, in their relationships, and in the community.

The cycle continues through the generations unless we take a stand and start teaching young children and adolescents that those behaviors and actions will not be tolerated in our schools and in our lives. Only by training children to think differently will we be able to influence their actions. It is by teaching children to take responsibility for all of their behaviors that we will begin the transformation that needs to occur.

Will bullying ever disappear? It is a hope! However, it must begin with what is acceptable in terms of behaviors in American society. The government cannot go invading other countries or bullying smaller nations into compliance to get economic growth and development. Children learn by example, so let us hope that the examples of the leaders of this country will be positive and humanistic ones. Future generations hopefully will have the benefit of our past mistakes and do things differently.

FIND OUT MORE

Resources

Bully B'ware, www.bullybeware.com.

Bully Free Kids, www.bullyfreekids.com.

Bully Police USA, www.bullypolice.org.

Bullying No Way (Australia), www.bullyingnoway.com.

Bullying.org (Canada), www.bullying.org.

Childline (United Kingdom), www.childline.org.uk.

Coalition for Children, www.safechild.org.

Committee for Children, "Steps to Respect: A Bully Prevention Program," www.cfchildren.org/programs/str/overview.

Department for Children, Schools, and Families, "Don't Suffer in Silence," www.dfes.gov.uk/bullying/index.shtml.

Hazelden, "No Bullying," www.hazelden.org/OA_HTML/ibeCCtpItmDspRte.jsp?item=3221.

Jared's Story, parent's point of view, www.jaredstory.com.

PTA, Safeguarding your children at school, www.pta.org/.

Stop Bullying Now (a national bullying prevention campaign), www.stopbullying now.hrsa.gov.

Stop Bullying Now, www.stopbullyingnow.com.

Books

Beane, A. L. 1999. *The bully free classroom*. Minneapolis, MN: Free Spirit Publishing.

Coloreso, B. 2004. *The bully, the bullied and the bystander from preschool to high school*. New York: Harper Resource.

Rigby, K. 2003. *Stop the bullying: A handbook for schools*. Camberwell, Victoria: ACER Press.

Zarzour, K. 1999. *The schoolyard bully: How to cope with conflict and raise an assertive child*. Toronto: HarperCollins.

Videos

Brown, Thomas, *The Broken Toy*.

Equity Institute, *Sticks and Stones and Stereotypes*.

National Center for Violence Prevention, *Bully Breath: How to Tame a Trouble-maker.*

National Center for Violence Prevention, *Don't Pick on Me.*

National Center for Violence Prevention, *No More Teasing.*

Sunburst Communications, *Real People: What Is Hate All About?*

Toronto School Board of Education, *Bullying at School.*

Women's Educational Media. *Let's Get Real.*

References

Center for Professional Development. 2008. *Bullying prevention.* Bloomington, IN: Phi Delta Kappa International.

U.S. Department of Education. 2006. Exploring the nature and prevention of bullying. U.S. Department of Education. www.ed.gov/admins/lead/safety/training/bullying/index.html (accessed February 4, 2008).

Wikipedia. 2008. Bullying. Wikipedia. www.en.wikipedia.org/wiki/bullying (accessed February 8, 2008).

Wright, J. 2003. Preventing classroom bullying: What teachers can do. Intervention Central. www.interventioncentral.com/htmdocs/interventions/bully/bully prevent.php.

Chapter Thirteen

Accidents

Cars, Bicycles, Fire, and Water Safety

Accidents are the leading cause of injury death of children aged one to twenty-four. The number one killer is motor vehicle accidents, followed by (depending on the age group) drowning and fire accidents. Some accidents are preventable, and certainly steps can be taken to keep children safe from these all-too-common accidents. This chapter explores the most dangerous and common accidents, those involving motor vehicles, bicycles, fire, and water, and discusses strategies to reduce the risk of serious harm or death for children.

> ASK: WHAT IS POTENTIALLY DANGEROUS OR PROBLEMATIC FOR CHILDREN? WHAT CAN I DO (OR WHAT CAN BE DONE) TO MAKE THIS CHILD (OR THESE CHILDREN) SAFER OR HEALTHIER OR MORE SUCCESSFUL IN THIS/THESE SITUATION/S (OR SIMILAR ONES)?

Motor vehicle accidents. Inexperienced or immature drivers are responsible for 40 percent of teen deaths from motor vehicle accidents. In addition, the failure to wear seat belts consistently and drinking alcohol and using other drugs make driving even more dangerous. Car seats and seat belts can help a great deal in reducing motor vehicle fatalities. For example, Osberg and DiScala (1992) showed that for children who died in car crashes, there was a significant difference between those who were restrained (2.4 percent) and those who were unrestrained (4.5 percent).

155

More recently, the Children's Hospital of Philadelphia released a paper demonstrating that just restraining children is insufficient. Even though evidence has shown that children dying in car accidents has declined dramatically in the past twenty years, authorities propose that we must focus on making sure restraint devices fit properly and are correctly used. Physicians interviewed in the Children's Hospital of Philadelphia piece suggest the following:

> For instance, infants should ride in a rear-facing child safety seat until they reach one year and 20 pounds. Children aged one to four, between 20 and 40 pounds, should ride in a forward-facing car seat, not in a seat belt. "Premature graduation to safety belts raises the risk of 'seat belt syndrome,' injuries to the abdomen and spinal cord from an improperly positioned seat belt," said Dr. Durbin. Children over 4 years and 40 pounds should use a booster seat until about age 8, when they can properly use a seat belt without a booster seat. And for all children 12 years old and younger, "the safest place is in a vehicle's rear seat," added Dr. Winston. (1999, para. 4)

The *Journal of the American Medical Association* (JAMA) (2006) showed that children in child safety seats (car seats or booster seats) were safer than those children wearing seat belts alone. Researchers at the University of Michigan found,

> Overall, approximately one in 1,000 children in a two-way crash died, with less than half (45 percent) of all children in restraint seats. One of six children (15.7 percent) were in the front seat, two thirds (67.6 percent) were in passenger cars, one of six (15.6 percent) were in pre-1990 model year vehicles and 4 percent of cars were driven by teenage drivers. Compared with seat belts alone, child safety seats were associated with a 21 percent reduction in risk of death. When excluding cases of serious misuse of safety seats or belts, the reduced risk of death was 28 percent.

Also, even though many children resist sitting in the middle of the back seat, researchers have found this space to be the safest for properly restrained children (University of Buffalo 2006). Consider the following scary "close calls" of a couple of college students:

> When I was little I was in a car accident in my dad's truck. I remember I was still in my car seat and we were only a minute from home. Some girl who

had just gotten her license pulled out and hit the side of the car that I was on. Luckily no was injured, but I know I was scared. (College sophomore)

I was in a car accident driving home one night from work. It was foggy and I lived on a country road. I was approaching a blind curve; I knew a car was approaching from the other direction because I could see headlights (even though I couldn't see the car). As I rounded the curve, the other car was completely in my lane, about 100 feet in front of me. We were both traveling 40–45 mph, so a collision was unavoidable. I was able to pull off the road prior to the collision so that the impact on my car was on the driver's side instead of head-on. I was cut in the head and face from some shattered glass and had a couple of bruises but was otherwise unhurt. I found out later that the other driver had been drinking but not enough to be considered legally drunk. (Twenty-year-old college sophomore)

Countless adolescents have high school experiences of loss like these:

Between 9th and 10th grade, four of my classmates were out driving in the summertime and were speeding. There were 2 15-year-olds and 2 16-year-olds. Two of the boys were fraternal twins. They were going too fast around a corner and lost control of the car. One of the twins was ejected from the car and died due to internal trauma. The driver had to be taken out of the car by the "jaws of life" and the other two boys were hurt rather badly as well. The fraternal twin who passed away was in a coma for about 2 days before he died. This was the saddest funeral I ever went to. During my graduation, there was a memorial about him and we had to relieve that tragic day all over again. (Twenty-year-old college sophomore)

Inexperience and driving while impaired contribute to the majority of fatal car crashes. As one of the examples above illustrates, having them in appropriate car seats reduces the risk for young children. But these children and adolescents can be harmed because of the inexperienced drivers on the road. Of our small sample of college-aged survey respondents, several had been in a car accident, and most of them were driving and still inexperienced.

A recent study commissioned by the Robert Wood Johnson Foundation (RWJF) found that "graduated teen driver's-licensing programs" were found to reduce deaths from car accidents. Graduate driver's-licensing programs include

- A learner's phase requiring a licensed driver to be in the vehicle for a young driver's first months of driving.

- An intermediate phase allowing new young drivers to drive only during daylight and early evening hours and/or with a limited number of passengers.
- Full licensure available after the intermediate phase and sometimes only at age 17 or older. (RWJF 2006)

These researchers credit the reduction in traffic deaths among young people also partly to the raising of the legal drinking age, mandating seat belt use, and stricter drunk-driving laws.

In addition to auto accidents, there are also concerns about children being backed over by vehicles (approximately twenty-five hundred children are treated for back-over injuries according to the CDC, 2005), hit by cars (research has shown that kids are at higher risk of being run over or hit by larger cars such as SUVs, kidsandcars.org, 2007), and harmed or killed by heatstroke from being left in vehicles (this number has been steadily rising, kidsandcars.org).

Bicycle accidents. Many young people have accidents on or falls from bicycles. The website for KidsHealth (www.kidshealth.org) reports that close to three hundred thousand children end up in the emergency room because of injuries from bike falls. And according to the Centers for Disease Control and Prevention, bike injuries made up 59 percent of emergency room visits for children aged fifteen and younger. Death from falls typically results from head injury (see chapter on brain injuries). The concern about head injury has resulted in states' adopting helmet laws. Laws mandating proper helmet wearing for youths riding bikes have helped to reduce the number of head injuries from bike crashes (although the evidence is inconsistent). For example, the bicycle and helmet statistics reported by the Bicycle Helmet Safety Institute (2008) found,

> Helmet use in the U.S. varies by orders of magnitude in different areas and different sectors of our society. White collar commuters probably reach 80 per cent, while inner city kids and rural kids would be 10 per cent or less. Overall, our best wild guess is probably no more than 25 per cent. Sommers Point, NJ, where a state helmet law is in effect, found that only 24 of the 359 students who rode to school in one week of the Winter of 2002 wore helmets (6 per cent) until the School District adopted a helmet rule. North Carolina observed 17 per cent statewide before their law went into effect in 2001.

Although the evidence is mixed on the impact of mandatory helmet laws on reducing fatalities, most generally studies report that for children aged four to twenty, there has been a reduction (National Highway Transportation Association 2006). As adults, we must be consistent in enforcing the wearing of helmets, not only for younger children but for older adolescents as well.

Fire injury and death. According to the Centers for Disease Control and Prevention's statistics, the third leading cause of injury death for one- to four-year-olds is "unintentional fireburn," and this is the second leading cause of injury death for children aged five to nine.

> I was 8 years old when my house burnt to the ground. I was staying over at my friend's house and my brother was supposed to stay at his friend's house. My mother had just served my father divorce papers and he was really upset. The only two people that were supposed to be in the house were my mom and dad. Years later, I found out that my father was trying to kill my mother the night our house burnt down. One fire was electrical and the other fire, my father started by flicking his cigarette on the living room carpet. It was devastating and we lost just about everything. If I was home that night, I would not be answering these questions on this survey because the electrical fire started in the room next to my bedroom. (Twenty-nine-year-old female)

This violent form of arson—with intent to harm or kill another—is rarer than the accidental or unintentional fires that start, but this example speaks to how devastating and deadly fires can be. The U.S. Fire Association (USFA) provided the following statistics about accidental fires for 2006:

- There were 3,245 civilians that lost their lives as the result of fire.
- There were 16,400 civilian injuries that occurred as the result of fire.
- There were 106 firefighters killed while on duty.
- Fire killed more Americans than all natural disasters combined.
- 81 percent of all civilian fire deaths occurred in residences.
- 1.6 million fires were reported. Many others went unreported, causing additional injuries and property loss.
- Direct property loss due to fires was estimated at $11.3 billion.
- An estimated 31,000 intentionally set structure fires resulted in 305 civilian deaths.
- Intentionally set structure fires resulted in an estimated $755 million in property damage. (USFA 2007a, p. 2)

The USFA provides the following statistics on arson injuries and costs:

- An estimated 31,000 intentionally set structure fires occurred in 2006.
- Intentionally set fires in structures resulted in 305 civilian deaths.
- Intentionally set structure fires also resulted in $755,000,000 in property loss.
- 20,500 intentionally set vehicle fires occurred, a decrease of 2.4 percent from a year ago, and caused $134,000,000 in property damage, an increase of 18.6 percent from a year ago. (USFA 2007b, p. iii)

Water accidents—drowning. The CDC reports that the second leading cause of injury death for children under fifteen is drowning. Three times as many children who drown go to the emergency room for "nonfatal submersion injuries," and in many cases these "nonfatal drownings" can result in "brain damage that may result in long-term disabilities including memory problems, learning disabilities, and permanent loss of basic functioning (i.e., permanent vegetative state)" (CDC 2008, para. 3).

My father is an EMT. I remember him coming home from work one day, a complete wreck. He had witnessed an infant who had fallen into her grandparent's indoor pool and drown to death. Ever since then, he became paranoid of my sister and I swimming. (Twenty-one-year-old college junior)

The CDC reports the following as the major risk factors for drowning:

- *Lack of barriers and supervision.* Children under one year most often drown in bathtubs, buckets, or toilets. Among children ages 1 to 4 years, most drownings occur in residential swimming pools. Most young children who drowned in pools were last seen in the home, had been out of sight less than five minutes, and were in the care of one or both parents at the time. Barriers, such as pool fencing, can help prevent children from gaining access to the pool area without caregivers' awareness.
- *Age and recreation in natural water settings (such as lakes, rivers, or the ocean).* The percent of drownings in natural water settings increases with age. Most drownings in those over 15 years of age occur in natural water settings.
- *Lack of appropriate choices in recreational boating.* In 2006, the U.S. Coast Guard received reports for 4,967 boating incidents; 3,474 boaters were reported injured, and 710 died. Among those who drowned, 9 out of

ten were not wearing life jackets. Most boating fatalities from 2006 (70%) were caused by drowning; the remainder were due to trauma, hypothermia, carbon monoxide poisoning, or other causes. Open motor boats were involved in 45% of all reported incidents, and personal watercraft were involved in another 24%.

- *Alcohol use.* Alcohol use is involved in up to half of adolescent and adult deaths associated with water recreation and about one in five reported boating fatalities. Alcohol influences balance, coordination, and judgment, and its effects are heightened by sun exposure and heat.

- *Seizure disorders.* For persons with seizure disorders, drowning is the most common cause of unintentional injury death, with the bathtub as the site of highest drowning risk. (CDC 2008, para. 3)

A research review of where children drown (published in the journal *Pediatrics*) found that roughly 60 percent of drownings happen among children under age five—with the overwhelming majority being boys (Brenner, Trumble, and Smith 2001). Nearly 88 percent of children were being supervised when they drowned—with a shocking 46 percent under parental supervision. The study by Brenner, Trumble, and Smith (2001) found that of reviewed drownings, a little over one-third happened in lakes, rivers, or ponds (37 percent), most happened in residential or community pools (39 percent), and 18 percent happened around the home (in baths, hot tubs, or buckets).

Those under five are at greater risk of drowning around the home, and older children (aged five to fourteen) are at greater risk of drowning in lakes, ponds, rivers, or other open bodies of water—with more than half of the older children (59 percent) choosing to be in the water. Another cause for concern is that parents and children often overestimate their swimming abilities and can easily get into trouble in the water.

BRING TOGETHER ALL ADVOCATES WHO CAN ASSIST IN MAKING CHILDREN SAFER IN THESE SITUATIONS

Preventing accidents is challenging. However, the same advocates will be able to help make children safer in the car, home, school, and around water—that is, adult care providers. These include parents, teachers, school administrators, law-enforcement officers, fire officials, lifeguards, day care providers, and other child-care workers (e.g., baby sitters). Any person charged with the care of children must be made aware of the importance of seat belts, proper car seats, helmet wearing, careful supervision in high-risk areas (e.g., around water and busy streets), and fire- and water-safety plans. Schools should educate students and parents about safety in cars, on bicycles, around water, and in the event of fire. In some cases, policy changes and law-enforcement vigilance are called for—as is described in the next section.

CONSIDER THE OPTIONS (PARTICULARLY ONES WITH DEMONSTRATED SUCCESS)

Although some of the specific recommendations may differ for preventing motor vehicle and bicycle accidents, fire-related injuries, and drowning, there are a few general recommendations. The first is awareness of the specific risk factors, and the second is adult vigilance. Each of these accidents is among the leading causes of unintentional injury death for young people, and all need to be addressed in systematic ways by caring adults.

Protection from motor vehicle accidents. Some preventative measures can be taken to reduce the chances of motor vehicle accidents. Consider the following:

- Make sure ability is not impaired by sleep deprivation, drugs (including over-the-counter, cold medication, or alcohol), or emotional state.
- Make sure driving conditions are appropriate for driving.
- Take advantage of driver's education courses, and give young drivers as much supervised driving experience as possible.
- Have parents closely monitor their inexperienced adolescents' driving—making sure that conditions are safe, that they are not driving with too many distractions (friends, music, telephones), and when possible that they drive with competent adult supervision as they gain experience.
- Determine that car seats and booster seats for younger children are properly installed and maintained and that seat belts for younger riders are being used and fit appropriately.

- Increase awareness and intervention for other forms of auto-related accidents, such children being backed over (install motion detectors on rear bumpers of cars), hit or run over by cars, or suffering heat stroke from being left in cars.
- Lobby for graduated driver's-licensing programs—particularly those that limit nighttime driving, have at least a six-month "learning period," and restrict the number of passengers until the driver has more experience.

Protection from bicycle accidents. The federal government has issued standards for helmet safety. Helmets should have a sticker from the Consumer Product Safety Commission (CPSC) indicating that it meets these standards. In addition to meeting helmet standards, helmets must fit properly—qualified personnel at bike stores or police stations can help determine if a helmet fits correctly if you are unsure. KidsHealth (2007) offers the following help in fitting helmets properly:

> Once you have the right helmet, you need to wear it the right way so it will protect you. It should be worn level and cover your forehead. Don't tip it back so your forehead is showing. The straps should always be fastened. If the straps are flying, it's likely to fall off your head when you need it most. Make sure the straps are adjusted so they're snug enough that you can't pull or twist the helmet around on your head.

There were many examples such as this one among our survey respondents:

> My friend's brakes gave out and she flipped over her bike damaging her teeth. (College junior)

Having good bike equipment, including a well-fitting helmet (and checking before riding to make sure the helmet is in good repair), is also critical to preventing accidents such as the one in this example.

Children are also at risk of being hit by cars when riding their bicycles beside or in the road. Parents should be aware of where their children are riding and encourage them to stay away from busy and/or narrow-shouldered streets. The BicycleSafe website (www.bicyclesafe.com) offers suggestions for how to avoid getting hit by cars while riding a bike, such as watching the way that you turn at a red light and signaling properly. The authors of the website also encourage getting a horn and a headlight, slowing down, and watching out for car doors opening as you ride by.

The KidsHealth website offers a section on bike safety for kids and gives reminders about road rules (e.g., stop and check traffic in both directions, cross at intersections, use proper hand signals), wearing bright-colored clothing, making sure the bike is safe (e.g., working brakes, properly inflated tires, no loose clothing to get caught in bike chains, and so on).

The National Highway Transportation and Safety Association (NHTSA) reports that "universal bicycle helmet use by children aged 4-15 would prevent 39,000 to 45,000 head injuries, and 18,000 to 55,000 scalp and face injuries annually." The NHTSA reports that currently fourteen states have no state or local helmet laws (Arkansas, Colorado, Idaho, Indiana, Iowa, Minnesota, Mississippi, Nebraska, North Dakota, South Dakota, South Carolina, Utah, Vermont, and Wyoming). Lobbying for mandatory helmet laws for children under age eighteen in these states could help save lives and prevent harm to children—as will more consistent enforcement of helmet laws in the states that have them.

Protection from fires. The U.S. Fire Administration (USFA) has a website for kids at www.usfa.dhs.gov/kids/flash.shtm. The site provides links to information about home fire safety, smoke alarms, and escaping from fires, as well as an opportunity to become a "junior fire marshal." The site also has more information on the USFA's fire prevention and safety campaigns. FireSafety.gov (2008), a website sponsored by the CDC, the CPSC, and the USFA, recommends the following to help prevent fires and to reduce injury and death in the event of a fire:

- Get a smoke alarm [approximately two thirds of fire deaths happen in homes without working smoke alarms, which should be on every level of the house, both outside and inside of all sleeping areas, and properly installed and maintained.]
- Make an escape plan [practice regularly, have two means of escape from every room, leave the house immediately, never open hot doors, create a meeting location away from the house that everyone knows about, and once you're out of the house, stay out.]
- Practice fire safety [firesafety.org offers strategies for practicing safety in the home, such as bedroom, kitchen, and fireplace safety.]

• Use fire sprinklers [studies by the USFA have demonstrated that sprinkler systems could perhaps have prevented thousands of injuries, saved thousands of lives, and prevented millions of dollars in damage to homes.]

Protection from drowning. Children should learn to swim and be taught water safety at a very young age—particularly if they live near or around water. Requiring young children to wear well-fitting life jackets whenever they are going to be playing in or near water can reduce the chances of drowning. The National Safe Kids Campaign's Splash into Safety program focuses on the following "water-safety wisdoms" for caregivers:

• *Supervision*—Designate a responsible adult to actively supervise kids around water.
• *Environment*—Ensure safe swimming environments by installing multiple layers of protection around pools and equipping all water recreation sites with appropriate signage and emergency equipment.
• *Gear*—Make sure the right safety gear is always used.
• *Education*—Teach children to swim and educate them about water safety. (Safe Kids USA 2004)

The Safe Kids Campaign also makes the following recommendations:

• Never leave a young child unsupervised in or around water, even for a moment.
• Never allow children to swim without adult supervision.
• Always designate a responsible adult to serve as the "water watcher"—a supervisor whose sole responsibility is to constantly observe children in or near the water. . . .
• Supervisors should maintain continuous visual and auditory contact with children in or near the water, and should stay in close proximity (waterside) so that they can effectively intervene if an emergency situation should arise.
• Supervisors should not engage in distracting behaviors such as talking on the phone, preparing a meal or reading.
• Supervisors should keep children who cannot swim within arm's reach at all times.
• While there is no specific recommended ratio of supervisors to child swimmers, the number of supervisors should increase when many children are swimming, younger or inexperienced swimmers are present, or the swimming area is large. (Safe Kids USA 2004, para. 4)

It is important for adults to remember that very young children can drown in only an inch or two of water, so always stay within reach of a very young child. The American Association of Pediatrics suggests the following safety tips for avoiding accidental drowning around the home:

- Empty all buckets, pails, and bathtubs completely after each use—do not leave them filled and unattended.
- Keep young children out of the bathroom unless they are closely watched. Teach others in the home to keep the bathroom door closed. Install a hook-and-eye latch or doorknob cover on the outside of the door.
- Never leave a child alone in a bathtub or in the care of another child, even for a moment.
- Use a rigid, lockable cover on a hot tub, spa, or whirlpool, or fence in all 4 sides as you would for a swimming pool.
- Set your water heater thermostat so that the hottest temperature at the faucet is 120°F to avoid burns.
- Throw away or tightly cover water or chemical mixtures after use.
- Watch children closely when they are playing near wells, open post holes, or irrigation or drainage ditches. Fill in empty holes or have fences installed to protect your child.
- Learn CPR and know how to get emergency help. (American Academy of Pediatrics 1994, para. 3)

A few words about falls and young children. Young children are at risk of falling, particularly as they are learning to walk or still mastering such skills as climbing stairs. Using protective gates around fireplaces, stairs, and other dangerous places can help. Also, protective buffers on sharp-edged tables or other corners can prevent head injury during falls.

Children are also at risk of being injured from toys—with the majority of major injuries occurring from falls off of toys (Children's Health Encyclopedia, childrenscentralcal.org). Carefully monitor children on riding toys, and be sure that all toys are developmentally appropriate. Also, windows in children's rooms should be carefully latched to prevent youngsters from falling out. And finally, as children graduate from cribs to toddler or "big kid" beds, be sure to use safety devices to keep them from falling out of bed.

DO WHAT YOU CAN

Motor vehicles accidents. Schools and communities need to invest in driver-training programs that teach young drivers defensive driving skills, the importance of wearing seat belts, and not to drive while under the influence of an impairing substance or to ride with anyone who is. As parents and/or adult caregivers, let adolescents know that they can be picked up any time, any place, no questions asked, to avoid their riding with unsafe peers. Also, communities and states need to invest in graduated driver's-licensing programs.

Bicycle accidents. Carefully monitor where children can ride bikes. Make sure places are safe from cars and that children wear helmets at all times. Be sure that bicycles are in working order and that an adult is always supervising younger riders carefully.

Fire safety. Children and adults need to be made aware of risks and safety strategies. Giving young children an opportunity to visit a fire station and see fire fighters in their uniforms can help (so they are not fearful if they see them during a fire). Also, children should know what to do in the event of a fire and practice — both at home and at school.

Water safety. Attentive, skilled adult supervision is essential. Always watch children carefully when they are near any kind of water source — from the bathtub to a river (be sure when there are multiple adults that at least one is charged with watching all children). When possible, put up gates or fences to keep children out of water sources unless supervised. Invest in swimming lessons — encourage community recreation programs to offer reduced-rate or sliding-fee-scale (or even free) swimming lessons with qualified instructors.

EVALUATE YOUR SUCCESS

Evaluation of prevention is difficult as knowing the number of accidents prevented is often merely conjecture. We can compare incidence, injuries, and emergency room visits for particular accidents from year to year to see if implementation of different prevention programs (e.g., helmet laws and fire safety workshops) has made a difference. For example, New Hampshire recently passed a boater-safety law requiring all boat drivers to pass a written exam about water safety. The evidence should be collected to determine if this measure has had an impact on childhood drowning in that state.

In addition to emergency room statistics, law-enforcement and fire marshal statistics may be useful to determine if changes in policies and practices are having an impact.

FIND OUT MORE

American Academy of Pediatrics (AAP). 1994. Home water hazards for young children. AAP. www.aap.org/family/homewatr.htm.

Bicycle Helmet Safety Institute (BHSI). 2008. Helmet related statistics from many sources. BHSI. www.helmets.org/stats.htm.

BicycleSafe.com. 2008. http://bicyclesafe.com.

Brenner, R., A. Trumble, and G. Smith. 2001. Where children drown, United States, 1995. *Pediatrics* 108, no. 1: 85–89.

Centers for Disease Control and Prevention (CDC). 2008. Water-related injuries: A fact sheet. CDC. www.cdc.gov/ncipc/factsheets/drown.htm#major%20risk%20factor.

Children's Hospital of Central California. 2008. Toy safety and injury statistics and incidents rates. Children's Hospital of Central California. http://children scentralcal.org/content.asp?id=1169&parent=1&groupid=G0066 (accessed June 10, 2008).

Children's Hospital of Philadelphia. 1999. Buckling up is not enough to protect children in auto accidents; seat belts and child safety seats must be used properly. *ScienceDaily*, June 9. www.sciencedaily.com/releases/1999/06/990607173710.htm (accessed June 6, 2008).

FireSafety.gov. 2008. www.firesafety.gov.

JAMA and Archives Journals. 2006. Child safety seats reduce risk of death in crashes more than seat belts alone. *ScienceDaily*, June 6. www.sciencedaily.com/releases/2006/06/060606092204.htm (accessed June 6, 2008).

Kids and Cars. 2008. www.kidsandcars.org.

KidsHealth.org. 2007. Bike safety. KidsHealth. http://kidshealth.org/kid/watch/out/bike_safety.html.

National Center for Injury Prevention and Control (NCIPC). 2006. Bicycle related injuries. NCIPC. www.cdc.gov/ncipc/bike.

National Highway Transportation and Safety Association (NHTSA). 2006. Kids and bicycle safety. NHTSA. www.nhtsa.dot.gov/people/injury/pedbimot/bike/KidsandBikeSafetyWeb/index.htm.

Osberg, J. S., and C. DiScala. 1992. Morbidity among pediatric motor vehicle crash victims: The effectiveness of seat belts. *American Journal of Public Health* 82, (3): 422–25.

Robert Wood Johnson Foundation (RWJF). 2006. Study finds that rigorous graduate teen driver licensing programs reduce traffic fatalities. RWJF. www.rwjf.org/reports/grr/048279.htm (accessed June 6, 2008).

Safe Kids USA. 2004. Clear danger: A national study of childhood drowning and related attitudes and behaviors. Safe Kids USA. www.usa.safekids.org/ NSKW.cfm.

University of Buffalo. 2006. A car's middle back seat may be least desirable, but it's the safest. *ScienceDaily*, June 27. www.sciencedaily.com/releases/2006/06/ 060627173902.htm (accessed June 6, 2008).

U.S. Fire Association (USFA). 2007a. QuickStats. www.usfa.dhs.gov/statistics/ quickstats/index.shtm.

U.S. Fire Association (USFA). 2007b. Arson. www.usfa.dhs.gov/statistics/ arson/index.shtm.

Chapter Fourteen

Abuse

Psychological, Sexual, and Physical

Child abuse casts a shadow the length of a lifetime.

—Henry Ward

The impact of being abused in any way has long-lasting effects. Every ten seconds a child is reported as being abused, and every day three children die at the hands of abusing adults. The goal of schools and society is to protect children and ensure a safe learning environment and community.

The National Clearinghouse on Child Abuse and Neglect (U.S. Department of Health and Human Services 2007) reported that nationally an estimated 906,000 children were victims of abuse or neglect, and more than 1,500 children died as a result of these incidents. Approximately 63 percent of those children suffered neglect, 19 percent were physically abused, 10 percent were sexually abused, and 5 percent were emotionally abused. Child protection agencies received 2.9 million referrals, which involved a total of 5.5 million children. Educators reported a total of 16.3 percent of these referrals.

Many factors come into play when a child becomes a victim of abuse. Abused children and youths who receive proper attention and support are more likely to survive the child maltreatment. Many of the reports from former abused children indicate that it is essential that the child have an adult that believes him or her. For many children, those adults are their teachers or school personnel who interact with them every day. It is of paramount importance that children have that safety connection at school or in the community.

Child abuse is divided into four types: physical, sexual, neglectful, and emotional. The types are often found in combination rather than alone. If a child is being sexually abused, chances are that there is emotional abuse happening at the same time. Teachers and school personnel are consistent observers of children. Indications of child abuse may be easily identified or hidden behind unusual behaviors. No one sign or symptom definitely indicates abuse or neglect. Educators should not attempt to be diagnostic but should report any suspected abuse.

One of my friends in middle school was constantly hit by his father. He was never seriously injured (no broken bones). His parents didn't get along at all and he would always tell me they would tell him and his younger brother that they were just "staying together for the kids." Once my friend and his brother graduated high school they planned on divorcing. I think them staying together only made things worse. His father would take all his anger out on my friend. I told my parents about this once but I don't think they really believed me because I was about 12 years old and was constantly getting in trouble for lying around that time. My friend ended up graduating high school but was placed in behavioral classes, and was always getting detention and in house suspensions. He started experimenting with drugs and getting in all kinds of legal trouble. He joined the army once he graduated high school to get away from his parents. Their parents are now divorced. (College sophomore)

> **ASK: WHAT IS POTENTIALLY DANGEROUS OR PROBLEMATIC FOR CHILDREN? WHAT CAN I DO (OR WHAT CAN BE DONE) TO MAKE THIS CHILD (OR THESE CHILDREN) SAFER OR HEALTHIER OR MORE SUCCESSFUL IN THIS/THESE SITUATION/S (OR SIMILAR ONES)?**

Children are vulnerable individuals because they rely on adults for many of their basic needs. They do not have the capacity to go to work, shop for food, pay bills, and so forth. As a teacher or parent, it is crucial that you become aware of the possible warning signs that a child is being abused. One factor that should trigger concern for a child is a change in the child's functioning, whether it is physical (soiling), behavioral (active to passive), or emotional (weepy or moody).

The following are factors that adults need to be aware of that may be in play for an abused child. There are several environmental factors worth noting that may place a child at risk:

- social isolation
- poverty
- domestic violence
- stress from financial problems, unemployment, inadequate housing, illness, and lack of child care
- parent with history of abuse
- parents who are emotionally immature, impulsive, or needy
- poor parenting skills and lack of knowledge about child development
- unrealistic parental expectations of a child
- disruptions to the early bonding process between parent and child
- a child who is difficult to care for (learning disabled, physically disabled, emotionally disturbed, or a behavior problem (American Psychological Association 2003)

> When I was young I was not allowed to stay home alone with my older brother, my parents were always worried that he would beat me so bad that something would happen, they were scared not only for me but what he would become. (College sophomore)

There is a series of indicators of physical, sexual, and emotional abuse and neglect. The important component is to recognize the behaviors and warning signs. Most states have a list that is used to gauge whether or not abuse is occurring. This list is not exhaustive, and the author highly suggests that you consult your local or state handbook on child abuse and neglect to have the checklist as a guide in your assessment of the situation.

Physical abuse refers to nonaccidental physical injury to a child. With physical abuse, look for a pattern or series of events. Be aware of frequent occurrences that alone may seem to have a reasonable explanation but, when taken as a whole, cause concern. Some of the indicators may be extensive bruises, burns, frequent complaints of injuries, sleep problems, headaches, enuresis, substance abuse, regression, social withdrawal, delinquency, stealing, running away, truancy, school learning, anxiety, depression, guilt, suicidality, anger, aggression, and tantrums.

When I was younger I had a baby sitter, well me and my brother had one. She seemed like a nice lady at first, walking us down to go and get movies and teaching us how to ride our bikes. But as the weeks went on she started to try and do things with my brother, she stole things and got me and my brother into trouble, she would lock me in my room because I could not do the bike signals and also she would whip me with my dad's weight belt whenever I did do anything out of order. She would throw things at me, my brother and I were just petrified to say anything to my parents, but finally they caught her stealing something and they did not hear about what happened to me till now. (College sophomore)

Sexual abuse refers to any sexual contact with a child or the use of a child for someone else's sexual pleasure. The signs of sexual abuse include a sudden and inexplicable fear of people and places, a severe interest in or avoidance of "all things of a sexual nature," nightmares, depression, withdrawal, secretiveness, delinquency, aggression, and suicidal behavior. Another large indicator is verbalization or physical reenactment of sexual activities, especially in a young child. Sexually abused children may not be able to say that they were sexually abused; instead, they often use words like dirty, damaged, and hurt to express pain.

I don't go to my grandparents house anymore because when I used to spend the weekends, my grandfather would make me do things I wasn't comfortable with, so I stopped going and never told anyone . . . come to find out he's not my real biological grandfather. (College junior)

Neglect refers to a failure to provide a minimum degree of care in supplying a child with adequate food, clothing, shelter, education, or medical care, resulting in physical, cognitive, or emotional impairment or danger of impairment. Some of the signs are failure to thrive, poor hygiene, poor health, malnutrition, rocking back and forth for self-soothing, begging or stealing food, crying easily, impaired socialization, falling asleep in class, being troublesome at school, lying, anxiety, withdrawal, hostility, anger, illnesses, infections, inappropriate clothing, aggression, and cruelty to others.

My aunt used to abuse my cousin until one day my cousin went to school with a bruise on her face. My aunt had my cousin when she was 19 and she was using many drugs and did not know how to be a parent. She had to go to parenting classes, but their relationship has never been close. Now, my cousin had her first child at 19 as well. She does not abuse him, but yells at him all the time. She had to go to parenting classes as well. (College junior)

Emotional abuse is a pattern of behavior that attacks a child's emotional development and sense of self-worth. The warning signs are delayed physical, cognitive, and emotional development, wetting of pants or bed, sleep disturbances, ulcers, poor physical appearance, habit disorders, inappropriate aggression, poor peer relations, bizarre or self-destructive acts, extreme need for perfection, emotional extremes, nightmares, clinging, fear of adults, tics, phobias, obsessions, depression, low self-esteem or confidence, and family and peer conflicts.

A report produced by the National Center on Child Abuse and Neglect showed that children with disabilities experience abuse and neglect 1.7 times more frequently than children without disabilities. Children with serious emotional disturbance, physical or cognitive disability, learning disability, and speech or language delay or impairment faired worse in terms of maltreatment. Young children under five years old are most at risk. Parents of special needs children are more stressed in caring for their children. Special needs children are more likely to be abused due to the following factors:

- As infants they may cry more, may be harder to soothe than other babies, or may need almost constant care.
- Infants with disabilities may not smile, give eye contact, or enjoy cuddling. It may be harder for parents to become attached and feel protective toward their children.
- Long hospital stays, especially soon after birth, take away important time parents usually have with their new child. This is when parents normally develop loving, protective feelings.
- Young children may not reach developmental milestones like other children. The general milestones of walking, talking, toilet training, and so forth, may not occur at the same rate as parents expect. Parents in turn may become very frustrated and angry and lash out.
- These children may have behaviors that are very difficult to handle.
- These children are more likely to go along with some of the inappropriate activities and are less likely to report or complain if someone hurts them.

- Special needs children may not always know what is right or wrong.
- Some of these children do not have the ability to communicate that something bad has happened to them (State of New Hampshire 2002).

> My cousins had their three children taken away from them because one of their baby twin girls had a broken leg. The parents were recently found not guilty, but have to take parenting classes. The great grandparents have the twins and another cousin has the older daughter. The girls were taken away almost a year ago and won't be given back for another 8 or 9 months. (College junior)

Helping parents of disabled children is vital to the protection of these children. Respite care is needed to give that temporary break. Support networks are crucial for understanding the disability, dealing with the loneliness, sadness, and frustration, and providing someone to share the joy of the child's accomplishments. Parents need to know that the Individuals with Disabilities Education Act provides for early intervention for infants and toddlers and special education for school-age children. Supplemental Security Income may be available to provide financial help to families with severely disabled children.

> I used to work with the Duke University Child Protection team and was an attorney in Juvenile Court, so the stories are so numerous. I can't begin to go into all of them. In one of the worst, the father of a family of four sexually abused all of the children, his wife and the dog, but the children were not believed when they told—the stories were so grotesque that no one believed (wanted to believe) that the children could really be enduring what they were enduring. He eventually went to prison. (Colleague of researcher)

BRING TOGETHER ALL ADVOCATES WHO CAN ASSIST IN MAKING CHILDREN SAFER IN THESE SITUATIONS

In the United States, each state has a law that corresponds to the reporting of suspected child abuse. Any physician, surgeon, county medical examiner, psychiatrist, intern, dentist, osteopath, optometrist, chiropractor, psychologist, therapist, registered nurse, hospital employee, teacher, school official, school nurse, school counselor, social worker, day care worker, law-enforcement official, priest, minister, or any other person having reason to suspect that a child has been abused or neglected shall report the suspected problem to the Central Intake Unit of the child protection agency of that state immediately. Failure to report suspected abuse or neglect is a misdemeanor offense under the state law.

Enormous responsibility is placed on classroom teachers and educators today to protect children. The Texas Department of Family and Protective Services (2005) suggest the following roles to help teachers bridge into the lives of abused children.

- *Observer:* First teachers must be good kid watchers. They must have awareness of the physical and behavioral signs of abuse or neglect. Teachers need to observe what is different in kids. When something does not feel right or is blatantly disclosed, they have the responsibility to report it immediately.
- *Listener:* Teachers need to listen to what kids are saying. Teachers can create a climate where children may speak directly to their teachers or may convey messages through what they say to others, through their play, in their writings, or in reaction to what they are learning.
- *Role model:* Teachers can model self-worth. By demonstrating actions and behaviors that reinforce the need to value one's self, body, spirit, and place in the community, they can teach kids acceptable behaviors. Modeling can show kids what a positive environment can look like. A child can begin to feel safe in this positive environment. If a child feels safe and can trust the adults, he or she is more likely to disclose the abuse.
- *Advocate:* Teachers can become advocates by remaining informed of and maintaining connections with local and state services for children. They must stay connected with the community. It is about creating relationships that provide support for all children to improve the condition of their lives.

Once a report has been made to the Child Protection Agency (CPA), several procedures are followed. The CPA begins to collect the following information to assess the situation:

- summary of suspected abuse and neglect (who, what, where, when, number of incidents, degree of current risk, medical attention, presence of domestic violence)

- the child (who, where, whom the child is with, school, grade, home address, child's relationship to offender, any disabilities, who is available for support)
- the alleged abuser/person (name, where he or she is now, place of employment, home address, current relationship with child, access to child, history of violence, mental health, criminal behavior, awareness of the referral)
- nonoffending parent (who, place of employment, contact information, current relationship to offender, any knowledge of abuse, does this person possess the ability to protect the child, extended family or support groups)
- siblings or other children in the home (names, schools, current whereabouts, other siblings being abused or who know of abuse)
- other household members (names, ages, genders, relationships, involvement in or knowledge of alleged abuse)
- referral source (name, relationship to the family, how the source knows about the abuse, whether he or she has directly observed the abuse or knows how the family will react to the assessment, why is the referral made now, any other individuals who know about the abuse, any other insights about the family)

If the concerns have been raised by an educator or school employee, that person's identity should be made known to the school principal; the school should be named as the reporter, but the identity of the individual school employee who raised the suspicions can be kept confidential. The only time the identity of the reporter is identified is when the reporter must be involved as a witness in court to uphold the petition so that the child receives the services needed to stay safe. The reporter will be served a subpoena to testify in court.

If the decision is made to further investigate the report and the case is accepted for assessment, it gets transferred from the Central Intake Unit to the local Division for Children, Youth and Families (DCYF) district office for an assessment and determination of services. If the report is not going to be investigated, the Central Intake Unit will help the school officials with suggestions for dealing with the family.

If a DCYF worker comes to the school, he or she must notify law-enforcement officials in cases of serious physical injury or sexual abuse of the child. DCYF workers must be accompanied by a police officer, or a police officer may come to the school alone to interview the child. DCYF workers are required by law to videotape in their entirety all interviews of children in a public setting including schools. The school must cooperate with the DCYF by providing information and assistance in the assessment process. In most cases the school will do the following:

• arrange access to the child
• arrange for a private location for interviews
• take every precaution to protect the child's privacy and confidentiality, allowing an absolute minimum of people to know what is transpiring
• make school staff available to quietly sit in on interviews only if the child requests them to be present
• make sure the child is emotionally prepared to return to the classroom before having him or her do so (State of New Hampshire 2002)

In addition, the DCYF will instruct the school personnel as to

• what information they can and cannot share with parents about the interviews
• how to handle the child's concerns about going home, parents finding out, or any other concerns regarding the assessment (State of New Hampshire 2002)

If the DCYF believes a child to be in imminent danger in such circumstances or surroundings and where immediate removal appears necessary to protect the child, the DCYF must contact a district court or family division court immediately for an ex parte order to remove the child. Ex parte means that due to the child's emergency circumstances, the DCYF requests that the court remove the child without involving or notifying the child's parents.

If the court finds reasonable cause to believe that the child is in such circumstances or surroundings as would present an imminent danger to the child's health or life and issues an ex parte order, the DCYF will be required to file a petition with the court within seventy-two hours of the issuance of the ex parte order. A preliminary hearing will be scheduled by the court within five calendar days from the date of the ex parte order. Parents will be served a copy of the petition and will receive notice of the preliminary hearing. Parents will also receive a copy of the ex parte order. The court may also grant temporary legal custody to the DCYF to place the child in a foster home or other substitute care setting.

Law-enforcement agencies may take a child into protective custody without the consent of the parents and without a court order. Law enforcement is permitted to do this when a child is in such circumstances or surroundings as would present imminent danger to the child's health or life unless immediate action is taken and there is not enough time to petition the court for an ex parte order. Whenever a child is taken into protective custody by law enforcement, the district court or family division must be notified immediately, and a court hearing must be scheduled within twenty-four hours of taking the child into protective custody.

All law-enforcement and agency personnel will cooperate in limiting the number of interviews of a child victim and, when appropriate, will conduct joint interviews of the child. DCYF workers will share with the investigating police officers all information in their possession that they may lawfully disclose to a law-enforcement agency. Investigating police officers shall not use or reveal any confidential information shared with them by the DCYF workers except to the extent necessary for the investigation and prosecution of the case.

CONSIDER THE OPTIONS (PARTICULARLY ONES WITH DEMONSTRATED SUCCESS)

When a child is being abused, there are really no options. You, the adult, must report it. It is the only thing to do. It is the only way to protect a child. All states mandate that educators report abuse to the Child Protection Agencies. It is very important that all educators be trained in protocols for reporting suspected cases of maltreatment and follow all guidelines so as to avoid penalties for not reporting. Teachers need to be aware of hotlines like the Childhelp USA National Child Abuse Hotline at (800-422-4453 to begin the process of protecting a child.

If a child discloses abuse, it is important that the educator remain calm and supportive. If the disclosure occurs during instruction, it is important that the educator acknowledge the disclosure but maintain strict confidentiality in the discussion and action of the disclosure. If teachers suspect abuse, they should not pressure the child to disclose but simply report what they have observed.

Teachers should remember the following guidelines when dealing with abuse:

- Follow your school's protocol for reporting.
- Remain calm, keep an open mind, and do not make judgments.
- Support the child with active listening.
- Find a quiet place to talk to the child.
- Reassure the child that he or she has done the right thing by telling someone.
- Listen to the child without interruptions. Let him or her talk openly about the situation, and record concrete information.
- Tell the child that there is help available.
- Reassure the child that you will do your best to protect and support him or her.
- Let the child know you must report the abuse to someone who has helped other children like him or her and their families.
- Report the incident to the proper authorities.
- Let the child know what will happen when the report is made, if you have the appropriate information.
- Seek out your own support persons to help you work through your feelings about the disclosure, if needed.
- Be aware of personal issues and how they affect your perception.
- Do not promise confidentiality.
- Remember that you are not responsible for investigating the claims, only reporting. Child Protective Services will do the investigations. (State of New Hampshire 2002).

Individual teachers are in a unique situation to recognize and report suspected cases of child abuse and neglect. Effective prevention programs reduce the number of victims, while educating a broader cross section of the public. Schools can become advocates for abuse-prevention education and student assistance. Programs and curricula that give children an understanding of appropriate and inappropriate behaviors, that incorporate information on sex and sexual health, and that share resources such as access to clinics and support groups are useful in the prevention of child abuse and neglect.

DO WHAT YOU CAN

Some recommendations. If a child who has been the victim of abuse and neglect is coming back to the classroom or school, what can an adult do? The classroom teacher can play a significant role in the reintegration of that child by acknowledging, but not dwelling on, the situation and then creating a supportive and safe environment for the child. It is important to remember that these children may require a high level of support and understanding from their teachers.

Teachers can provide a safe environment for children. Children need to know they can trust someone. Talk to the child one on one, show interest, and let the child know that you are there for him or her. Don't pressure the child to talk; take their lead as to the depth and breadth of the discussion. Work closely with the school counselor, social worker, or psychologist.

Teachers can create a sense of structure in their classrooms, which in turn gives a message of security for the child. Children will need very clear guidelines and instructions for any task that is asked of them. Adults need to be consistent but not overly controlling. Clear structure provides consistency, which helps a child feel safer and more secure.

Teachers can give the child lots of positive feedback. Give many encouraging statements to build a sense of self-worth. Let the child express a variety of emotions without receiving advice; always keep an open mind and provide many encouraging strategies.

Teachers need to be predictable in their behavior and clear about their expectations regarding behavior and academic performance. It is important to share information about new or upcoming situations. The child will need to be corrected in the same way as his or her peers for common classroom behaviors. The child needs to know that you will be fair in how you deal with all the students. The child needs to know that your expectations are the same for all students and that you have the belief that they can and will behave appropriately when in your room. These parameters help the student to know the limits.

Teachers need to make sure that all students feel included in the classroom. Strategies and grouping can be used to make sure that all children have an association with one or many children within the classroom.

EVALUATE YOUR SUCCESS

The measure of success with abused children is the elimination of all abuse so that all children can lead safe and protected lives. It would be wonderful if children's lives were not touched by abuse; however, we know that as long as there are social and environmental factors present in our society, we will have neglect and abuse. The key is prevention and education. We need to be able to provide support for families in trouble emotionally, socially, and economically.

Educators play a huge role in the protection of children. It is vital that educators be knowledgeable and proactive in dealing with issues around abuse. It is only through commitment, training, and action that we can begin to break the cycle of abuse. It is by bringing abuse out of the shadows that can we address it. We need to be able to be positive in our responses to this issue. We need to protect children and give the adults who abuse the skills to change their behaviors. Abuse is a cycle that, if unbroken, attacks each future generation. We have to be diligent in our efforts to help the abusers as well as the abused. It begins with one small step, one person at a time.

FIND OUT MORE

The following compilations can be found at www.childabuse.com/capubs .htm.

Child Neglect: A Guide for Intervention—Understanding the Causes of Neglect
    Most studies of child maltreatment include both neglectful and abusive families and fail to differentiate between the groups, thus making it impossible to identify results specifically related to neglect.
Children with Sexual Behavior Problems: Assessment and Treatment—Table 1— Child Demographic Information
    001 No 31 18 No Answer/Don't Know 73 18 Average Age at Experience of Sexual Abuse Mean 4 Years, 8 months 5 years, 6 months ns (Std. (2.27) (2.53) Number Reported Experiencing Emotional abuse.

The Risk and Prevention of Maltreatment of Children with Disabilities

Child maltreatment, also known as abuse and neglect, affects all types of children, but children with disabilities may be at even greater risk of being maltreated than children without disabilities.

Solutions: IN FOCUS: The Risk and Prevention of Maltreatment of Children with Disabilities

Child maltreatment, also known as abuse and neglect, affects all types of children, but children with disabilities may be at even greater risk of being maltreated than children without disabilities.

Child Sexual Abuse—Treatment of Child Sexual Abuse

Treatment of child sexual abuse is a complex process. In this chapter, case-management issues and treatment modalities are discussed, and a model for understanding why adults sexually abuse children is proposed.

Risk-Assessment Protocols for Child Sexual Abuse

I. Type of sexual abuse: 1. sexual talk comments, 2. exposure/voyeurism comments, 3. fondle outside clothing comments, 4. fondle underclothing/digital comments, 5. oral sex/genital/anal penetration and copulation.

Crisis Intervention in Child Abuse and Neglect—Glossary of Terms

Case planning: This is the stage of the child-protection intervention process when the Child Protective Services (CPS) caseworker and other service providers develop a case plan with the family members. Evaluation of Family Progress.

Crisis Intervention in Child Abuse and Neglect—Understanding Special Family Situations

Crisis workers need to be especially sensitive to how child maltreatment may occur in response to divorce, stepfamilies, single-parent families, drug dependence and drug-related behavior, spousal abuse, and mental illness.

Developmental Disabilities and Child Maltreatment

This database search is a product of the National Clearinghouse on Child Abuse and Neglect Information. CD-27683 Reporting Abuse and Neglect of Children with Disabilities: Early Childhood Service Programs.

Treatment for Abused and Neglected Children: Infancy to Age 18—Notes

Kazdin, A. E. "Developmental Psychopathology: Current Research, Issues, and Directions." *American Psychologist* 44 (1989): 180–87; Handbook of Child Psychology: Social and Personality Development.

Treatment for Abused and Neglected Children: Infancy to Age 18—Consequences of Abuse and Neglect

Child maltreatment is a multidimensional and interactive problem involving the child and the multiple environments in which the child exists.

Protecting Children in Substance-Abusing Families—Children of Chemically Involved Parents: Special Risks

This chapter describes the health and development of children exposed prenatally to alcohol and/or other drugs. However, among infants who have been prenatally exposed to these substances, there is a wide, random study group.

Protecting Children in Substance-Abusing Families—Reporting Child Maltreatment in Cases Involving Parental Substance Abuse

Determining if and when parental substance abuse should be reported to a CPS agency is a difficult but important issue. State laws, policies, guidelines, and definitions govern the reporting of child abuse.

Protecting Children in Substance-Abusing Families—Notes

Child Welfare League of America, *Highlights of Questions from the Working Paper on Chemical Dependency*. Washington, D.C.: Child Welfare League of America, 1989. UCLA Medical Center, "Suspected Child Abuse."

Child Sexual Abuse—Investigation of Child Sexual Abuse

This chapter describes the role of CPS in the investigation of cases of sexual abuse, the structure of the investigation, and risk assessment in child sexual abuse.

Child Sexual Abuse—Interview Data Gathered from the Offender

Information rationale: (1) past history of physical abuse, neglect, and so forth, and potential for deficits in nurturing skills and lack of empathy with victim; (2) past history of sexual abuse and propensity to become an abuser. This outline assists the examiner.

Child Sexual Abuse—Interview Data Gathered from the Mother

Information rationale: (1) past history of physical abuse, neglect, and so forth, and potential for problems in parenting; (2) past history of sexual abuse and possible propensity to choose a sexual abuser as a partner, placing children in marriage at risk. This outline assists the examiner.

Child Neglect: A Guide for Intervention—Prevention of Neglect

The tragic consequences of child neglect suggest that significantly greater efforts should be directed toward prevention. Tertiary prevention entails targeting services to neglecting parents through development of a range of services to parents at risk of neglect and their children, who are potential victims.

Child Protective Services—Philosophy of Child Protective Services

The legal authority and the mandates that evolved from child abuse laws are described in *A Coordinated Response to Child Abuse and Neglect: A Basic Manual*. The philosophy provides sound professional CPS practice guidelines.

Child Protective Services—Overview of the Manual

Child abuse and neglect are community concerns. CPS, a division within state and local social service agencies, is at the center of every community's child-protection efforts.

Child Protective Services—Comprehensive Child and Family Assessment

The purposes of child and family assessment are to study the nature, extent, and causes of risk factors identified during the initial assessment and to assess any effects of maltreatment.

Maltreatment of Children with Disabilities Training and Prevention Program Resources

Training audience: parents and professionals who work with children with disabilities. *Intended usage:* material for trainers. *Format:* trainers' guide, transparencies, and participant handouts.

Prevention in Action

For example, a lack of effective parenting skills and understanding of child development may contribute to parental difficulties in providing appropriate care to children and could result in abusive behavior.

Substance Abuse

A comprehensive collection of more than thirty-one thousand documents related to child maltreatment and child welfare issues, such as CD-25656, *HIV Risk-Behavior in Poor Urban Women with Serious Mental Disorders: Association with Childhood Physical and Sexual Abuse*. The categories of HIV-related risk factors included adult sexual and physical assault or abuse.

Drug-Exposed Infants

The Impact of Drug-Exposed Children on Family Foster Care

Training the Child Welfare Workforce (Excluding Preprofessional Education)

The primary focus of this search is child welfare professional training in the United States. Training is for child-protective and child welfare services staff for collaboration and community-based agencies.

Solutions: Maltreatment of Children with Disabilities Training and Prevention Program Resources

Abuse and Neglect of Children with Disabilities: A Curriculum for Educators, Law Enforcement, Child Protective Services and Parents. Training audience: parents and professionals who work with children with disabilities.

Thirteen of the Best Books and Articles on Child Abuse Prevention

1. Barker, Judy, and Deborah T. Hodes. 2003. *The Child in Mind: A Child Protection Handbook*. New York: Routledge.

2. Gilbert, Neil. 1997. *Combating Child Abuse: International Perspectives and Trends.* New York: Oxford University Press.
3. Wurtele, Sandy K., and Cindy L. Miller-Perrin. 1993. *Preventing Child Sexual Abuse: Sharing the Responsibility.* Lincoln: University of Nebraska Press.
4. Roberts, Jennifer A., and Raymond G. Miltenberger. 1999. "Emerging Issues in the Research on Child Sexual Abuse Prevention." *Education & Treatment of Children* 22, 84–102.
5. Justice, Blair, and Rita Justice. 1990. *The Abusing Family* (see especially ch. 9, "Primary Prevention of Child Abuse"). New York: Insight Books
6. Landsberg, Gerald, and Corrine Wattam. 2001. "Differing Approaches to Combating Child Abuse: United States vs. United Kingdom." *Journal of International Affairs* 55, 111–24.
7. Bolen, Rebecca M. 2003. "Child Sexual Abuse: Prevention or Promotion?" *Social Work* 48(2): 174–85.
8. Rothery, Michael, and Gary Cameron. 1990. *Child Maltreatment: Expanding Our Concept of Helping* (see especially ch. 11, "Preventing Child Abuse and Neglect"). New York: Lawrence Erlbaum.
9. Westman, Jack C. 2002. *Licensing Parents: Can We Prevent Child Abuse and Neglect?* New York: DaCapo Press.
10. Osofsky, Joy D. 1997. *Children in a Violent Society* (see especially part II, "Prevention and Intervention Programs for Children and Families Exposed to Violence"). New York: Guilford Press.
11. Bensley, Lillian, Katrina Wynkoop Simmons, Deborah Ruggles, Tammy Putvin, Cynthia Harris, Melissa Allen, and Kathy Williams. 2004. "Community Responses and Perceived Barriers to Responding to Child Maltreatment." *Journal of Community Health* 29, 141–55.
12. Walker, Bonnie L. 1996. *Injury Prevention for Young Children: A Research Guide* (see especially ch. 3, "Child Abuse and Firearms"). Westport, CT: Greenwood Press.
13. Maney, Ann, and Susan Wells. 1988. *Professional Responsibilities in Protecting Children: A Public Health Approach to Child Sexual Abuse* (see especially ch. 1, "Professional Involvement in Public Health Strategies for the Prevention and Control of Child Sexual Abuse"). New York: Praeger Publishers.

Helpful Websites

Child Abuse Prevention Network, http://child-abuse.com/
ChildAbuse.com, www.childabuse.com

Childsafetykits.com, www.childsafetykits.com
PANdora's Box, www.prevent-abuse-now.com
Suite101.com, www.suite101.com
Tennyson Center for Children, www.childabuse.org
The Prevention Researcher, www.tpronline.org

References

American Psychological Association (APA). 2003. Protecting our children from abuse and neglect. Washington, DC: APA.

State of New Hampshire, Office of the Attorney General, Task Force on Child Abuse and Neglect. 2002. *Child abuse and neglect: Guidelines for New Hampshire school employees: Recognizing and reporting suspected child abuse and neglect*. 2nd ed. Concord, NH: Department of Education.

Texas Department of Family and Protective Services (DFPS). 2005. Your role regarding child abuse. DFPS. www.dfps.state.tx.us (accessed February 26, 2008).

U.S. Department of Health and Human Services. 2007. Mental health: A report of the surgeon general. National Mental Health Information Center. www.mentalhealth.org (accessed February 26, 2008).

Chapter Fifteen

Environmental Threats

Lead Poisoning and Other Environmental and Household Toxins

Hidden toxic dangers in the environment surround our children. One such danger is poisoning. Perhaps the most pervasive threat to the health and safety of children is lead poisoning, although certainly children are also at risk of poisoning from other environmental and common household elements. This chapter discusses the most dangerous and widespread environmental poisoning threats that face our children (including lead, mercury, radon, and DEET), as well as household products. Educators, parents, and other caregivers need to be on the lookout for hazardous substances for children and possible cognitive and/or physical effects from accidental poisoning.

> ## ASK: WHAT IS POTENTIALLY DANGEROUS OR PROBLEMATIC FOR CHILDREN? WHAT CAN I DO (OR WHAT CAN BE DONE) TO MAKE THIS CHILD (OR THESE CHILDREN) SAFER OR HEALTHIER OR MORE SUCCESSFUL IN THIS/THESE SITUATION/S (OR SIMILAR ONES)?

Lead poisoning. According to the Centers for Disease Control (CDC), unintentional poisoning is the fourth leading cause of injury death for children aged fifteen to twenty-four. As the American Academy of Pediatrics (AAP) wrote, "Of all the health problems caused by the environment, lead poisoning is the most preventable. Despite this, almost 1 million children in the United States have elevated levels of lead in their blood. Any child can be at risk for lead poisoning" (2005, para. 1).

Lead poisoning has been on the decline since 1991 when the CDC reported that as many as one in eleven American children had significantly elevated lead levels. Since that time, airborne lead from the use of leaded gasoline has been virtually eliminated. Currently, much lead poisoning in children happens from lead paint in the form of dust or in the soil. Also, lead poisoning can be transferred from mother to child through the placenta and/or breast milk, and lead can be ingested by drinking tap water from lead plumbing (AAP Policy Statement 2005)

U.S. News & World Report (2008) stated that lead poisoning "afflicts an estimated 890,000 American preschoolers [and] can be a threat in any house or apartment with lead paint, even if fresh paint is layered over it."

Children can be exposed not only through paint on houses but, as has recently been discovered, through paint on recalled toys, as well as through the following:

* soils
* household dusts
* leaded paints
* gasoline

The report features the research of Theodore Lidsky and Jay Schneider, who studied fifty children with dangerous levels of lead in their blood and found that the following were warning signs:

* fine motor skills problems
* memory problems
* concentration problems
* behavioral problems that look like attention deficit hyperactivity disorder
* reduction in IQ scores, according to some studies

Some of the signs look similar to attention deficit disorder. Adult caregivers, teachers, or anyone else working with children should encourage lead-poisoning blood tests for children. Some studies have shown that even very low levels of lead in the blood of young children can produce problematic effects like the ones listed above, as well as trouble with balance, coordination, problem solving, and movement (Schmidt 1999). There are treatment agents that can reduce lead levels in the blood. Prevention is obviously preferable—as is catching problems early in childhood.

Mercury poisoning, immunizations, and autism. A study published in 2006 showed a decline in certain kinds of neurodevelopmental disorders (such as those discussed in an earlier chapter on the brain and learning) after thimerosal (which contains mercury) was removed from childhood vaccines in the United States. Despite evidence of the harmful effects of mercury, however, it is a primary ingredient in many dental fillings (mercuryexposure.org). And another study in 2006 in Texas showed that as environmental mercury levels increased, so did rates of autism and special education services (Palmer et al. 2006). In addition, another study has shown that mercury exposure in utero and in early childhood from eating mercury-exposed fish is linked to some deficits among children with higher mercury levels (Davidson et al. 2006). A study conducted by D. A. Geier and M. R. Geier (2007) urine-tested seventy-one children with autism and found that these children had significantly higher (toxic) mercury levels than their siblings and other control group members. It is important to note that these studies are hotly contested and that there have been no causal links—the studies are typically correlational (showing relationships between two things), and no studies show a direct causal relationship. However, the evidence bears mentioning here so that parents and other caregivers can make informed decisions.

DEET and other insecticides. The AAP's position on the use of insect repellents containing DEET (N,N-diethyl-m-toluamide, also known as N,N-diethyl-3-methylbenzamide) on children is as follows:

> DEET-containing products are the most effective mosquito repellents available. DEET also is effective as a repellent against a variety of other insects, including ticks. It should be used when there is a need to prevent insect-borne disease. The concentration of DEET in products may range from less than 10% to over 30%. The efficacy of DEET plateaus at a concentration of 30%, the maximum concentration currently recommended for infants and children. The major difference in the efficacy of products relates to their duration of action. Products with concentrations around 10% are effective for periods of approximately two hours. As the concentration of DEET increases, the duration of activity increases; for example, a concentration of

about 24% has been shown to provide an average of 5 hours of protection. (AAP 2003, para. 2)

The AAP does not recommend using DEET products on children under the age of two months, and other organizations suggest avoiding the use of DEET products on children under two years of age. According to the Sierra Club, Canada legally banned products with more than 30 percent DEET because some research has shown that in high doses neurological problems can occur from excessive DEET exposure in rats (www.sierra club.ca). However, the stance among the medical community is that the benefits of avoiding diseases transmitted by biting insects from the effective use of DEET outweigh the risks.

Radon. According the Environmental Protection Agency (EPA), radon is responsible for an estimated fourteen thousand preventable lung cancer deaths per year (with estimates ranging between seven thousand and thirty thousand) (EPA 2008). The EPA states,

Radon is a cancer-causing natural radioactive gas that you can't see, smell or taste. Its presence in your home can pose a danger to your family's health. Radon is the leading cause of lung cancer among non-smokers. Radon is the second leading cause of lung cancer in American and claims about 20,000 lives annually. (2008, para. 1)

The EPA encourages families to test their homes for radon. Schools should also test for radon and provide education to families to promote testing (perhaps raising money to assist low-income families). January is the designated National Radon Awareness/Action Month, and states are encouraged to promote educational campaigns. Drinking water can also carry radon and should be tested.

Other household chemicals and poisons. An article about childhood poisoning by Hingley (1996) states, "Iron containing products remain the biggest problem by far when it comes to childhood poisoning. Most people regard their home as a safe haven, a calming oasis in a stormy world. But home can be a dangerous place when it comes to accidental poisoning, especially accidental poisoning of children. One tablet of some medicines can wreak havoc on or kill a child."

Some of the other nonpharmacological substances that the American Association of Poison Control Centers reported were

- glues
- alcohols (ethanol, isopropanol, methanol)
- art supplies
- batteries
- automotive/boat products (e.g., ethylene glycol)
- building products
- other chemicals (acids, acetone, pool products, cleaning solvents/chemicals, cosmetics)
- fertilizers/herbicides/insecticides
- gases
- paints/varnishes
- plants
- stings
- tobacco products

Pharmaceutical substances. The following commonly found elements in medicine cabinets were among the most responsible for pediatric poisonings:

- analgesics (aspirin, acetaminophen, ibuprofen)
- analgesics with other narcotic substances such as codeine, oxycodone, and so forth
- topical anesthetics
- antianxiety agents
- antidepressants
- antihistamines
- antimicrobials (e.g., antibiotics)
- cold medications
- sedatives
- stimulants/street drugs
- vitamins (including iron and fluoride)

Many adults may consider drugs such as aspirin, acetaminophen, and ibuprofen to be relatively benign, but the truth is they are among the drugs most commonly associated with overdose deaths (often in cases of suicide) and toxic levels brought to emergency rooms. We must be especially careful with these common household substances to be sure caps are on tightly and that they are out of reach of children.

BRING TOGETHER ALL ADVOCATES WHO CAN ASSIST IN MAKING CHILDREN SAFER IN THESE SITUATIONS

Adult caregivers, physicians, emergency medical personnel (e.g., first responders and EMTs), teachers, child-care workers, school administrators, and counselors should all be educated about the cognitive and physical signs of environmental poisoning, such as that due to lead or other household medications or items (more on psychoactive medications will be discussed in a later chapter).

Schools are the logical spaces for community-awareness campaigns about the impact of lead and other environmental toxins. Also, hospitals or community medical centers can work with communities and their members to highlight the signs of environmental toxins and to offer free lead-screening programs.

Education and screening will help, but considering the possibility of poisoning when a child shows signs of cognitive shortcomings will also help with the diagnosis—which means those on the front lines of a child's cognitive development (e.g., teachers and parents) need to be aware of the warning signs.

CONSIDER THE OPTIONS (PARTICULARLY ONES WITH DEMONSTRATED SUCCESS)

Lead poisoning. Consider the following recommendations to reduce risk of lead poisoning among children:

- Educate parents, teachers, and other caregivers that lead poisoning can be invisible and can harm children when they put dust or toys in their mouths.
- Ask parents and school personnel to do an inventory of possibly hazardous, lead-containing material around the house. The Department of Health can do assessments at schools or homes where lead hazards are thought to exist.
- School personnel, physicians, and parents should know the laws about universal screening—and eligibility for screening under Medicare.

- Early lead screening should ideally take place when a child is one year old—and those at higher risk should be tested again at age two.
- Parents should consider their own exposure to lead to determine if they (particularly mothers) can pass along lead poisoning to their infants.
- The Department of Housing and Urban Development does have funds to improve old homes with substantial lead paint threats.

The AAP recommends the following prevention strategies:

Environmental lead-based threat	*Prevention strategy*
Paint	Identify and abate
Dust	Wet mop (assuming abatement)
Soil	Restrict play in area, plan ground cover, wash hands frequently
Drinking water	Flush cold-water pipes by running the water until it becomes as cold as it will get (a few seconds to two minutes or more). Use cold water for cooking and drinking (AAP 2005, table 3).

The AAP also recommends avoiding any possible folk remedies, cosmetics, toys, or mineral substances that have lead in them. In addition, if parents have jobs or hobbies where they come into contact with lead, they need to be careful with their work clothing (remove it at work and wash separately, and store hobby items carefully).

Radon testing. The EPA calls the radon threat a "health hazard with a simple solution" (EPA 2008). We know that radon is a carcinogen. We know that some homes have dangerous levels of radon. We do not know which homes unless they have been tested. There are do-it-yourself home test kits, or you can have your home professionally tested. If excessive levels are found, radon-abatement programs can be installed to reduce the levels of radon in the home. The EPA has a website where you can check your risk by state at www.epa.gov/radon/zonemap.html#more%20about%20the%20map.

DO WHAT YOU CAN

As a parent or caregiver. Educate yourself about the impact of these toxic chemicals on your own and your growing child's body and brain. Be sure to work with a physician to have children screened as early as possible, and be aware of cognitive delays.

As a school teacher, administrator, or counselor. If you notice any of the warning signs, like cognitive delays or other signs, be sure to encourage the child's parents to seek medical attention as soon as possible, which should include a blood test to screen for toxic agents such as lead or mercury.

As a physician or other health care professional. Conduct assessments of risk for lead and mercury poisoning. Urge parents to have their young children screened, and rule out poisoning when presented with cognitive or other constellations of symptoms that indicate possible poisoning.

Other poisonings, radon, and DEET. Educate yourself and your community about the need to take precautions to protect children from toxic substances in the home as well as the importance of having your home tested for radon. As far as using DEET, use as needed with percentages less that 30 percent with children older than age two. Educational campaigns set forth by day care providers, preschool centers, and schools can be really useful for increasing awareness on these topics—as can public service announcements on television or radio. Educating children on the dangers of radon, for example, in the same way we educate them about the dangers of smoking, can be effective as well.

Environmental threats for children around the world. According to the United Nations Environmental Program (UNEP), children around the world are at risk in utero, after they are born, and throughout their lives from a variety of environmental threats, such as lack of safe water and sanitation, chemical pollution and radiation, indoor and outdoor air pollution, and natural resource degradation. While some parts of the world have greater risks than others, we must work together in our global community to improve these threatening conditions.

EVALUATE YOUR SUCCESS

Certainly medical records will show declines in lead poisoning and increases in screening if education and outreach are reducing rates. Reduction in emergency room visits and 911 calls related to household chemical and pharmaceutical poisonings will also show the success of any educational or outreach campaign to increase awareness of these all-too-common dangers for children. Also, increasing the number of radon tests conducted in a community—and determining policy changes that make testing for radon a legal mandate for the sale of a home as well as a part of paying homeowner's insurance (providing proof of testing)—will also be a sign of improvement in the risk to children and adults posed by radon exposure. And finally, lobbying for vaccines that are mercury-free in all areas of the world may also have some impact in prompting vaccine manufacturers to create safer vaccines.

We must determine if we are improving the overall quality of our air, water, and earth in general for our children. UNEP has some recommendations and programs with some demonstrated successes (these are too numerous to mention here, but they can be found on their website at www.UNEP.org). For example, they recommend starting with a "climate-friendly lifestyle" that seeks to "kick the CO_2 habit," suggesting that we can make a difference and improve our planet for its future inhabitants.

FIND OUT MORE

American Academy of Pediatrics (AAP). 2005. Policy statement: Lead exposure in children: Prevention, detection and management. *Pediatrics* 116, (4): 1036–46.

American Academy of Pediatrics (AAP) Patient Education Online. 2008. Lead screening for children. AAP Patient Education Online. http://patiented.aap .org/content.aspx?aid=5568 (accessed June 6, 2008).

Davidson, P., G. Myers, B. Weiss, C. Shamlaye, and C. Cox. 2006. Prenatal methyl mercury exposure from fish consumption and child development: A review of evidence and perspectives from the Seychelles Child Development Study. *Neurotoxicology* 27, (6): 1106–109.

Environmental Protection Agency. 2008. Radon. EPA. www.EPA.gov/radon (accessed October 22, 2008).

Geier, D. A., and M. R. Geier. 2007. A prospective study of mercury toxicity biomarkers in autistic spectrum disorders. *Journal of Toxicology and Environmental Health, Part A* 70, (20): 1723–30.

Hingley, Audrey T. 1996. Preventing childhood poisoning: Iron-containing products remain the biggest problem by far when it comes to childhood poisoning.

BNET. http://findarticles.com/p/articles/mi_m1370/is_n2_v30/ai_18175435? tag=content;col1.

Palmer, R. F., S. Blanchard, Z. Stein, D. Mandell, and C. Miller. 2006. Environmental mercury release, special education rates, and autism disorder: An ecological study of Texas. *Health and Place* 12, (2): 203–209.

Schmidt, Charles W. 1999. Poisoning young minds. *Environmental Health Perspectives* 107, (6). www.ehponline.org/docs/1999/107-6/focus.html.

Sierra Club of Canada. DEET fact sheet. Sierra Club of Canada. www.sierraclub.ca/atlantic/programs/healthycommunities/pesticides/factsheets/deet.pdf (accessed June 8, 2008).

U.S. News and World Report. 2008. Health tip: Get children tested for lead poisoning. U.S. News and World Report Online. www.usnews.com/usnews/health/healthday/080104/health-tip-get-children-tested-for-lead-poisoning.htm (accessed October 22, 2008).

Chapter Sixteen

Healthy Lifestyle Choices

Reducing Childhood Obesity and Inactivity and Improving Childhood Nutrition

Worldwide, concerns about children's adequate nutritional needs as well as their intake of healthy and safe drinking water are great. Inadequate nutrition, fast and processed food, and overreliance on sodas and other high-calorie beverages instead of healthy water and food, as well as a lack of physical activity, have resulted in an epidemic of overweight children.

Childhood obesity poses one of the greatest long-term health threats to our nation's children. Part of the growing trend of obesity is the result of poor nutrition, and part is from inactivity. The number one killer of adult Americans is that "silent killer" of heart disease—and obesity contributes to risk factors for heart disease.

The best predictor of adult obesity is childhood obesity, as a recent, comprehensive study following nearly ten thousand children into adulthood found (Freedman, Khan, and Dietz 2001). There are ways that adult caregivers can reduce the risk later in life for children and adolescents. The primary ways are through the promotion of a healthy diet low in fat and processed foods, plenty of healthy water (and reduction of sodas or other drinks high in sugar), reduced stress/anxiety, involvement in food decisions (shopping, preparation, and so forth), and regular exercise.

> ### ASK: WHAT IS POTENTIALLY DANGEROUS OR PROBLEMATIC FOR CHILDREN? WHAT CAN I DO (OR WHAT CAN BE DONE) TO MAKE THIS CHILD (OR THESE CHILDREN) SAFER OR HEALTHIER OR MORE SUCCESSFUL IN THIS/THESE SITUATION/S (OR SIMILAR ONES)?

Poor nutrition. Poor nutrition is perhaps one of the greatest worldwide health concerns, one that will affect as many as one billion of the world's children in the future. The United Nations has reported that "malnourishment could stunt and handicap an estimated 1 billion children worldwide by 2020 unless a more focused nutrition campaign is launched" (CNN 2000). In addition to inadequate nutrition affecting children, poor nutrition harms the fetus in women who are malnourished. Direct links have been made between malnourishment and diseases, including chronic diseases (such as diabetes) and learning problems/deficiencies and delays. Some studies have shown that children who do not get proper nutrition are at higher risk of behavioral disorders or problems. And some recent studies have shown that those who eat a healthy breakfast perform better academically (Mahoney et al. 2005).

In the United States, a study with the U.S. Department of Agriculture and Harvard University found that

> U.S. children who ate fast food, compared with those who did not, consumed more total calories, more calories per gram of food, more total and saturated fat, more total carbohydrate, more added sugars and more sugar-sweetened beverages, but less milk, fiber, fruit and nonstarchy vegetables. The study also revealed out of the two days surveyed, those children who consumed fast food on only one day showed similar nutrient shortfalls on the day they had fast food. But they did not show these shortfalls on the other day. (Bliss 2004, para. 3)

Our increased reliance on fast and processed foods is resulting in a generation of poorly nourished children; some studies have estimated that daily meals from fast food establishments have increased from 2 percent to 10 percent since the late 1970s (Bliss 2004). One of the many concerns associated with poor nutrition, including greater reliance on fast and processed foods, is an increase in childhood obesity.

Childhood obesity. Why should we care so much about childhood obesity? Children who are obese risk long-term health risks (such as heart disease), but they can also develop more immediate health problems such as type 2 diabetes, high blood pressure, asthma/respiratory or other breathing problems, early puberty, skin infections, eating disorders, sleep disturbances/disorders, and even liver disease. In addition, children who are extremely overweight are often at higher risk of being bullied and harassed and suffer lowered self-esteem, leading to learning problems and/or depression.

BRING TOGETHER ALL ADVOCATES WHO CAN ASSIST IN MAKING CHILDREN SAFER IN THESE SITUATIONS

Parents, children, community members, school counselors and administrators, physicians, nutritionists, physical education and other teachers, school board members, health care professionals, community center personnel, and organizations (such as parent-teacher organizations) should work together to create local campaigns to get kids outside (creating safe spaces to be outside where adults can be watching vigilantly) exercising, playing, and active. These advocates should also determine ways to assure that all children have regular access to nutritious meals and snacks every day.

CONSIDER THE OPTIONS (PARTICULARLY ONES WITH DEMONSTRATED SUCCESS)

Diet at home. Children need to eat healthy food. The guidelines are available on the updated food pyramid (promoted by the U.S. Department of Agriculture). An individualized "pyramid," or plan, depends on age, gender, weight, and physical activity level. To create an individualized plan for a child or children, visit the U.S. Department of Agriculture at www.mypyramid.gov for more information. For example, for the typically developing eight-year-old female who gets less than thirty minutes of physical exercise, the plan is for fourteen hundred calories per day: 5 ounces of grains (preferably whole grains), 1.5 cups of vegetables, 1.5 cups of fruits, 2 cups of milk, and 4 ounces of meat and beans. The information on the website promotes at least sixty minutes of physical activity every day, limiting oils to less than four tablespoons per day. Extra fats and sugars should be limited to 170 calories or less, with the following variation in the veggies: 1.5 cups of dark green/leafy vegetables weekly, 1 cup of orange vegetables, 1 cup of dry beans and peas weekly, 2.5 cups of starchy vegetables, and 4.5 cups of other vegetables, all at least weekly. More information can be found on the U.S. Department of Agriculture's website at www.mypyramid.gov.

School breakfast and lunch programs. As school-aged children spend much of their waking hours in school, schools have become places where low-income children are consistently able to receive free or reduced-price lunches and breakfasts. Mahoney et al. found that children who took advantage of the school breakfast program had improved academic performance in school. School lunches and breakfasts in low-income areas are still often highly processed; were they made even more nutritious, they would likely yield even greater cognitive and physical results. Another concern about children eligible for school lunches is the lack of healthy food available to children on the weekends and during school vacations. Communities need to work together to ensure proper nutrition is made available to all children every day.

Drinking water. There have been campaigns to assure fresh, safe drinking water in schools. The EPA reports that many schools have lead in their school drinking water, even if the community water supply meets EPA regulations, due to lead plumbing and seasonal use patterns. The U.S. EPA oversees the Safe Drinking Water Act, which guarantees safe drinking water (www.epa.gov). For the good of our environment and because of new health discoveries showing the negative impact of plastic bottles, we need to promote healthy drinking water from the faucet.

Providing safe drinking water to the world's children is also a high priority for the World Health Organization and the United Nations as dehydration is a leading cause of death and other physical and learning problems in high-poverty areas of the world. The United Kingdom has instituted a program called Water Is Cool in School to promote providing healthy drinking water to children in school (www.wateriscoolinschool.org).

A Welsh study in which students in 275 elementary schools were provided fresh water and encouraged to drink adequate amounts of water daily found the following:

In research carried out by the Welsh Assembly Government's Health Promotion Division in schools using PHS Waterlogic's machines, teachers reported that they believed children's concentration was improved and that they were less tired in class. Teachers also reported that children were not drinking so many sugary fizzy drinks. Teachers felt that the children enjoyed having drinking water available, and increased the amount of water that they drank during the school day. (PHS Group 2005, para. 3)

Depending on size, weight, physical activity, and the weather, children should drink as many as eight to ten glasses of water per day. Suffice it to say, very few children drink that much water, and many are dehydrated in schools. The brain needs sufficient water to function effectively, and children need to be encouraged to drink more water, and they should have safe water close and available.

Childhood obesity and activity. Physical activity is an important factor in reducing health risks from obesity in children. Parents and other caregivers can help children by promoting physical fitness, reducing television and video game (and other sedentary activities) time, and encouraging outside active play. For example, a study published in 2006 by Gable, Chang, and Krull found,

Children who watched more television and ate fewer family meals were more likely to be overweight for the first time at spring semester of third grade. Children who watched more television, ate fewer family meals and lived in neighborhoods perceived by parents as less safe for outdoor play were more likely to be persistently overweight. Child aerobic exercise and opportunities for activity were not associated with a greater likelihood of weight problems. . . . This study supports theories regarding the contributions of television watching, family meals and neighborhood safety to childhood weight status. (2006, 53)

Clearly, the results of this study and the several that these authors reviewed show that parents need to reduce the television watching of their children. They also need to work to create time for family meals—and to learn about nutrition to provide healthy meals.

Making exercise fun and part of the daily routine (even in bad weather) is critically important for children and adolescents. Young people need to get at least sixty minutes of cardiovascular exercise every day. Given the very busy lives of families and young people, finding time for this kind of activity can be difficult. And this can be particularly challenging in areas where the weather can be extreme.

Important things to consider include the following:

- Ensure that an adult always supervises children playing outside.
- Always use sunscreen any time a child is outside (SPF of fifty preferably).
- Ensure that there is time for free play.
- Ensure that there is time for structured physical activities to make sure children are moving around.
- Ensure that children wear clothing appropriate for the climate.
- In cold weather climates, check for signs of frostbite on any exposed areas.
- If children must remain indoors because of the weather, find a safe place where they can be active—in a gymnasium at school, or a spot in the house where they can jog in place, do jumping jacks, and so forth. Consider having an age-appropriate workout video or music.
- Find safe places to go for walks (parks, woods, sidewalks, and so on)—this is good for adults and children. Sometimes children need to build up their stamina; start with shorter walks and build up to longer ones. For younger children, think of ways to make it interesting—go on a "treasure hunt" for the prettiest leaves or see how many seconds a child can run or walk like an elephant.
- Make a set time every day to exercise, and make it part of the family routine, like eating dinner. Going for an after-dinner walk can be very helpful for metabolizing this large meal.

Exercise is a good way to reduce stress and anxiety. However, sometimes children and adolescents have extreme levels of stress and anxiety. See the chapter on anxiety for some of the warning signs.

Physical fitness in schools. Research reports have shown that with the increased emphasis on test score performance, schools have been dramatically reducing, and sometimes even eliminating altogether, physical education and fitness programs, as well as recess, particularly in low-income neighborhoods (Kozol 2006). Low-income neighborhoods have the highest rates of childhood obesity and perhaps need even more physical education and fitness in schools—as schools are often the safest places in the neighborhood.

DO WHAT YOU CAN

Demand clean drinking water and nutritious food for all children. We need to protect our environment and work together to reduce contaminants put into the ground water and other water sources. We also need to work with authorities to test and provide clean drinking water in schools and homes—and we need to be particularly vigilant in low-income areas. Also, we need to continue to fund and work to improve the quality of food provided through such programs as the federal free and reduced-price lunch and breakfast programs, as well as to assure all children access to healthy foods consistent with their individual needs.

Obesity. The Mayo Clinic (2008, para. 27) recommends the following to prevent childhood obesity:

- *Schedule yearly well-child visits.* Take your child to the doctor for well-child checkups at least once a year. During this visit, the doctor measures your child's height and weight and calculates his or her body-mass index (BMI). Increases in your child's BMI or in his or her percentile rank over one year, especially if your child is older than 4, is a possible sign that your child is at risk of becoming overweight.
- *Set a good example.* Make sure you eat healthy foods and exercise regularly to maintain your weight. Then, invite your child to join you.
- *Avoid food-related power struggles with your child.* You might unintentionally lay the groundwork for such battles by providing or withholding certain foods—sweets, for instance—as rewards or punishments. As a general rule, foods aren't recommended for behavior modification in children.
- *Emphasize the positive.* Encourage a healthy lifestyle by highlighting the positive—the fun of playing outside or the variety of fresh fruit you can get year-round, for example. Emphasize the benefits of exercise apart from helping to manage their weight, for example, it makes their heart, lungs and other muscles stronger. If you foster your child's natural inclination to run around, explore and eat only when hungry—not out of boredom—a healthy weight should take care of itself.

- *Be patient.* Many overweight children grow into their extra pounds as they get taller. Realize, too, that an intense focus on your child's eating habits and weight can easily backfire, leading a child to overeat even more, or possibly making him or her more prone to developing an eating disorder.

Demand regular physical activity and education in school. As many school districts are cutting physical education (PE) time and recess/play time, children are getting far less of the activity they need in a given week. As parents and teachers or other concerned community members, lobby for more time spent in PE courses and after-school intramural activities and organized athletics. Children should strive toward sixty minutes of physical activity per day. As most of their waking time is spent in schools, this is the logical place for this to happen.

EVALUATE YOUR SUCCESS

Test drinking water and see how much kids are drinking. First, test your school's water fountains to determine the water's quality—test for lead and other pathogens. Determine if the drinking water is safe—if not, work with the EPA to be sure that your school offers quality water. Also, test drinking water in the homes within a community. After launching campaigns for fresh, clean water and promoting sufficient drinking of water, retest the water at various locations and different times to ensure that it is still safe. Also, observe children and ask teachers how much children are actually drinking.

Take children for basic yearly physicals to determine BMI and nutritional intake. After improving the amount and quality of physical education and activity for children, be sure to measure the fitness and BMI of children to determine if there is some improvement in the overall fitness and reduction in obesity levels in your school. As parents, you can work with your child's pediatrician to determine a plan and measure progress toward lowered BMI and increased levels of fitness.

Examine absences and test scores. Perhaps one of the best and easiest measures of improved nutrition and fitness is examining changes in absenteeism in schools as well as test scores. If children are living and eating better, they will feel better, be healthier, and attend school more regularly—and ultimately they will perform better.

FIND OUT MORE

Nutrition

Child nutrition: HealthCorps, www.healthcorps.org.

Child nutrition and health: U.S. Department of Agriculture, www.usda.gov.

Child nutrition, health, and physical activity: International Food Information Council, www.ific.org/nutrition/kids/index.cfm.

Childhood nutrition: Keep Kids Healthy, www.keepkidshealthy.com/nutrition/childhood_nutrition.html.

Kids nutrition resources: KidsHealth, www.kidshealth.org.

Nutrition education: MyPyramid, www.mypyramid.gov.

School nutrition: School Nutrition Association, www.schoolnutrition.org.

School nutrition programs: USDA Economic Research Service, www.ers.usda.gov/Briefing/ChildNutrition.

State information on child nutrition programs: USDA Food and Nutrition Service, www.fns.usda.gov/cnd/Contacts/StateDirectory.htm.

World Health Organization nutrition disorders: World Health Organization, www.who.int/topics/nutrition_disorders/en.

Water

Keidel.com. no date. Wellness and water intake. Keidel.com. www.keidel.com/resource/wellness/h20.htm.

KidsHealth. 2006. Dehydration. KidsHealth, http://kidshealth.org/teen/safety/first_aid/dehydration.html.

Morris, Suzanne Evans. no date. Water intake for health and well-being, Olin College Faculty, faculty.olin.edu/~jcrisman/Service/KWTWebNews/Nutrition/water.htm

Petter, L. P., J. O. Hourihane, and C. J. Rolles. 1995. Is water out of vogue? A survey of drinking habits of 2-7 year olds. PubMed Central. www.pubmedcentral.nih.gov/articlerender.fcgi?artid=1511032.

Water Is Cool in School. 2005. FAQ. Water Is Cool in School. www.wateriscoolinschool.org.uk/faq.html.

Obesity

American Obesity Association, http://obesity1.tempdomainname.com/subs/childhood.

Centers for Disease Control and Prevention, www.cdc.gov/nccdphp/dnpa/obe
   sity/childhood.
KidSource, www.kidsource.com/kidsource/content2/obesity.html.
Mayo Clinic, www.mayoclinic.com/health/childhood-obesity/DS00698.
Medline Plus, www.nlm.nih.gov/medlineplus/obesityinchildren.html.
Office of the Surgeon General, www.surgeongeneral.gov/topics/obesity/callto
   action/fact_adolescents.htm.

Exercise

American Heart Association, www.americanheart.org/presenter.jhtml?identifier=
   3007589
CDC BAM! www.bam.gov/sub_physicalactivity
KidsHealth, www.kidshealth.org/parent/nutrition_fit/fitness/exercise.html
Medline Plus, www.nlm.nih.gov/medlineplus/exerciseforchildren.html

References

Bliss, R. M. 2004. Survey links fast food, poor nutrition among U.S. children.
   U.S. Department of Agriculture Research Service. www.ars.usda.gov/is/pr/
   2004/040105.htm (accessed June 12, 2008).
CNN. 2000. U.N.: Poor nutrition could handicap 1 billion children. CNN. March
   20. http://archives.cnn.com/2000/WORLD/europe/03/20/nutrition.report (accessed June 12, 2008).
Freedman, D. S., L. K. Khan, and W. H. Dietz. 2001. Relationship of childhood
   obesity to coronary heart disease risk factors in adulthood: The Bogalusa heart
   study. *Pediatrics* 108: 712–18.
Gable, Sara, Yiting Chang, and Jennifer L. Krull, 2007. Television watching and
   frequency of family meals are predictive of overweight onset and persistence
   in a national sample of school-aged children. *Journal of the American Diatetic
   Assocation* 107 (1): 53–61.
Kozol, Jonathan. 2006. *Shame of the nation: The restoration of apartheid schools
   in America*. New York: Random House.
Mahoney, C. R., H. A. Taylor, R. B. Kanarek, and P. Samuel. 2005. Effect of
   breakfast composition on cognitive processes in elementary schoolchildren.
   Psychology and Behavior 85: 635–45.
Mayo Clinic. 2008. Childhood obesity. MayoClinic.com. www.mayoclinic.com/
   health/childhood-obesity/DS00698.
PHS Group. 2005. Drinking water provision boosts brainpower in Welsh primary
   schools. PHS Waterlogic. www.phs.co.uk/waterlogic/1444.html.

Chapter Seventeen

Alcohol and Other Drugs

Experimentation and Problem Use

According to the 2006 National Survey on Drug Use and Health (NS-DUH), more than 8 million adolescents aged 12 to 17 drank alcohol in the past year, nearly 5 million used an illicit drug, and more than 4 million smoked cigarettes. In addition, on an average day during the past year, adolescents aged 12 to 17 used the following substances:

- 1,245,240 smoked cigarettes.
- 630,539 drank alcohol.
- 586,454 used marijuana.
- 49,263 used inhalants.
- 26,645 used hallucinogens.
- 13,125 used cocaine.
- 3,753 used heroin.

The 2006 NSDUH also indicates that

- adolescents who used alcohol in the past month drank an average of 4.7 drinks per day on the days they drank.
- adolescents who smoked cigarettes in the past month smoked an average of 4.6 cigarettes per day on the days they smoked.

—Office of Applied Studies 2007, para. 5

Alcohol and other drug experimentation and use (including misuse of prescription drugs and illegal recreational drugs) in childhood and adolescence pose a double threat. Not only is the use of these substances harmful (and potentially lethal) to the developing brains and bodies of children and adolescents, but their combined use increases dangers resulting from poor decision making, such as in sexual promiscuity and driving/car accidents.

ASK: WHAT IS POTENTIALLY DANGEROUS OR
PROBLEMATIC FOR CHILDREN? WHAT CAN I
DO (OR WHAT CAN BE DONE) TO MAKE THIS
CHILD (OR THESE CHILDREN) SAFER OR
HEALTHIER OR MORE SUCCESSFUL IN
THIS/THESE SITUATION/S (OR SIMILAR ONES)?

First: The Dangers in Their Own Right

Late childhood and early adolescence are critical periods for the developing body and brain. There is evidence to suggest that use of drugs, such as prescription drugs, alcohol, marijuana, and others, can have a long-term impact on learning and memory. In addition to causing physical and psychological dependence, adolescents and young adults can die from overdosing on many of these drugs.

Prescription drugs. Recently, a number of prescription drugs have been found to be among the drugs of choice for adolescents. For example, Ritalin (a stimulant used to treat attention problems like attention deficit disorder) is abused by a variety of young people—sometimes they are trying to improve their performance in school or sporting events—much in the same way that caffeine is abused. Other drugs include depressants such as Valium, Xanax, and other sleep aids and narcotic/opiate pain-killers, such as OxyContin, Percodan, and Vicodin.

Sometimes adolescents have prescription drug parties where they take their parents' prescriptions drugs and put them in a giant bowl and take them—often washing them down with alcohol and using them with other recreational drugs such as marijuana. These "pharm parties" are extremely dangerous. At the time of writing this book, one of my graduate students had a student of his die from an overdose at one of these parties (KW).

In an article published by the Boston Public Health Commission titled "Teen Prescription Drug Abuse: An Invisible Epidemic," A. Raynor and J. Payne (2004) report that young women are about twice as likely to become dependent from abusing prescription medication as young men (with women between the ages of twelve and twenty-five showing increases in prescription drug abuse).

Sometimes abusing prescription medication may start because the user is trying to lose weight or reduce stress/anxiety, is experimenting or indulging curiosity, or is trying to fit in. It can be very difficult for teens to talk about prescription drug abuse. Also, young people may also not realize the dangers of prescription drugs, mistakenly assuming that these drugs must be safer than street drugs as they are prescribed by doctors.

Caffeine: Legal for all. Caffeine is a popular and often-abused drug— but it is a drug, a stimulant that affects the brain and body by speeding up physiological processes. Caffeine affects sleep cycles. Children who drink caffeine products, such as energy drinks and sodas, may have difficulty sleeping, show signs and symptoms similar to attention deficit disorder, and have learning difficulties (as REM sleep cycles are critical to effective learning).

A position paper published in *Monitor on Psychology* called "A Sip into Dangerous territory" states,

> "Caffeine can stimulate immature neurological systems beyond children's ability to tolerate it, which can have serious effects," says APA Div. 43 (Family) President Terence Patterson, EdD, of the University of San Francisco. "Excessive caffeine use damages the attention capacity that children need to cooperate in play, family and school environments." . . . Leading caffeine researcher Roland Griffiths, PhD, of Johns Hopkins University, deems the drug the most widely used mood-altering drug in the world, with usage far exceeding that of alcohol and nicotine. "Research has shown that the dose of caffeine delivered in a single can of soft drink is sufficient to produce mood and behavioral effects," he says. "Children who haphazardly consume caffeine are at risk for going through alternating cycles of withdrawal and stimulation." (O'Connor 2001, para. 3)

Nicotine. Nicotine in any form is illegal to purchase until the age of eighteen. Nicotine's effects are quite well known (increased adult risk of cancer, heart attack, and stroke). Despite a gradual decline of tobacco use among adolescents, there are still over four million children between twelve and seventeen who smoke—a third of high school graduates are actively smoking (Leshner 2005). The National Institute on Drug Abuse (NIDA) wrote of nicotine abuse and teens:

> Nicotine is a powerfully addictive drug. Once your teen is addicted, it will be very difficult to quit. The cause of addiction is simple. Nicotine goes straight to the brain. The human brain has circuits that control feelings of

pleasure. Dopamine—a brain chemical—contributes to the desire to consume drugs. Nicotine spikes an increase in dopamine. When your teen
smokes, he or she inhales the nicotine. It goes quickly to the brain. In just
10 seconds, the pleasurable effects of smoking reach peak levels. Within a
few minutes, the pleasure is gone, and the craving for a cigarette begins a
new cycle. A teen can easily get hooked on nicotine, although it takes much
more effort to quit. Many kid smokers, they find it hard to stay away from
the drug's effects. (Leshner 2005, para. 7-10)

NIDA has nicotine listed as one of the most addictive psychoactive substances. They list the following as the health concerns:

Nicotine is highly addictive. The tar in cigarettes increases a smoker's risk
of lung cancer, emphysema, and bronchial disorders. The carbon monoxide
in smoke increases the chance of cardiovascular diseases. Secondhand
smoke causes lung cancer in adults and greatly increases the risk of respiratory illnesses in children. (NIDA 2008c, para. 2)

New evidence suggests that

people who start [smoking cigarettes] in their teens are more likely to become life-long smokers than those who first light up as adults . . . and when
compared with nonsmoking peers, young smokers are more likely to be
abusers of other drugs: In 2002, the National Survey on Drug Use and
Health reported that roughly half (48.1 percent) of youths aged 12–17 who
smoked cigarettes in the past month also used an illicit drug whereas only
6.2 percent of nonsmoking youths reported using an illicit drug in the past
month. (Zickler 2004, para. 2)

Alcohol. The U.S. has had a love-hate relationship with alcohol. With
prohibition in the early part of the twentieth century, to the repeal of this
constitutional amendment years later (the only constitutional amendment
to be repealed in our nation's history), so much of our culture is affected
by alcohol. We socialize with alcohol. We celebrate with alcohol. We
grieve with alcohol. We recognize the many health risks of alcohol—damage to our bodies and brains, as well as to unborn fetuses, and the impairments leading to accidents that occur under the influence, killing thousands of people per year.

It is no wonder that young people experiment with this drug that is so prevalent and accepted in our culture. In addition, this drug targets powerful pleasure chemicals in our brains and lowers our stress/anxiety levels (albeit temporarily).

But alcohol is a central nervous system depressant—it is an illicit drug if you are under the age of twenty-one. It is dangerous. The National Institute on Alcohol Abuse and Alcoholism (NIAAA) reports that young people who drink are at higher risk of becoming victims of violent crime (e.g., rape, assault, and battery), having problems at school, being in car accidents, having unprotected sex, and developing drinking problems as adults.

As the young brain is developing rapidly during adolescence until about age twenty-five, alcohol can harm some of that development—the cognitive impairments are still being researched. The NIAAA provides a list titled "Warning Signs of a Drinking Problem":

Although the following signs may indicate a problem with alcohol or other drugs, some also reflect normal teenage growing pains. Experts believe that a drinking problem is more likely if you notice several of these signs at the same time, if they occur suddenly, and if some of them are extreme in nature.

- Mood changes: flare-ups of temper, irritability, and defensiveness.
- School problems: poor attendance, low grades, and/or recent disciplinary action.
- Rebelling against family rules.
- Switching friends, along with a reluctance to have you get to know the new friends.
- A "nothing matters" attitude: sloppy appearance, a lack of involvement in former interests, and general low energy.
- Finding alcohol in your child's room or backpack, or smelling alcohol on his or her breath.
- Physical or mental problems: memory lapses, poor concentration, bloodshot eyes, lack of coordination, or slurred speech. (NIAAA 2006, para. 3)

Other Popular Recreational Drugs

Marijuana. According to the results of the "Monitoring the Future Study" (a national survey of a sample of students in grades eight, ten, and twelve), marijuana use has been steadily declining since the late 1990s, but the study still shows that nearly 40 percent of those in twelfth grade had used the drug at least once. The National Survey on Drug Use and Health reported in 2006 that 14.8 million people aged twelve or older used marijuana at least once a month.

Marijuana can be smoked (in a carved out cigar called a blunt, a pipe, a water bong, or a cigarette/joint) or ingested (in bread or brownies or in tea). As R. A. Nicoll and B. N. Alger in their *Scientific American* article titled "The Brain's Own Marijuana" write,

> Marijuana is a drug with a mixed history. Mention it to one person, and it will conjure images of potheads lost in a spaced-out stupor. To another, it may represent relaxation, a slowing down of modern madness. To yet another, marijuana means hope for cancer patients suffering from the debilitating nausea of chemotherapy, or it is the promise of relief from chronic pain. The drug is all these things and more, for its history is a long one, spanning millennia and continents. It is also something everyone is familiar with, whether they know it or not. Everyone grows a form of the drug, regardless of their political leanings or recreational proclivities. That is because the brain makes its own marijuana, natural compounds called endocannabinoids (after the plant's formal name, Cannabis sativa). (2004, para. 1)

Because marijuana targets cannabinoid receptors of the brain, it is believed that the parts of the brain that have more of these receptors are affected most by marijuana use. These areas include pleasure centers and coordination centers for memory, concentration, perception of time, and movement. The drug affects these areas and also dopamine neurons that affect pleasure and reward. NIDA reports that there is an "addictive potential" from long-term marijuana use, as well as "an association between chronic marijuana use and increased rates of anxiety, depression, suicidal ideation, and schizophrenia" (NIDA 2008b). Earlier ages of first use tend to lead to greater problems in these areas (see NIDA, www.drugabuse.gov/Infofacts/marijuana.html).

Other health (emotional and physical) risks from marijuana smoking are as follows (according to NIDA):

Effects on the Heart
    One study found that an abuser's risk of heart attack more than quadruples in the first hour after smoking marijuana. The researchers suggest that such

an outcome might occur from marijuana's effects on blood pressure and heart rate (it increases both) and reduced oxygen-carrying capacity of blood.

Effects on the Lungs

Numerous studies have shown marijuana smoke to contain carcinogens and to be an irritant to the lungs. In fact, marijuana smoke contains 50 to 70 percent more carcinogenic hydrocarbons than tobacco smoke. Marijuana users usually inhale more deeply and hold their breath longer than tobacco smokers do, which further increases the lungs' exposure to carcinogenic smoke. Marijuana smokers show dysregulated growth of epithelial cells in their lung tissue, which could lead to cancer; however, a recent case-controlled study found no positive associations between marijuana use and lung, upper respiratory, or upper digestive tract cancers. Thus, the link between marijuana smoking and these cancers remains unsubstantiated at this time.

Nonetheless, marijuana smokers can have many of the same respiratory problems as tobacco smokers, such as daily cough and phlegm production, more frequent acute chest illness, a heightened risk of lung infections, and a greater tendency toward obstructed airways. A study of 450 individuals found that people who smoke marijuana frequently but do not smoke tobacco have more health problems and miss more days of work than nonsmokers. Many of the extra sick days among the marijuana smokers in the study were for respiratory illnesses.

Effects on Daily Life

Research clearly demonstrates that marijuana has the potential to cause problems in daily life or make a person's existing problems worse. In one study, heavy marijuana abusers reported that the drug impaired several important measures of life achievement including physical and mental health, cognitive abilities, social life, and career status. Several studies associate workers' marijuana smoking with increased absences, tardiness, accidents, workers' compensation claims, and job turnover. (NIDA 2008b, para. 9-12)

Cocaine. Cocaine is a central nervous system stimulant that mimics the brain's natural pleasure chemicals. Cocaine can be snorted or eaten in powdered form, injected, or smoked (in the form of crack freebasing). There is some concern that adolescent use of cocaine "could alter the normal growth of brain regions affected by cocaine, specifically the reward system" (Catlow and Kirstein 2007, para. 1). However, researchers Catlow and Kirstein note that "very little is known about how repeated exposure to drugs of abuse during adolescence alters normal brain development" (2007, para. 2). Yet consistent research has shown that the impact of drugs of abuse on adolescent rats' brains is far more severe than it is on adult rats' brains.

The negative impact of cocaine can depend somewhat on the way it is used. For example, if smoked, damage to the lungs and throat and other respiratory problems can occur. If snorted, loss of smell, chronic nosebleeds, difficulty swallowing or speaking, and general irritation to the nose and throat can occur. Intravenous use can result in easier overdose, track marks, and possibly allergic reactions. Some of the general effects of cocaine are

> heart attacks, respiratory failure, strokes, and seizures. Large amounts can cause bizarre and violent behavior. In rare cases, sudden death can occur on the first use of cocaine or unexpectedly thereafter. The short-term physiological effects of cocaine include constricted blood vessels; dilated pupils; and increased temperature, heart rate, and blood pressure. Large amounts (several hundred milligrams or more) intensify the user's high, but may also lead to bizarre, erratic, and violent behavior. These users may experience tremors, vertigo, muscle twitches, paranoia, or, with repeated doses, a toxic reaction closely resembling amphetamine poisoning. Some users of cocaine report feelings of restlessness, irritability, and anxiety. In rare instances, sudden death can occur on the first use of cocaine or unexpectedly thereafter. Cocaine-related deaths are often a result of cardiac arrest or seizures followed by respiratory arrest. Use of cocaine in a binge, during which the drug is taken repeatedly and at increasingly high doses, leads to a state of increasing irritability, restlessness, and paranoia. This may result in a full-blown paranoid psychosis, in which the individual loses touch with reality and experiences auditory hallucinations. (CocaineDrugAddiction.com 2008, para. 5)

Interestingly, new drug research suggests that adolescents are much more likely to "become addicted and relapse more easily than adults because developing brains are more powerfully motivated by drug-related cues" (APA 2008, para. 2). Comparing adolescent rats to adult rats, researchers have found that the adolescents were more likely to continue to seek out cocaine than adults—and even after they quit using, they were more apt to start using again when given the chance than the adult rats (Brenhouse and Andersen 2008).

Other stimulants. Amphetamines, methamphetamine, and Ritalin are all stimulants. Methamphetamine (typically comes in a form of powder or clear crystals that can be dissolved, then snorted, smoked, or injected) is made in illegal labs from easily available items such as battery acid, antifreeze, and drain cleaner. The other two are typically prescribed medications. Ritalin is prescribed for attention deficit disorder. They share similar effects with other stimulants in that they speed the user up—including heart rate, blood pressure, energy level, and so forth—and when abused, they share similar effects to cocaine (in high doses) and caffeine (in low doses).

Inhalants. Inhalants exist all around the home and even in schools. These often toxic substances, such as glues, gasoline, nitrous oxide, and some household cleaners, are sniffed or huffed using a bag, rag, or balloon (in the case of nitrous oxide).

These drugs are typically classified into three basic categories:

Solvents include:

- Certain industrial or household products, such as paint thinner, nail polish remover, degreaser, dry-cleaning fluid, gasoline, and glue
- Some art or office supplies, such as correction fluid, felt-tip marker fluid, and electronic contact cleaner

Gases include:

- Some household or commercial products, such as butane lighters, propane tanks, whipped cream dispensers, and refrigerant gases
- Certain household aerosol propellants, such as those found in spray paint, hair spray, deodorant spray, and fabric protector spray
- Medical anesthetic gases, such as ether, chloroform, halothane, and nitrous oxide

Nitrites include:

- Cyclohexyl nitrite (found in substances marketed as room deodorizers)
- Amyl nitrite (used for medical purposes)
- Butyl nitrite (previously used in perfumes and antifreeze but now an illegal substance) (NIDA for Teens 2008, para. 3-5)

According to NIDA, nearly twenty-three million young people admitted to having used inhalants at least once—with numbers increasing. These chemicals are widely available, making them an easy high for youngsters. Because these chemicals are often toxic, they have very harmful effects on the developing brain, including harming nerve cells and fibers as well as memory centers. Regular abusers may show harm not only to the brain but also to the heart, liver and kidneys, and muscles.

Steroids. Anabolic steroids are substances that mimic the hormone testosterone. These should not be confused with corticosteroids, which are prescribed to treat skin reactions and reduce inflammation. Anabolic steroids can be taken orally (in pill form) or injected, typically intramuscularly. Some abusers "stack" their use by taking two or more different kinds at once—or "pyramid" doses in weekly cycles—altering doses. The numbers of adolescents using steroids according the Monitoring the Future survey ranges from 2.5 percent of eighth graders to 4 percent of high school seniors.

The effects can range from increased acne on the face and body to increased body and facial hair (on girls and boys). Boys may develop breasts. Liver and heart complications can occur. Another serious concern is what are called "'roid rages," which are violent, angry outbursts. In my career as professor and counselor (KW), I have encountered a handful of adolescents abusing steroids—all with consistent stories of these angry, uncontrollable outbursts—sometimes resulting in fighting or hurting another person. One student was removed from college for such outbursts and threats made against fellow students. In all cases, the reasons were the same—to "get bigger and stronger." In some cases, they were athletes wanting to get better, but in more cases, they were young men wanting to enhance their appearance. Because hormone levels are fluctuating in adolescents and the brain is developing and working toward finding a balance of hormones, adding synthetic hormones to the mix is profoundly problematic for developing bodies and brains.

Club Drugs

Ecstasy/MDMA. The scientific name for Ecstasy is 3,4-methylenedioxymethamphetamine. It is created in illicit labs with no safety controls, so it is difficult to know what is in the pills. Sometimes these pills involve all kinds of other compounds from caffeine to amphetamine to cocaine. Drops in usage were seen earlier in this decade with a huge drop among high school seniors (from 11.7 percent to 5.4 percent between 2001 and 2005) according to the NIDA "High School and Youth Trends" survey.

Ecstasy has been called a "rave" or "party" or "dance" drug because it gives users the energy to dance for hours. Some people experience an increase in body temperature (some have died from overheating as MDMA interferes with the body's ability to regulate temperature). In addition, some experience dehydration, sweating, chills, anxiety, agitation, muscle tension, confusion, depression, sleep problems, clenching of teeth, blurry vision, fainting, and increases in heart rate and blood pressure (NIDA for Teens 2008). Ecstasy has also been called the "love drug" because users claim they feel closer to other people. Adolescents are more likely to have more and unprotected sex with several partners under the influence of such a drug.

There are other club drugs such as "Special K" (ketamine), LSD, and GHB (gamma hydroxy butyrate). Surveys of adolescent drug use have shown an increase in GHB abuse in the U.S. since 1992. Like ketamine, GHB was initially used as an anesthetic (ketamine for veterinary use). It is a colorless, tasteless, and odorless liquid but can be available in powder or capsule/pill form. Users claim that it causes a euphoric feeling, increased sex drive, and lowered inhibitions. Some side effects are nausea/vomiting, dizziness, drowsiness, and seizure activity. In higher doses, loss of consciousness, irregular or lowered respiration, tremors, or even coma can occur.

Opiates: Opium, heroin. In 2006 over a half a million people aged twelve and older had used heroin at least once in the past year (www.monitoringthefuture.org). Opium and heroin can both be injected or smoked. As with the other drugs mentioned, adolescent use of these substances is particularly problematic as users' brains and bodies are still developing, and abuse of these chemicals may result in lifelong health consequences. Some more immediate consequences are poor mental functioning, shallow breathing, difficulty moving (heavy feeling in extremities), dry mouth, and infections at injection sites; more serious effects include infectious diseases from sharing needles (HIV/AIDS, hepatitis), collapsed veins, or fatal overdoses. The 2007 Monitoring the Future study showed that there was a slight increase (from 0.2 to 0.3 percent) among eighth graders, and use without a needle among twelfth graders increased from 0.6 percent to 1 percent. Vicodin and OxyContin, which are both opiates in prescription pill form, were reportedly used by 2.7, 7.2, and 9.6 percent of eighth, tenth, and twelfth graders, respectively.

Second: Poor Decision Making Made Poorer

New research on the adolescent brain has shown that the way teenagers make decisions can be fundamentally different from the way adults make decisions. Some cutting-edge research comparing the adolescent and adult brains using fMRI technology has shown not only that different areas of the brain are involved in making decisions about potentially harmful ideas (e.g., swimming with sharks), but it takes teenagers longer to arrive at these sometimes dangerous decisions (e.g., swimming with sharks is a good idea) (Baird and Bennett, in Powell 2006). The brain is still growing, maturing, and developing until about age twenty-five, researchers are finding, and part of that maturation is an improved ability to make complex decisions. Drugs affect decision making in teens two ways. First, teens tend to make poorer decisions than adults about risk-taking behaviors—including those about drugs. Second, teens will likely make even poorer decisions under the influence of drugs, like the above, that lower inhibitions and reduce cognitive functioning. This means that decisions about sexual activity, driving, and other risk-taking behaviors will be worsened under the influence.

Third: Poor Driving Made Poorer

Drinking and drugging while driving. The National Highway Traffic Safety Administration (NHTSA) reported in 2007 that in the prior year over seventeen thousand people died in alcohol-related car crashes. And according to the National Survey on Drug Use and Health,

- In 2006, an estimated 13.3 percent of persons age 12 and older drove under the influence of an illicit drug or alcohol at least once in the past year. This percentage has dropped since 2005, when it was 14.1 percent. The 2006 estimate corresponds to 32.8 million persons.
- Driving under the influence of an illicit drug or alcohol was associated with age. In 2006, an estimated 7.3 percent of youth age 16 drove under the influence. This percentage steadily increased with age to reach a peak of 31.8 percent among young adults age 22. Beyond the age of 22, these rates showed a general decline with increasing age.
- Also in 2006, among persons age 12 and older, males were nearly twice as likely as females (17.6 percent versus 9.3 percent) to drive under the influence of an illicit drug or alcohol in the past year.

In recent years, drugs other than alcohol that act on the brain have increasingly been recognized as hazards to road traffic safety. Some of this research has been done in other countries or in specific regions within the United States, and the prevalence rates for different drugs vary accordingly. Overall, the research indicates that marijuana is the most prevalent illegal drug detected in impaired drivers, fatally injured drivers, and motor vehicle crash victims. Other drugs also implicated include benzodiazepines, cocaine, opiates, and amphetamines. (NIDA 2008a, para. 5-6)

Drugs impair cognition for drivers, and inexperienced drivers need all of their mental focus to be able to drive effectively. Car accidents are one of the leading causes of death for adolescents, and drugs (including alcohol) have been found to play a major role in these accidents. The Monitoring the Future survey found that 13 percent of twelfth graders reportedly drove under the influence of marijuana in the two weeks before the survey. When inexperienced teen drivers get behind the wheel, we are all in danger. The upside is that that the percentage of teens dying in drugged-driving crashes has declined 63 percent since 1982 and 10 percent since 2000 (NHTSA 2007). But the numbers are still unacceptable as nearly six thousand teenage drivers die in car crashes each year, and over a third of them are under the influence of alcohol or other drugs.

BRING TOGETHER ALL ADVOCATES WHO CAN ASSIST IN MAKING CHILDREN SAFER IN THESE SITUATIONS

Certainly all adults in our society should be concerned about teenage substance use and abuse. However, some key advocates should be included when attempting to reduce drug use and abuse in your home, school, or larger community. First are educators—teachers, parents, administrators, school counselors, community program workers. Second are social workers or other community agencies working with youth as caseworkers and Child Protective Services agents. Third are emergency personnel, such as EMTs and police officers, and other health care providers, such as physicians and nurses. Community members including school board members and shop owners who sell nicotine and alcohol products, as well as pharmacy workers and owners, must make sure that youngsters do not have access to different prescription and over-the-counter substances that are potentially problematic.

CONSIDER THE OPTIONS (PARTICULARLY ONES WITH DEMONSTRATED SUCCESS)

Raynor and Payne (2004, p. 2) recommend the following tips for parents in their article about teen prescription drug abuse:

- Parents can make a difference in their child's life!
- Be sure to listen more to your child
- Spend time together
- Share your family values
- Talk to your child, but not at them
- Agree to disagree and be respectful
- Help build your child's self-esteem
- Keep the lines of communication open

Caffeine and nicotine. Eliminate altogether or severely limit any intake of caffeine in the diets of young people. Schools should avoid having any caffeinated beverages available in vending machines or in the cafeteria and should treat caffeinated beverages like other drugs in school—they are not allowed without parental consent. Adults need to be educated (as do young people) about the problems associated with caffeine.

Unlike caffeine, which is not illegal for youth to consume, nicotine is illegal for those under age eighteen to use. All nicotine products, including gums, patches, and chewing tobacco, are illegal—but also dangerous—as are cigarettes, the obvious and most widely abused form of nicotine. Talk to kids about the dangers of smoking—preventing them from even trying tobacco is the best form of prevention. But once they start, getting kids to quit is also important. Groups like the NIDA are looking at strategies to help adolescents quit effectively.

Alcohol. The National Institute on Alcohol Abuse and Alcoholism of the National Institutes of Health has a helpful guide for parents about ways to talk with their children about alcohol. They recommend several points in their publication (available for download at http://pubs.niaaa.nih

.gov/publications/MakeADiff_HTML/makediff.htm#TakingAction). The highlights of their recommendations are as follows:

- Develop an open, trusting relationship.
- Encourage open conversations; ask open-ended questions and control your emotions if you don't agree or if something your child says upsets you.
- Try not to lecture but to have a sharing of ideas. Ask your child what he or she thinks or knows about alcohol and share the facts about alcohol, providing good reasons to avoid drinking.

The above recommendations can help young people stay away from all other drugs too—not just alcohol. Teenagers need to be carefully monitored by caring adults who give them increased freedom as they earn it by showing responsible behavior. If you as an adult suspect a problem with a young person with any drug, get help as soon as possible. The school's counselor or psychologist, the child's physician, or another health care professional can be helpful in determining the extent and nature of any drug problem.

DO WHAT YOU CAN

Parents and prescription drugs. Carefully monitor any prescription medication you own. Count the number of tablets and destroy any unused portions, particularly of narcotic medication.

Alcohol. The NIAAA recommends the following to prevent teen abuse of alcohol:

Monitor Alcohol Use in Your Home.

If you keep alcohol in your home, keep track of the supply. Make it clear to your child that you don't allow unchaperoned parties or other teen gatherings in your home. If possible, however, encourage him or her to invite friends over when you are at home. The more entertaining your child does in your home, the more you will know about your child's friends and activities.

Connect with Other Parents.

Getting to know other parents and guardians can help you keep closer tabs on your child. Friendly relations can make it easier for you to call the parent of a teen who is having a party to be sure that a responsible adult will be present and that alcohol will not be available. You're likely to find out that you're not the only adult who wants to prevent teen alcohol use—many other parents share your concern.

Keep Track of Your Child's Activities.

Be aware of your teen's plans and whereabouts. Generally, your child will be more open to your supervision if he or she feels you are keeping tabs because you care, not because you distrust him or her.

Develop Family Rules about Youthful Drinking.

When parents establish clear "no alcohol" rules and expectations, their children are less likely to begin drinking. Although each family should develop agreements about teen alcohol use that reflect their own beliefs and values, some possible family rules about drinking are:

- Kids will not drink alcohol until they are 21.
- Older siblings will not encourage younger brothers or sisters to drink and will not give them alcohol.
- Kids will not stay at teen parties where alcohol is served.
- Kids will not ride in a car with a driver who has been drinking.

Set a Good Example.

Parents and guardians are important role models for their children—even children who are fast becoming teenagers. Studies indicate that if a parent uses alcohol, his or her children are more likely to drink as well. But even if you use alcohol, there may be ways to lessen the likelihood that your child will drink. Some suggestions:

- Use alcohol moderately.
- Don't communicate to your child that alcohol is a good way to handle problems. For example, don't come home from work and say, "I had a rotten day. I need a drink."
- Let your child see that you have other, healthier ways to cope with stress, such as exercise; listening to music; or talking things over with your spouse, partner, or friend.
- Don't tell your kids stories about your own drinking in a way that conveys the message that alcohol use is funny or glamorous.
- Never drink and drive or ride in a car with a driver who has been drinking.

- When you entertain other adults, serve alcohol-free beverages and plenty of food. If anyone drinks too much at your party, make arrangements for them to get home safely.
- Don't support teen drinking.
- Help your child build healthy friendships.
- Encourage healthy alternatives to alcohol. (NIAAA 2006, p. 15-18)

Cocaine. The best approach is prevention, using many of the same strategies as for the other drugs. Signs of a cocaine problem can be sudden weight loss, sleep disturbance, attention problems, and extreme energy followed by periods of exhaustion. Cocaine dependency is typically treated using psychological interventions rather than medical or pharmaceutical ones. Because many cocaine-addicted young people also are addicted to alcohol, treating the alcohol dependence medically to avoid harmful withdrawal is important. Seeking medical treatment for a young person struggling with addiction is very important. The bottom line is that to break the pattern of addiction, adolescents or young adults need to change their lifestyles and patterns of behavior—as well as their friends and associates. This can be very challenging and requires a great deal of support.

Preventing All Drug Problems: Some General Rules

Open Parenting/Open Teaching: The Basic ABCs

Authentic and open. Parents and teachers—in fact, any adult interested in raising healthy and safe youngsters—need to be authentic—that is, real. As we invite young people to be open and honest with us, they need to know that they can trust us, no matter what. Parents wonder, should I be honest about my own experiences as a child or adolescent? It depends on the message you want to send.

But don't flinch. Keep emotions in check when listening—and ask good questions to get children to be honest about what they are doing, with whom they are doing it, and their fears and concerns. You must stay neutral to achieve this kind of safe space where kids will talk with you honestly.

Care no matter what. Make it clear to your child that you care, and no matter what he or she tells you, your feelings will not change—you will still care, unconditionally. Your child must believe this—and you must convey this level of care. Make it clear, for example, by saying to your child, "I'll pick you up any time, any place, no questions asked."

EVALUATE YOUR SUCCESS

Most school districts engage in some kind of regular survey of student attitudes and use of alcohol and other drugs. One measure of success would be a reduction in the number of children experimenting with different drugs—as well as a reduction in regular users and abusers. Police reports of accidents involving alcohol and other drugs should also decline. It is important for communities to monitor (anonymously) the amount and nature of alcohol and other drug use among adolescents.

FIND OUT MORE

American Psychological Association (APA). 2008. Rat study suggests why teens get hooked on cocaine more easily than adults. *ScienceDaily.* www .sciencedaily.com/releases/2008/04/080421133021.htm (accessed June 13, 2008).

Brenhouse, H. C., and S. L. Andersen. 2008. Delayed extinction and stronger reinstatement of cocaine conditioned place preference in adolescent rats, compared to adults. *Behavioral Neuroscience* 122(2): 460–65.

Catlow, B. J., and C. L. Kirstein, 2007. Cocaine during adolescence enhances dopamine in response to a natural reinforcer. *Neurotoxicology* 29 (1): 57–65.

CocaineDrugAddiction.com. 2008. Cocaine addiction facts: What is cocaine addiction? CocaineDrugAddiction.com. www.cocainedrugaddiction.com.

Leshner, A. I. 2005. Parents: Nicotine is a real threat to your kids. National Institute on Drug Abuse.www.drugabuse.gov/Published_Articles/Nicotinethreat.html (accessed June 12, 2008).

National Highway Traffic Safety Administration (NHTSA). 2007. Traffic safety annual assessment: Alcohol-impaired driving fatalities. www-nrd.nhtsa.dot .gov/Pubs/811016.pdf (accessed October 22, 2008).

National Institute on Alcohol Abuse and Alcoholism (NIAAA). 2006. Make a difference—talk to your child about alcohol. http://pubs.niaaa.nih.gov/ publications/MakeADiff_HTML/makediff.htm#TakingAction (accessed June 12, 2008).

National Institute on Drug Abuse (NIDA). 2008a. NIDA InfoFacts: Drugged Driving. www.drugabuse.gov/Infofacts/driving.html.

——. 2008b. NIDA InfoFacts: Marijuana. www.drugabuse.gov/Infofacts/marijuana.html.

——. 2008c. Tobacco/nicotine. www.drugabuse.gov/drugpages/nicotine.html.

Nicoll, R. A., and B. N. Alger. 2004. The brain's own marijuana. *Scientific American* (November), www.sciam.com/article.cfm?id=0008F53F-80F7-119B-80F783414B7F0000 (accessed June 12, 2008).

NIDA for Teens. 2008. Inhalants. NIDA for Teens. http://teens.drugabuse.gov/facts/facts_inhale1.asp.

O'Connor, E. 2001. A sip into dangerous territory. *Monitor on Psychology* 32, (5): www.apa.org/monitor/jun01/dangersip.html (accessed June 12, 2008).

Office of Applied Studies (OAS). 2007. A day in the life of American adolescents: Substance use facts. October 18. www.oas.samhsa.gov/2k7/youthFacts/youth.pdf (accessed June 14, 2008).

Powell, K. 2006. Neurodevelopment: How does the teenage brain work? *Nature* 442 (August 23): 865–67.

Raynor, A., and J. Payne. 2004. Teen prescription drug abuse: An invisible epidemic. Boston Public Health Commission. www.bphc.org/reports/pdfs/report_193.pdf (accessed June 12, 2008).

Zickler, P. 2004. Early nicotine initiation increases severity of addiction, vulnerability to some effects of cocaine. *NIDA Notes* 19, (2) (July), www.nida.nih.gov/NIDA_notes/NNvol19N2/Early.html (accessed June 13, 2008).

NIAAA Recommended Resources

Join Together
One Appleton St., 4th Floor
Boston, MA 02116
Phone: (617) 437-1500
Website: www.jointogether.org
Serves as a national resource center for communities across the nation that are working to prevent alcohol and other drug abuse.

National Council on Alcoholism and Drug Dependence (NCADD)
22 Cortlandt St., Ste. 801
New York, NY 10007
Phone: (800) NCA-CALL (622-2255)
(toll-free; twenty-four-hour affiliate referral)
Website: www.ncadd.org

Provides educational materials on alcohol abuse and alcoholism as well as phone numbers for local NCADD affiliates, who can supply information about local treatment resources.

National Institute on Alcohol Abuse and Alcoholism
5635 Fishers Ln., MSC 9304
Bethesda, MD 20892-9304
Phone: (301) 443-3860
Website: www.niaaa.nih.gov
Makes available free informational materials on many aspects of alcohol use, alcohol abuse, and alcoholism.

Substance Abuse and Mental Health Services Administration
National Drug Information Treatment and Referral Hotline
Phone: (800) 662-HELP (4357) (toll-free)
Website: www.findtreatment.samhsa.gov
Provides information, support, treatment options, and referrals to local rehab centers for drug or alcohol problems. Operates twenty-four hours a day, seven days a week.

Chapter Eighteen

Mental Health

*Depression, Anxiety, and
Posttraumatic Stress Disorder*

DEPRESSION

> ### ASK: WHAT IS POTENTIALLY DANGEROUS OR PROBLEMATIC FOR CHILDREN? WHAT CAN I DO (OR WHAT CAN BE DONE) TO MAKE THIS CHILD (OR THESE CHILDREN) SAFER OR HEALTHIER OR MORE SUCCESSFUL IN THIS/THESE SITUATION/S (OR SIMILAR ONES)?

The word "depression" evokes a variety of responses in people. For some it is a personal experience that brings up emotions of dark places full of isolation and misery. The American Heritage Dictionary defines a depressed person as being low in spirits, dejected, and suffering from psychological depression. What exactly is psychological depression? It is the journeys into these faraway places within the mind that hold many anxieties and feelings of helplessness and worthlessness. For others, this word represents a journey traveled alongside a significant other, a colleague, or a relative. Everyone has been touched by depression in some capacity. It is only now in the twenty-first century that we are beginning to truly understand the magnitude of its grasp and influence on the lives of the affected individuals.

> I have had many experiences with mental illness. One that comes to mind is one of my best friend's mother had bi-polar disorder. When my friend was 16 her parents broke up, she lived with her mom for a while and then got her own apartment. It wasn't good—she quit school herself, got involved in drugs and ended up in a rehab facility herself. This was many years ago. Her mom is now o.k. as far as I know. My friend is doing well. (College junior)

Statistical Information about Children with Depression

"According to epidemiological studies, about 2.5% of prepubertal children and up to 8.3% of adolescents in the United States have depression" (Voelker 2003).

"About 5% of children and adolescents in the general population suffer from depression at any given point of time. Children under stress, who experience loss, or have attentional, learning, conduct or anxiety disorders, are at a higher risk for depression. Depression also tends to run in the families" (American Academy of Child and Adolescent Psychiatry 2008).

"In any given 1-year period, 9.5% of the population, or about 18.8 million American adults, suffers from a depressive illness. The economic cost for this disorder is high, but the cost for human suffering cannot be estimated" (National Institute of Mental Health 2005).

"In 2000, 29,350 people died in the United States due to suicide" (National Institute of Mental Health 2005).

Many people in my family are bipolar, depressed or alcoholic or maybe a combination. There are people like my cousin who tried to commit suicide, he had a hard life because his father was a sick person who would do things to his son and daughter, and record them. My aunt who is that cousin's mother, is very depressed and also bipolar, she was an alcoholic at one point in her life and does not drink anymore. My father was an alcoholic and was put on Prozac for a while, but he had a bad reaction to it and got even more aggressive so was taken off, but he has matured and is not anything like he used to be. My grandfather was also an alcoholic, he also had lung cancer. It is very scary to see all these people around me with all these problems. Also see my friends drink so much and see them turn into different people. (College junior)

Depression in children has some common symptoms with that in adults; however, children's inability to articulate exactly the cause of the unhappiness or depression is to be expected. It is important to recognize that not all depression is manifested in depressive behaviors, such as withdrawal or destructive acts toward oneself and others.

It is particularly difficult for children experiencing depression to be able to explain to adults what it is that they are living through or with. It becomes even more complex with teenagers, who already feel a sense of alienation from adults. They often fear that by speaking out, they will be perceived as incompetent, unbalanced, and dysfunctional. They also fear placement in settings that may limit their individuality or freedom. The price of speaking out is often seen as too high, so many suffer in silence, until an action or a behavior brings their depression to the forefront of their lives and/or impacts the lives of those around them.

Adolescent depression occurs in a time of emotional upheaval, raging hormones, great drama, and heightened sensitivity. It is a time when a youth believes he or she is no longer a child but a young adult who should have the freedom to make his or her own choices.

The following checklists were developed by Dr. Marcel Lebrun and adapted from the National Association of Mental Health. They are to be used to collect information about the child and brought to professionals who can interpret them in a way that will lead to clinical treatment.

BRING TOGETHER ALL ADVOCATES WHO CAN ASSIST IN MAKING CHILDREN SAFER IN THESE SITUATIONS

Parents and teachers are on the front line when it comes to recognizing the manifestations of depression. Often, a child will receive excellent care and attention because of a zealous teacher or parent who will not give up on the child, no matter how rude or standoffish the child is. The adult is keenly aware of the existence of a potential problem and will search out answers and/or seek professional help through collaboration with other educators or mental health professionals.

CONSIDER THE OPTIONS (PARTICULARLY ONES WITH DEMONSTRATED SUCCESS)

The first line of defense is your family physician. She or he knows the family's history, has probably seen the child since birth, and has knowledge of the physical health of the child. Be careful not to assume that your general practitioner can diagnose depression. He or she is more likely to recognize the physical aspects of the depression. The physician may prescribe medication, which may merely alter or mask the symptoms. However, it is necessary to obtain a referral to a mental health practitioner trained to work with a child or adolescent who is manifesting depression.

Major Depression in Children Checklist #1

Name: _____   Date: _____

Observer: _____   Time: _____

Answer Criteria: Circle yes or no to each criteria/symptom if it has been observed for the categories shown in the box below.

Abbreviate (F) for Frequency (D) Duration (I) Intensity

Frequency:	**Duration:**	**Intensity:**
(a) Every 5 min.	(a) 5 min.	(a) Mild
(b) Every 15 min.	(b) 15 min.	(b) Average
(c) Hourly	(c) 30 min.	(c) Extreme
(d) Daily	(d) More than 30 min.	
(e) Too frequent to count	(e) More than 1 hr.	

1. Displays irritability   Yes or No   (F)_____   (D)_____   (I)_____

2. Displays aggressiveness   Yes or No   (F)_____   (D)_____   (I)_____

3. Displays combativeness   Yes or No   (F)_____   (D)_____   (I)_____

4. Feels angry all the time   Yes or No   (F)_____   (D)_____   (I)_____

5. Sullen   Yes or No   (F)_____   (D)_____   (I)_____

6. Has complaints about headaches   Yes or No   (F)_____   (D)_____   (I)_____

7. Has complaints about stomachaches   Yes or No   (F)_____   (D)_____   (I)_____

8. Experiences drop in grades   Yes or No   (F)_____   (D)_____   (I)_____

9. Refuses to do homework   Yes or No   (F)_____   (D)_____   (I)_____

10. Refuses to attend school   Yes or No   (F)_____   (D)_____   (I)_____

11. Feels extreme anxiety about tests   Yes or No   (F)_____   (D)_____   (I)_____

12. Has developed negative self-judgments   Yes or No   (F)_____   (D)_____   (I)_____

13. Is down on him or herself   Yes or No   (F)_____   (D)_____   (I)_____

14. Believes he or she is weird and ugly   Yes or No   (F)_____   (D)_____   (I)_____

15. Picked on by others	Yes or No	(F)_____	(D)_____	(I)_____
16. Has thought of death	Yes or No	(F)_____	(D)_____	(I)_____
17. Hyper-sensitive to criticism	Yes or No	(F)_____	(D)_____	(I)_____
18. Overreacts to disappointment and frustration	Yes or No	(F)_____	(D)_____	(I)_____
19. Becomes tearful	Yes or No	(F)_____	(D)_____	(I)_____
20. Gives up easy	Yes or No	(F)_____	(D)_____	(I)_____
21. Unable to have fun	Yes or No	(F)_____	(D)_____	(I)_____
22. Withdrawn	Yes or No	(F)_____	(D)_____	(I)_____
23. Moping	Yes or No	(F)_____	(D)_____	(I)_____
24. No involvement in activities	Yes or No	(F)_____	(D)_____	(I)_____
25. Becomes lethargic	Yes or No	(F)_____	(D)_____	(I)_____
26. Apathetic	Yes or No	(F)_____	(D)_____	(I)_____
27. Dispirited	Yes or No	(F)_____	(D)_____	(I)_____
28. Has difficulty sleeping	Yes or No	(F)_____	(D)_____	(I)_____
29. Oversleeps	Yes or No	(F)_____	(D)_____	(I)_____
30. Can't get up in morning	Yes or No	(F)_____	(D)_____	(I)_____
31. Sleeping in school	Yes or No	(F)_____	(D)_____	(I)_____
32. Has hallucinations (Seeing/hearing things)	Yes or No	(F)_____	(D)_____	(I)_____
33. Delusions (false beliefs)	Yes or No	(F)_____	(D)_____	(I)_____
34. Paranoia (suspiciousness)	Yes or No	(F)_____	(D)_____	(I)_____
35. Puts on a good face in public and displays symptoms at home	Yes or No	(F)_____	(D)_____	(I)_____

(adapted from Nami, 2001)

Major Depression in Adolescence Checklist #2

Name: _____ Date: _____

Observer: _____ Time: _____

Answer Criteria: Circle yes or no to each criteria/symptom if it has been observed for the categories shown in the box below.

Abbreviate (F) for Frequency (D) Duration (I) Intensity

Frequency:	**Duration:**	**Intensity:**
(a) Every 5 min.	(a) 5 min.	(a) Mild
(b) Every 15 min.	(b) 15 min.	(b) Average
(c) Hourly	(c) 30 min.	(c) Extreme
(d) Daily	(d) More than 30 min.	
(e) Too frequent to count	(e) More than 1 hr.	

1. Feels sad   Yes or No   (F)_____ (D)_____ (I)_____

2. Hopelessness   Yes or No   (F)_____ (D)_____ (I)_____

3. Feels empty   Yes or No   (F)_____ (D)_____ (I)_____

4. Cries in class   Yes or No   (F)_____ (D)_____ (I)_____

5. Appears lethargic   Yes or No   (F)_____ (D)_____ (I)_____

6. Slow moving   Yes or No   (F)_____ (D)_____ (I)_____

7. Sleepy   Yes or No   (F)_____ (D)_____ (I)_____

8. Inability to control hyperactivity   Yes or No   (F)_____ (D)_____ (I)_____

9. Extreme sensitivity in interpersonal relationships   Yes or No   (F)_____ (D)_____ (I)_____

10. Highly reactive to rejection   Yes or No   (F)_____ (D)_____ (I)_____

11. Highly reactive to criticism   Yes or No   (F)_____ (D)_____ (I)_____

12. Drops friends that are in conflict with them   Yes or No   (F)_____ (D)_____ (I)_____

13. Grouchy   Yes or No   (F)_____ (D)_____ (I)_____

14. Prefers to sulk and cannot be cajoled into a better mood   Yes or No   (F)_____ (D)_____ (I)_____

15. Overacts to disappoint- Yes or No   (F)_____   (D)_____   (I)_____
    ment or failure

16. Takes months to recover Yes or No   (F)_____   (D)_____   (I)_____
    from setbacks

17. Feels restless and   Yes or No   (F)_____   (D)_____   (I)_____
    aggressive

18. Becomes antisocial:

    (a) lies to parents   Yes or No   (F)_____   (D)_____   (I)_____

    (b) cuts school   Yes or No   (F)_____   (D)_____   (I)_____

    (c) shoplifts   Yes or No   (F)_____   (D)_____   (I)_____

19. Believes they are   Yes or No   (F)_____   (D)_____   (I)_____
    different

20. No one understands   Yes or No   (F)_____   (D)_____   (I)_____
    them

21. Everyone looks down   Yes or No   (F)_____   (D)_____   (I)_____
    on them

22. Isolated from

    (a) family   Yes or No   (F)_____   (D)_____   (I)_____

    (b) schoolmates   Yes or No   (F)_____   (D)_____   (I)_____

23. Finds a new main-   Yes or No   (F)_____   (D)_____   (I)_____
    stream of friends and
    peer groups

24. Hangs out exclusively Yes or No   (F)_____   (D)_____   (I)_____
    with one friend

25. Becomes self-destructive Yes or No   (F)_____   (D)_____   (I)_____

26. Self-medicated with   Yes or No   (F)_____   (D)_____   (I)_____
    drugs or alcohol

27. Stops caring about their Yes or No   (F)_____   (D)_____   (I)_____
    appearance

28. Regularly has morbid   Yes or No   (F)_____   (D)_____   (I)_____
    imaginings and thoughts
    of death
    adapted from Nami, 2001)

Early-Onset Bipolar Disorder Checklist #3

Name: _____   Date: _____

Observer: _____   Time: _____

Answer Criteria: Circle yes or no to each criteria/symptom if it has been observed for the categories shown in the box below.

Abbreviate (F) for Frequency (D) Duration (I) Intensity

Frequency:	**Duration:**	**Intensity:**
(a) Every 5 min.	(a) 5 min.	(a) Mild
(b) Every 15 min.	(b) 15 min.	(b) Average
(c) Hourly	(c) 30 min.	(c) Extreme
(d) Daily	(d) More than 30 min.	
(e) Too frequent to count	(e) More than 1 hr.	

1. Hair-trigger arousal system is set off by the slightest irritant or change   Yes or No   (F)_____   (D)_____   (I)_____

2. Overreaction takes form of: (A) irritable   Yes or No   (F)_____   (D)_____   (I)_____

      (B) oppositional   Yes or No   (F)_____   (D)_____   (I)_____

      (C) negative behavior   Yes or No   (F)_____   (D)_____   (I)_____

3. Multiple mood shifts   Yes or No   (F)_____   (D)_____   (I)_____

4. Child acts like two different people (angel/devil)   Yes or No   (F)_____   (D)_____   (I)_____

5. Rage is controlled in school   Yes or No   (F)_____   (D)_____   (I)_____

6. Rage is uncontrolled at home   Yes or No   (F)_____   (D)_____   (I)_____

7. Hyperactive   Yes or No   (F)_____   (D)_____   (I)_____

8. Highly distractible   Yes or No   (F)_____   (D)_____   (I)_____

9. Inattentive   Yes or No   (F)_____   (D)_____   (I)_____

10. Decreased need for sleep   Yes or No   (F)_____   (D)_____   (I)_____

11. Grandiose behavior   Yes or No   (F)_____   (D)_____   (I)_____

12. Control-seeking behavior   Yes or No   (F)_____   (D)_____   (I)_____

13. Highly directive toward adults (bossy)   Yes or No   (F)_____   (D)_____   (I)_____

14. Harasses other children/ adults   Yes or No   (F)_____   (D)_____   (I)_____

15. Overt hypersexual activities and communicate them in the classroom — Yes or No — (F)_____ — (D)_____ — (I)_____

16. Great sensitivity to temperature and heat — Yes or No — (F)_____ — (D)_____ — (I)_____

17. Insatiable craving for carbohydrates and sweets — Yes or No — (F)_____ — (D)_____ — (I)_____

18. Psychotic episodes of auditory hallucinations (common) may be reported — Yes or No — (F)_____ — (D)_____ — (I)_____

19. Ragged sleep cycles — Yes or No — (F)_____ — (D)_____ — (I)_____

20. Night terrors — Yes or No — (F)_____ — (D)_____ — (I)_____

21. Violent nightmares — Yes or No — (F)_____ — (D)_____ — (I)_____

22. First reaction to any request is no — Yes or No — (F)_____ — (D)_____ — (I)_____

23. Severe separation anxiety — Yes or No — (F)_____ — (D)_____ — (I)_____

24. School refusal — Yes or No — (F)_____ — (D)_____ — (I)_____

25. Has rages as seizures

    (a) wild-eyed — Yes or No — (F)_____ — (D)_____ — (I)_____

    (b) violent tantrums — Yes or No — (F)_____ — (D)_____ — (I)_____

    (c) kicking — Yes or No — (F)_____ — (D)_____ — (I)_____

    (d) hitting — Yes or No — (F)_____ — (D)_____ — (I)_____

    (e) biting — Yes or No — (F)_____ — (D)_____ — (I)_____

    (f) screaming — Yes or No — (F)_____ — (D)_____ — (I)_____

    (g) foul language — Yes or No — (F)_____ — (D)_____ — (I)_____

    (h) thrashing — Yes or No — (F)_____ — (D)_____ — (I)_____

26. Sleep disturbance — Yes or No — (F)_____ — (D)_____ — (I)_____

27. Hard to rouse in am — Yes or No — (F)_____ — (D)_____ — (I)_____

28. Gains energy throughout day — Yes or No — (F)_____ — (D)_____ — (I)_____

29. Hyperactivity(acting out) by the end of school day — Yes or No — (F)_____ — (D)_____ — (I)_____

30. Reports extreme physical sensitivity to:

    (a) clothes — Yes or No — (F)_____ — (D)_____ — (I)_____

    (b) food — Yes or No — (F)_____ — (D)_____ — (I)_____

31. Child acts worse at home than school — Yes or No — (F)_____ — (D)_____ — (I)_____

(adapted from Nami, 2001)

Bipolar Disorder in Adolescence Checklist #4

Name: _____   Date: _____

Observer: _____   Time: _____

Answer Criteria: Circle yes or no to each criteria/symptom if it has been observed for the categories shown in the box below.

Abbreviate (F) for Frequency (D) Duration (I) Intensity

Frequency:	Duration:	Intensity:
(a) Every 5 min.	(a) 5 min.	(a) Mild
(b) Every 15 min.	(b) 15 min.	(b) Average
(c) Hourly	(c) 30 min.	(c) Extreme
(d) Daily	(d) More than 30 min.	
(e) Too frequent to count	(e) More than 1 hr.	

Criteria
Manic Phase

1. Difficulty sleeping   Yes or No   (F)_____   (D)_____   (I)_____

2. High activity level late at night   Yes or No   (F)_____   (D)_____   (I)_____

3. Increased goal setting   Yes or No   (F)_____   (D)_____   (I)_____

4. Unrealistic expectations of skills   Yes or No   (F)_____   (D)_____   (I)_____

5. Rapid and insistent speech   Yes or No   (F)_____   (D)_____   (I)_____

6. All-or-nothing mentality   Yes or No   (F)_____   (D)_____   (I)_____

7. Spending sprees   Yes or No   (F)_____   (D)_____   (I)_____

8. Aggressiveness   Yes or No   (F)_____   (D)_____   (I)_____

9. Touchy, irritable "in your-face" manner   Yes or No   (F)_____   (D)_____   (I)_____

10. Reckless driving   Yes or No   (F)_____   (D)_____   (I)_____

11. Drinking and driving   Yes or No   (F)_____   (D)_____   (I)_____

12. Repeated car accidents   Yes or No   (F)_____   (D)_____   (I)_____

13. Hyper-sexuality   Yes or No   (F)_____   (D)_____   (I)_____

14. Provocativeness   Yes or No   (F)_____   (D)_____   (I)_____

15. Lack of concerns for harmful consequences   Yes or No   (F)_____   (D)____   (I)_____

16. Lying   Yes or No   (F)_____   (D)_____   (I)_____

17. Making up stories   Yes or No   (F)_____   (D)_____   (I)_____
18. Sneaking out of class   Yes or No   (F)_____   (D)_____   (I)_____
19. Sneaking out of house   Yes or No   (F)_____   (D)_____   (I)_____
    at night to party
20. Psychotic episodes

    (a) delusions (False   Yes or No   (F)_____   (D)_____   (I)_____
        beliefs)

    (b) hallucinations   Yes or No   (F)_____   (D)_____   (I)_____
        (seeing/hearing
        things)

    (c) paranoia   Yes or No   (F)_____   (D)_____   (I)_____
        (suspiciousness)

    (d) omantic delusions   Yes or No   (F)_____   (D)_____   (I)_____
        about teachers

Depressive Phase

1. Crying   Yes or No   (F)_____   (D)_____   (I)_____
2. Gloominess   Yes or No   (Г)_____   (D)_____   (I)_____
3. Moodiness   Yes or No   (F)_____   (D)_____   (I)_____
4. Irritability   Yes or No   (F)_____   (D)_____   (I)_____
   (picks fights with others)
5. Tremendous fatigue   Yes or No   (F)_____   (D)_____   (I)_____
6. Oversleeping   Yes or No   (F)_____   (D)_____   (I)_____
7. Lethargy   Yes or No   (F)_____   (D)_____   (I)_____
8. Carbohydrate-craving   Yes or No   (F)_____   (D)_____   (I)_____
9. Insecurity   Yes or No   (F)_____   (D)_____   (I)_____
10. Separation anxiety   Yes or No   (F)_____   (D)_____   (I)_____
11. Low self-esteem   Yes or No   (F)_____   (D)_____   (I)_____
12. School avoidance   Yes or No   (F)_____   (D)_____   (I)_____
13. Feigning sickness   Yes or No   (F)_____   (D)_____   (I)_____
    to stay home from school
14. Constant physical   Yes or No   (F)_____   (D)_____   (I)_____
    complaints
15. Self-isolation   Yes or No   (F)_____   (D)_____   (I)_____
    Pushing people away
16. Suicidal thoughts   Yes or No   (F)_____   (D)_____   (I)_____
17. ADHD symptoms

    (a) inattention   Yes or No   (F)_____   (D)_____   (I)_____
    (b) impulsivity   Yes or No   (F)_____   (D)_____   (I)_____

(adapted from Nami, 2001)

The school guidance counselor is another good resource if the depression is reactional or situational. School can be a wonderful place for children, but it can also be a source of great stress and anxiety. The fear of failure and being socially rejected or isolated may lead to depression manifesting itself within the classroom. This professional can provide coping, management, and problem-solving skills, which can empower the child or adolescent to be less reactive in the school setting.

The child can learn new strategies for being included, communicating, and voicing concerns in a way that will lead to proactive change. Contact with a school counselor may prevent academic failure. He or she can also be a liaison to the rest of the school faculty and communicate your concerns so as not to aggravate the situation for the child. The school nurse is another daily resource for the child. The nurse will dispense medications if necessary but may also provide some well-needed care, nurturing, and/or daily advice and attention.

Paraprofessionals or paraeducators are often found in the classroom and work primarily with children with special needs. They may also form a close emotional bond with these children and serve as a support within the classroom by facilitating and managing the daily workload and helping children maneuver academics and homework.

Psychiatrists are also key in the treatment of depression. They are medical doctors who provide both physical and mental evaluations. Many psychiatrists follow a specific treatment modality, so it is important to ask specific questions about what modality they employ. Psychiatrists believe that depression is chemically based and is treated by medication alone. The best treatments are those that combine both medication and talk therapy (cognitive behavioral therapy). Be wary of those who only refill prescriptions, as is sometimes the case for adults.

Psychologists serve as very useful resources for treating depression. They are generally based more in therapy than in medication. There are a few states that allow psychologists to prescribe antidepressants. Generally speaking, the majority of these professionals follow a therapeutic model as well. Many psychologists will follow one or a combination of the following approaches. The four main approaches focus on social skills, self-control, helplessness, and cognitive strategies. These approaches will be discussed later in the treatment section.

Social workers are often included in the treatment of depressed children because of the effects that depressed children may have on the dynamics of families. Social workers provide some community services for both parents and children. They access services, which may provide financial, emotional, medical, and other basic needs for families distraught by the fact that their depressed child is creating enormous chaos.

Mental health counselors can also provide support and therapy for the individual child, as well as for the family. Many counselors are licensed and regulated. They cannot prescribe medications but may make referrals to physicians. Health maintenance organizations often pay for the services of one of these professionals. It is important to check whether or not one's health policy will pay for the counseling visits and/or cover some of the prescriptions. At times, the bureaucracy may be daunting; however, with determination, one can ensure that the depression of the child and the accompanying costs do not overwhelm the family and create more stress or worry.

Community mental health centers also offer services for individuals and families. Centers often offer specialized programs that deal with grief, depression, and addictions. It is vital to find a center that will provide services that recognize the specific needs of a depressed child. Many centers do very well with adults; however, they are less efficient in dealing with children. Find a center that specializes in children and is better able to deliver quality programming meant for that specific audience.

Hospital psychiatry departments and outpatient clinics are another source of support if the child or adolescent may need to be admitted to the hospital due to a risk of committing suicide. These facilities provide twenty-four-hour supervision and health care. They are often lockup facilities and provide short-term solutions for children in crisis. University- or medical school–affiliated programs include the client as training for their medical students. A depressed child can receive treatment free of charge, but he or she will be required to agree to act as a teaching model for student medical practitioners. These practitioners are supervised and often can deliver quality programming. This is a viable option for lower-income families, provided there is one nearby.

Private clinics and facilities provide services for depressed individuals; however, they tend to be expensive. Many of these institutions run quality programs that may cost thousands of dollars. Very few offer short-term treatment plans, and they usually cater to the population that can afford them. They follow a variety of treatment modalities and are located throughout the United States. Many offer residential facilities.

Employee-assistance programs are another source of help. Many individuals have these programs at work. These plans offer short-term help (usually a maximum of six visits) with a professional within their network of service providers. This is often a great beginning to discussing the possibility that depression may be affecting the whole family. Usually, once the allotted visits have been used, a referral is made to a local provider, and the family or individual decides whether or not to continue with the treatment or explore other options.

Clergy have also been trained in mental health counseling and can offer support for the individual and/or family, depending on the family's spiritual beliefs. Clergy cannot prescribe medication but can offer spiritual guidance and possibly different perspectives on the life events occurring at that moment. This type of help can be excellent for situational depressions but is ineffective for biochemical depressions, which require medication to alter the functioning in the brain.

DO WHAT YOU CAN

The best solution for working with depressed children is first of all to identify what the causes are of the depression, seek out professional help, and evaluate how the child is responding to the treatments and supports.

EVALUATE YOUR SUCCESS

Your success will be evidenced by the child's returning to daily tasks and basic functioning that is developmentally appropriate. The child will

- return to activities that he or she previously enjoyed
- have increased social interaction
- be able to solve problems effectively
- make decisions
- seem more positive in outlook
- be able explain feelings and emotions and how they are tied to specific problem areas
- experience success in most aspects of daily living

Additional Information

Internet Search Topics: Childhood Depression or Adolescent Depression

Childhood Depression, www.childhood-depression.com
DepressionFreeChildren.com, www.depressionfreechildren.com
KidsHealth, www.kidshealth.org/teen/your_mind/mental_health/depression.html
National Alliance on Mental Illness, www.nami.org/helpline/depression-child.htm
PsychCentral, www.psychcentral.com/disorders/depressionchild.htm

ANXIETY

> ASK: WHAT IS POTENTIALLY DANGEROUS OR PROBLEMATIC FOR CHILDREN? WHAT CAN I DO (OR WHAT CAN BE DONE) TO MAKE THIS CHILD (OR THESE CHILDREN) SAFER OR HEALTHIER OR MORE SUCCESSFUL IN THIS/THESE SITUATION/S (OR SIMILAR ONES)?

Anxiety disorders are illnesses of the mind that, from the outsider's perspective, seem easily fixed by just being stronger and controlling one's thoughts. Unfortunately, it is not that simple. Anxiety disorders are broken down into four types:

1. *Phobias:* About 12 percent of Americans experience phobias in their lifetime. The victim feels dread or panic when confronted with a feared object, situation, or activity.
2. *Panic disorder:* About 1.5 million Americans may experience panic disorder in any six-month period. The victim feels overwhelming terror for no apparent reason.
3. *Posttraumatic stress disorder:* The victim has witnessed or experienced a life-threatening or traumatic situation and reexperiences the event through nightmares and flashbacks.
4. *Obsessive-compulsive disorder (OCD):* About 2.8 million Americans experience OCD during any six-month period. Victims attempt to cope with anxiety by associating it with obsessions, defined as repeated, unwanted thoughts or compulsive behaviors or rituals. A child can have obsessive disorder without compulsive behaviors. However,

most people who engage in compulsive behaviors also suffer from obsessions (Anxiety Disorders Association of America 2008).

Children and adolescents can suffer from any one of these disorders, which significantly impact their daily lives, school attendance, daily functioning, and movement in and out of the home. Anxiety symptoms can be so severe that the child or adolescent can be almost totally disabled, too terrified to leave home, enter a elevator, attend a social event, or even go shopping for food. The good news is that 70 percent of anxiety disorders can be treated successfully. The cause of anxiety disorders is a combination of physical and environmental factors.

BRING TOGETHER ALL ADVOCATES WHO CAN ASSIST IN MAKING CHILDREN SAFER IN THESE SITUATIONS

Treatment for anxiety disorders is best formulated by mental health professionals, such as psychologists, psychiatrists, and mental health counselors specializing in children with mental health issues. The Anxiety Disorders Association of America (ADAA) publishes lists of therapists to help families find specialists in their home area. The ADAA also operates a self-help network that may be able to assist in finding local support groups.

CONSIDER THE OPTIONS (PARTICULARLY ONES WITH DEMONSTRATED SUCCESS)

The following are the most common treatments available for anxiety disorders:

- A number of antianxiety and antidepressant medications are effective in controlling anxiety. Medications are usually required for at least a year.
- Behavior therapy works by trying to change the way the individual acts. The therapist seeks to develop the child's anxiety-reduction skills and teach new ways to express emotions.

- Relaxation techniques such as controlled breathing, meditation, and yoga can be effective.
- Exposure therapy is the most common treatment. Patients are gradually introduced to the anxiety-provoking situation and taught that they can cope.
- Cognitive therapy aims to change the way clients view themselves and their fears. The child or youth learns to assess the situation in a more positive way and is trained to analyze feelings and separate realistic from unrealistic assumptions.

DO WHAT YOU CAN

Once you, the parent, have made a connection with a mental health practitioner and a medical doctor to establish that there is no physical cause for the anxiety, then you, the parent, can begin helping your child with specific daily routines to manage the anxiety. It is important that regular practice sessions for relaxation occur and that regular calming breathing exercises that lessen the general anxiety and muscle tension take place daily. Sometimes therapy entails the child's returning to the site of the anxiety and becoming used to that environment. Make sure the child gets adequate exercise, sleep, and nutrition. It is important to reduce the amount of caffeine, soft drinks, and other highly chemically concentrated foods.

Keeping a stress diary also helps in evaluating where the anxiety is manifesting from. In this diary, the following information can be kept and brought to the mental health professional for analysis and possible treatment interventions:

- time
- amount of anxiety felt (1 to 10)
- emotions at the time
- nature of the event
- when and where it occurred
- factors that caused the anxiety
- how the anxiety was handled
- means of tackling the cause of the anxiety
- whether the anxiety was dealt with effectively and proactively

The following are specific strategies to help children and youth with anxiety symptoms:

- Laugh more.
- Be flexible.
- Breathe.
- Say no.
- Make mistakes.
- Play with a pet.
- Simplify.
- Get active.
- Eat well.
- Face difficulties.
- Talk to others.
- Cut down on caffeine.
- Journalize.
- Take up a hobby.
- Garden and perform other nature activities.
- Take bubble baths.
- Have massages.
- Listen to relaxing music.
- Practice aromatherapy.
- Daydream.
- Catch a movie.
- Read a book. (ADAA 2008)

Laughter is one of the most effective ways to manage anxiety and stress. In fact, there are researchers called psychoneuroimmunologists who study the stress-reducing impact of laughter. Laughter can boost immune system functioning, which in turn makes you more resistant to diseases and impaired cognitive thoughts.

EVALUATE YOUR SUCCESS

The key is to be able to understand the level of anxiety that an individual is happiest with and at which he or she can still function. The other key is to know the main sources of anxiety in the individual's present life. The individual should understand what circumstances make the anxiety particularly unpleasant and should begin to understand whether the strategies used for handling the anxiety are effective or not.

POSTTRAUMATIC STRESS DISORDER

> **ASK: WHAT IS POTENTIALLY DANGEROUS OR PROBLEMATIC FOR CHILDREN? WHAT CAN I DO (OR WHAT CAN BE DONE) TO MAKE THIS CHILD (OR THESE CHILDREN) SAFER OR HEALTHIER OR MORE SUCCESSFUL IN THIS/THESE SITUATION/S (OR SIMILAR ONES)?**

Posttraumatic stress disorder (PTSD) is a psychological response to a disaster or other type of traumatic event. Perhaps the individual has experienced a flood, hurricane, tornado, or earthquake. Or maybe the individual has been in a serious car accident or the victim of a crime. Traumatic events such as these tend to be sudden and overwhelming. In many cases, there are no outwardly visible signs of physical injury, but there is nonetheless a serious emotional toll. It is very common for people who have been traumatized to have very strong emotional reactions. Understanding normal responses to these abnormal events can aid in coping effectively with feelings, thoughts, and behaviors and slowly moving back to normal emotional and behavioral reactions.

A few studies of the general population have been conducted that examine rates of exposure and PTSD in children and adolescents. Results from these studies indicate that 15 to 43 percent of girls and 14 to 43 percent of boys have experienced at least one traumatic event in their lifetime. Of those children and adolescents who have experienced a trauma, 3 to 15 percent of girls and 1 to 6 percent of boys could be diagnosed with PTSD.

Rates of PTSD are much higher in children and adolescents recruited from at-risk samples. The rates of PTSD in these at-risk children and adolescents vary from 3 to 100 percent. For example, studies have shown that as many as 100 percent of children who witness a parental homicide or sexual assault develop PTSD. Similarly, 90 percent of sexually abused children, 77 percent of children exposed to a school shooting, and 35 percent of urban youth exposed to community violence develop PTSD (Hamelin 2007).

Signs to Watch for in Child and Adolescent Behavior after a Disaster

- Shock and denial are typical responses.
- Feelings become intense and are sometimes unpredictable.
- More irritability is accompanied by drastic mood changes.
- Anxiety, nervousness, and depression are often manifested.
- Thoughts and behavior patterns are affected by the trauma.
- The victim has repeated and vivid memories of the event.
- Flashbacks may lead to a rapid heartbeat or sweating.
- The victim has difficulty concentrating or making decisions.
- The victim is easily confused.
- Sleep and eating patterns are disrupted.
- Recurring emotional reactions are common, especially on anniversary dates.
- Interpersonal relationships often become strained.
- There is increased conflict and frequent arguing.
- Some individuals may become withdrawn and isolate themselves from all activities previously enjoyed.
- Physical symptoms may accompany the extreme stress.
- The victim experiences increased headaches, nausea, and chest pains. (ADAA 2008)

It is important to know that there is not one standard pattern of reaction to the extreme stress of a traumatic experience. Some people respond immediately, while others have delayed reactions, sometimes months or even years later. Some have adverse effects for a long time, while others recover quickly. Reactions can change over time. Some who have suffered from trauma are energized initially by the event, which helps them with the challenge of coping, only to become discouraged or depressed later.

A number of factors tend to affect the length of time for recovery. The first is the degree of intensity and loss. Events that last longer and pose a greater threat, and which involve loss of life or substantial loss of property, often take longer to resolve. The second factor is a child's general ability to cope with emotionally challenging situations. The third factor involves whether other stressful events preceded the traumatic experience.

BRING TOGETHER ALL ADVOCATES WHO CAN ASSIST IN MAKING CHILDREN SAFER IN THESE SITUATIONS

The intense anxiety and fear that often follow a disaster or traumatic event can be especially troubling for children. The involvement of mental health personnel and parents' ability to deal with the traumatic event themselves will influence the child's resolution of his or her own stress.

Children may regress and demonstrate younger behaviors, such as thumb sucking or bed-wetting. Children may be prone to nightmares and fear of sleeping alone. Performance in school may suffer. Children may manifest changes in behavior patterns, which may include throwing tantrums more frequently or withdrawing and becoming more solitary.

School personnel, local mental health practitioners, doctors, social workers, or specific aid agency personnel may be available to provide support and guidance in the realm of psychological treatment.

CONSIDER THE OPTIONS (PARTICULARLY ONES WITH DEMONSTRATED SUCCESS)

Parents, psychologists, and mental health personnel can guide the therapy and interactions of the child on a daily basis. Parents and others who care for the child can do several things. The parents or caregivers can spend more time with the child and let him or her be more dependent on them during the months following the trauma. Parents can exhibit more physical affection to reassure the child and provide play experiences to help relieve tension, encouraging the child to draw and play games. Parents need to encourage an older child to speak about his or her thoughts and feelings, and they need to respond to questions in terms that the child can understand. The parent needs to reassure the child repeatedly that they care about him or her and understand the child's fears and concerns. It is imperative that regular schedules for activities like eating, playing, and going to bed be maintained so as to help restore a sense of security and normalcy.

Several therapeutic options are available: cognitive behavioral therapy, play therapy, psychological first aid, twelve-step approaches, eye movement desensitization and reprocessing, and finally medication.

DO WHAT YOU CAN

A family and child can take a number of steps to help restore emotional well-being and a sense of control following a disaster or other traumatic experience, including the following:

- Give yourself time to heal and mourn the loss; be patient with changes in emotional state.
- Ask for support from people who care about you and who will listen and empathize with the situation.
- Communicate experiences in ways that feel comfortable.
- Find local support groups, which are often available. Find groups led by trained and experienced professionals. Group discussion can help people realize that other individuals in the same circumstances often have similar reactions and emotions.
- Engage in healthy behaviors. Eat well-balanced meals, get plenty of rest, use relaxation techniques, and avoid alcohol and drugs.
- Establish or reestablish routines.
- Avoid major life decisions.
- Become knowledgeable about what to expect as a result of the trauma.

EVALUATE YOUR SUCCESS

Success will be measured when the dysfunctional behaviors have disappeared or the child has the ability to work through the episodes with the proper psychological, cognitive, and behavioral responses. The child will no longer display PTSD-like symptoms. He or she will be able to function normally in all aspects of life.

FIND OUT MORE

State Mental Health Resources

The authors do not recommend one agency over another. These resources are provided for informational purposes only, and it is up to the reader to learn the particulars of specific agencies or programs.

Alabama

Alabama Department of Mental Health and Mental Retardation
RSA Union Building
100 N. Union St.
Montgomery, AL 36130-1410
Phone: (334) 242-3454
Secondary phone: (800) 367-0955
Fax: (334) 242-0725
Website: www.mh.state.al.us.

Spectracare Mental Health System
Barbour/Henry County Day Treatment
403 Dothan Rd.
Abbeville, AL 36310-2903
Phone: (334) 585-6864
Type of organization: Residential treatment centers for children

Spectracare Mental Health System
Adolescent Residential Center
1539 Sweetie Smith Rd.
Ashford, AL 36312-7422
Phone: (334) 691-3978
Type of organization: Residential treatment centers for children

Laurel Oaks Behavioral Health Center
700 E. Cottonwood Rd.
Dothan, AL 36301-3644
Phone: (334) 794-7373
Type of organization: Residential treatment centers for children

Alaska

North Slope Borough
Community Mental Health Center
PO Box 669
Barrow, AK 99723-0669
Phone: (907) 852-0260
Type of organization: Outpatient clinics

Arizona

Arizona Division of Behavioral Health Services, Department of Health Services
150 N. Eighteenth Ave., 2nd Floor
Phoenix, AZ 85016
Phone: (602) 364-8507
Fax: (602) 364-4570
Website: www.hs.state.az.us/bhs
Type of organization: State mental health agency

Mental Health Association of Arizona
6411 E. Thomas Rd.
Scottsdale, AZ 85251
Phone: (480) 994-4407
Fax: (480) 994-4744
Website: www.mhaarizona.org
Type of organization: Services include free mental health screenings, support
    groups, referrals, mentoring programs, education, and advocacy.

Mentally Ill Kids in Distress (MIKID)
755 E. Willetta St., Ste. 128
Phoenix, AZ 85006
Phone: (602) 253-1240
Secondary phone: (800) 35-MIKID
Fax: (602) 523-1250
Website: www.mikid.org
Type of organization: Parent advocacy group. Provides education and a resource
    center for parents as well as information on relevant support groups.

Horizon Human Services
Outpatient, Children, and Family Services
5497 W. McCartney Rd.
Casa Grande, AZ 85222-7423
Phone: (520) 723-9800
Type of organization: Multisetting mental health organizations

Community Behavioral Health Services
145 S. Main St.
Fredonia, AZ 86022

Phone: (928) 645-7230

Arkansas

Arkansas Division of Mental Health Services
Department of Human Services
4313 W. Markham St.
Little Rock, AR 72205-4096
Phone: (501) 686-9164
Fax: (501) 686-9182
Website: www.state.ar.us/dhs/dmhs
Type of organization: State mental health agency. Provides mental health services
  for the state of Arkansas. Oversees nonprofit community mental health centers.

Arkansas Federation of Families for Children's Mental Health
5800 W. Tenth, Ste. 101
Little Rock, AR 72204
Phone: (888) 682-7414
Secondary phone: (501) 537-9060
Fax: (501) 537-9062
Type of organization: Parent advocacy group

Health Resources of Arkansas
Youth Center
1355 E. Main St.
Batesville, AR 72501-3100
Phone: (870) 793-8910
Type of organization: Multisetting mental health organizations

Ozark Guidance Center
208 Highway 62 W.
Berryville, AR 72616
Phone: (870) 423-2758
Type of organization: Residential treatment centers for children

Counseling Associates
McCormack Place Apartments
855 S. Salem Rd.
Conway, AR 72034-8365

Phone: (479) 968-1298
Type of organization: Residential treatment centers for children

California
Alameda Community Support Center and Children's Outpatient Services
2226 Santa Clara Ave.
Alameda, CA 94501-4417
Phone: (510) 522-4668
Type of organization: Outpatient clinics

Crestwood Behavioral Health
Crestwood Geriatric
295 Pine Breeze Dr.
Angwin, CA 94508-9620
Phone: (209) 965-2461
Type of organization: Residential treatment centers

Because I Love You Parent Support Group
PO Box 2062
Winnetka, CA 91396-2062
Phone: (310) 659-5289
Secondary phone: (818) 882-4881
Fax: (805) 493-2714
Website: www.becauseiloveyou.org
Type of organization: Free support group for parents of children with any type of
    behavioral or emotional problem. Offered in twenty-one states.

California Council of Community Mental Health Agencies
1127 Eleventh St., Ste. 925
Sacramento, CA 95814
Phone: (916) 557-1166
Fax: (916) 447-2350
E-mail: mher@cccmha.org
Website: www.cccmha.org
Type of organization: State legislative body for mental health agencies

California Department of Mental Health
1600 Ninth St., Rm. 150
Sacramento, CA 95814
Phone: (800) 896-4042
Secondary phone: (916) 654-3565

Fax: (916) 654-3198
Website: www.dmh.cahwnet.gov
Type of organization: State mental health agency

Colorado
Colorado Child and Adolescent Psychiatric Society
6000 E. Evans Ave.
Bldg. 1, Ste. 140
Denver, CO 80222-5412
Phone: (303) 692-8783
Fax: (303) 692-8823
Type of organization: The organization is the contact point in Colorado for information about the activities of the American Academy of Child and Adolescent Psychiatry. They can provide referrals to child/adolescent psychiatrists in the state.

Colorado Mental Health Services
3824 W. Princeton Circle
Denver, CO 80236
Phone: (303) 866-7400
Fax: (303) 866-7428
Website: www.cdhs.state.co.us/ohr/mhs/index.html
Type of organization: State mental health agency

Colorado West Mental Health
Aspen Counseling Center
405 Castle Creek Rd., Ste. 9
Aspen, CO 81611-3125
Phone: (970) 920-5555
Type of organization: Residential treatment centers for children

Pikes Peak Mental Health Center
Child and Family Center
179 Parkside Dr.
Colorado Springs, CO 80910-3130
Phone: (719) 572-6300
Type of organization: Multisetting mental health organizations

Connecticut
Community Education—Connecticut Department of Mental Health
410 Capitol Ave., Fourth Floor
PO Box 341431

Hartford, CT 06134-7000
Phone: (800) 446-7348
Secondary phone: (860) 418-6948
TDD: (888) 621-3551
Fax: (860) 418-6786
Website: www.dmhas.state.ct.us
Type of organization: This organization provides information about mental health
    and other support services at the state level and is active in addressing and ad-
    vocating for mental health system issues. Provides information about con-
    sumer activities.

Families United for Children's Mental Health
PO Box 151
New London, CT 06320-0151
Phone: (860) 439-0710
Fax: (860) 715-7098
Website: www.ctfamiliesunited.homestead.com
Type of organization: The Connecticut chapter of the Federation of Families for
    Children's Mental Health. They are a support and advocacy group for families
    of children with mental health needs. They provide information, referrals, and
    training for family advocates.

Child Guidance Center of Greater Bridgeport
1081 Iranistan Ave.
Bridgeport, CT 06604-3713
Phone: (203) 367-5361
Type of organization: Outpatient clinics

Family and Children's Aid
75 West St.
Danbury, CT 06810-6528
Phone: (203) 748-5689
Type of organization: Residential treatment centers for children

The Village for Family and Children
1680 Albany Ave.
Hartford, CT 06105-1099
Phone: (860) 236-4511
Type of organization: Residential treatment centers for children

Delaware

Children and Families First
Claymont Community Center
3301 Green St.
Claymont, DE 19703-2052
Phone: (302) 792-2757
Type of organization: Residential treatment centers for children

Brenford Place Residential Treatment Center
136 Waterview Ln.
Dover, DE 19904-1049
Phone: (302) 653-6589
Type of organization: Residential treatment centers for children

Children and Families First
903 S. Governors Ave., Ste. 1
Dover, DE 19904
Phone: (302) 674-8384
Type of organization: Residential treatment centers for children

Middletown Residential Treatment Center
495 E. Main St.
Middletown, DE 19709-1463
Phone: (302) 378-5238
Type of organization: Residential treatment centers for children

Terry Children's Psychiatric Center
10 Central Ave.
New Castle, DE 19720-1152
Phone: (302) 577-4270
Type of organization: Residential treatment centers for children

Delaware Guidance Services for Children and Youth
1213 Delaware Ave.
Wilmington, DE 19806-4707
Phone: (302) 652-3948
Type of organization: Outpatient clinics

Florida

DMDA—Greater Jacksonville
6271-24 St. Augustine Rd. 3126
Jacksonville, FL 32217
Phone: (904) 730-8291
Secondary phone: (904) 737-6788
Fax: (904) 448-8965
Type of organization: Seeks to educate patients, families, professionals, and the public concerning the nature of depressive and manic-depressive illness as treatable medical diseases; to foster self-help for patients and families; to eliminate discrimination and stigma; to improve access to care; and to advocate for research toward the elimination of these illnesses.

DMDA Fellowship for Depression and Manic-Depression
919 SE Fourteenth St.
Ocala, FL 34471-3917
Phone: (352) 732-0879
Type of organization: Seeks to educate patients, families, professionals, and the public concerning the nature of depressive and manic-depressive illnesses as treatable medical diseases; to foster self-help for patients and families; to eliminate discrimination and stigma; to improve access to care; and to advocate for research toward the elimination of these illnesses. Meetings are from September to May on the first and third Wednesday of each month. They take place at 7 p.m. at the Shoney's Restaurant at 3631 SW College Rd. (State Rd. 200), Ocala, FL.

Florida Department of Children and Families
1317 Winewood Blvd.
Bldg. 1, Rm. 202
Tallahassee, FL 32399-0700
Phone: (850) 487-1111
Fax: (850) 922-2993
Website: www.state.fl.us/cf_web
Type of organization: The state department for alcohol, drug abuse, and mental health services. They provide information and referrals to the public. The department oversees state legislative affairs such as rules, statutes, and revisions.

Manatee Children's Services
The Flamiglio Center
439 Cortez Rd. W.

Bradenton, FL 34207-1544
Phone: (941) 345-1200
Type of organization: Residential treatment centers for children

Manatee Palms Youth Services
4480 Fifty-first St. W.
Bradenton, FL 34210-2857
Phone: (941) 792-2222
Type of organization: Private psychiatric hospitals

Harbor Behavioral Health Care Institute
Doris Cook Smith Counseling Center
14527 Seventh St.
Dade City, FL 33523-3102
Phone: (352) 521-1474
Type of organization: Residential treatment centers for children

Georgia

Carter Center Mental Health Programs
1 Copenhill
453 Freedom Parkway
Atlanta, GA 30307
Phone: (404) 420-5165
Fax: (404) 420-5158
Website: www.cartercenter.org
Type of organization: The Carter Center Mental Health Program addresses public policy issues surrounding mental health and mental illnesses through the Carter Center Mental Health Task Force and the annual Rosalynn Carter Symposium on Mental Health Policy. The task force identifies major mental health issues and develops initiatives to reduce stigma and discrimination against people with mental illnesses. The symposium provides a forum for national mental health organizations and their leaders to coordinate their efforts on issues of common concern.

Child and Adolescent Outpatient
Piedmont Hall
22 Piedmont Ave. SE
Atlanta, GA 30303-3057
Phone: (404) 616-2218
Type of organization: Outpatient clinics

Coastal Harbor Treatment Center
1150 Cornell Ave.
Savannah, GA 31406-2797
Phone: (912) 692-4285
Type of organization: Residential treatment centers for children

Georgia Mountains Community Services
Habersham MRSC—Mountain Industries
451 Roper Dr.
Clarkesville, GA 30523-6618
Phone: (706) 754-9423
Type of organization: Residential treatment centers for children

Georgia Mountains Community Services
Union MRSC—Trackrock Industries
10 Hughes St., #B
Blairsville, GA 30512-3552
Phone: (706) 745-5231
Type of organization: Residential treatment centers for children

Highland Rivers Mental Health Center
Fannin Child and Adolescent
3828 Appalachian Hwy.
Blue Ridge, GA 30513-4404
Phone: (706) 632-0236
Type of organization: Multisetting mental health organizations

Hillside
690 Courtenay Dr. NE
Atlanta, GA 30306-3421
Phone: (404) 875-4551
Type of organization: Residential treatment centers for children

Lighthouse Care Center of Augusta
3100 Perimeter Pkwy.
Augusta, GA 30909-4583
Phone: (706) 651-0005
Type of organization: Residential treatment centers for children

National Mental Health Association of Georgia
100 Edgewood Ave. NE, Ste. 502
Atlanta, GA 30303
Phone: (404) 527-7175
Fax: (404) 527-7187
Website: www.nmhag.org
Type of organization: The National Mental Health Association of Georgia serves people with mental illness and their families by promoting mental health, preventing mental illness, and ensuring access to appropriate treatment through advocacy, education and training, research, service provision, and the reduction of stigma.

Three Springs Augusta
3431 Mike Padgett Hwy.
Augusta, GA 30906
Phone: (706) 772-9053
Type of organization: Residential treatment centers for children

Idaho
Region VI Family and Children's Services
Child Mental Health Services
502 Tyhee Ave.
American Falls, ID 83211-1224
Phone: (208) 226-5186
Type of organization: Outpatient clinics

Northwest Children's Home
Syringa House
1306 E. Karcher Rd.
Nampa, ID 83687-3074
Phone: (208) 467-5223
Type of organization: Residential treatment centers for children that are mentally ill or delinquent

North Idaho Behavioral Health
2003 Lincoln Way
Coeur d'Alene, ID 83814
Phone: (800) 221-5008

Weeks and Vietri
818 S. Washington
Moscow, ID
Phone: (208) 882-8514
Type of organization: Outpatient counseling center for adolescents and children
   with depression

Illinois
Black Network in Children's Emotional Health (BNICEH)
6951 N. Sheridan Rd.
Chicago, IL 60626-3527
Phone: (773) 338-1090
Fax: (773) 493-1510
Type of organization: BNICEH is a global, family-centered organization. This or-
   ganization is a chapter of the Federation of Families for Children's Mental
   Health. They are also a member of Chicago Together, the Child Welfare and
   Juvenile Justice Consortium, and Urban Art Retreat Coalition.

DBSA—Fox Valley
2365 Coach and Surrey Ln.
Aurora, IL 60506
Phone: (630) 859-8035
Website: www.geocities.com/foxvalleydmda
Type of organization: Seeks to educate consumers, families, professionals, and
   the public concerning the nature of depressive and manic-depressive illness as
   treatable medical diseases; to foster self-help for patients and families; to eliminate discrimination and stigma; to improve access to care; and to advocate for
   research toward the elimination of these illnesses.

Lutherbrook Children's Center of Lutheran Child and Family Services
343 W. Lake St.
Addison, IL 60101-2599
Phone: (630) 543-6900
Type of organization: Residential treatment centers for children

Resurrection Behavior Health
1820 S. Twenty-fifth Ave.
Broadview, IL 60155-2864
Phone: (708) 681-2324
Type of organization: Residential treatment centers for children

Indiana

Park Center
Decatur Counseling Services
809 High St.
Decatur, IN 46733-2324
Phone: (260) 724-9669
Type of organization: Residential treatment centers for children

Oaklawn Association
Dr. Tim McFadden
330 Lakeview Dr.
Goshen, ID 46527
Phone: (800) 282-0809
Type of organization: Inpatient and outpatient facilities for children and adolescents who are mentally ill

Bowen Center
PO Box 497
Warsaw, ID 46581-0497
Phone: (800) 342-5653
Website: www.bowencenter.org

Indiana Federation of Families for Children's Mental Health
55 Monument Circle, Ste. 455
Indianapolis, IN 46204
Phone: (800) 555-6424, ext. 228
Secondary phone: (317) 638-3501
Fax: (317) 638-3540
Website: www.mentalhealthassociation.com/IFFCMH.htm
Type of organization: Statewide parent advocacy organization

Iowa

Iowa Federation of Families for Children's Mental Health
303 W. Main
PO Box 362
Anamosa, IA 52205
Phone: (319) 462-2187
Secondary phone: (888) 400-6302 (family only)
Fax: (319) 462-6789
Website: www.iffcmh.org
Type of organization: Parent advocacy group

Des Moines Child and Adolescent Guidance Center
1206 Pleasant St.
Des Moines, IA 50309
Phone: (515) 244-2207
Type of organization: Residential treatment centers for children

Gerard Treatment Programs
104 S. Seventeenth St.
Fort Dodge, IA 50501-5028
Phone: (515) 574-5492
Type of organization: Residential treatment centers for children

Kansas

Johnson County Mental Health Center
6000 Lamar Ave., Ste. 130
Mission, KS 66202-3299
Phone: (913) 831-2550
Type of organization: Residential treatment centers for children

Johnson County Mental Health Center
Olathe Office
1125 W. Spruce
Olathe, KS 66061-3123
Phone: (913) 782-2100
Type of organization: Residential treatment centers for children

Johnson County Mental Health Center
Adolescent Center for Treatment
301 N. Monroe St.
Olathe, KS 66061-3162
Phone: (913) 782-0283
Type of organization: Residential treatment centers for children

DMDA—Southwest Kansas
706 W. Fair
Garden City, KS 67846
Phone: (620) 276-2198
Secondary phone: (620) 279-0901
Type of organization: Seeks to educate patients, families, professionals, and the
   public concerning the nature of depressive and manic-depressive illness as

treatable medical diseases; to foster self-help for patients and families; to eliminate discrimination and stigma; to improve access to care; and to advocate for research toward the elimination of these illnesses.

Mental Health Association of South Central Kansas
555 N. Woodlawn, Ste. 3105
Wichita, KS 67208
Phone: (316) 685-1821
Fax: (316) 685-0768
Website: www.mhasck.org
Type of organization: Affiliated with the NMHA

Kentucky
Nelson County Child Development Program
327 S. 3rd St.
Bardstown, KY 40004-1032
Phone: (502) 348-0585
Type of organization: Multisetting mental health organizations

Communicare
Adult and Children's Crisis Stabilization
100 Gray St.
Elizabethtown, KY 42701-2608
Phone: (270) 360-0419
Type of organization: Multisetting mental health organizations

Kid's Care Child Development Center
1308 Woodland Dr.
Elizabethtown, KY 42701-2612
Phone: (270) 737-5676
Type of organization: Multisetting mental health organizations

Louisiana
Abbeville Mental Health Clinic
111 E. Vermilion St.
Abbeville, LA 70510-4709
Phone: (337) 898-1290
Type of organization: Outpatient clinics

Broadway—K Bar B Youth Ranch
31294 Highway 190
Slidell, LA 70458
Phone: (985) 641-1425
Type of organization: Residential treatment centers for children

DePaul/Tulane Behavioral Health Center
1040 Calhoun
New Orleans, LA 70118
Phone: (504) 899-8282
Secondary phone: (504) 582-7852
Fax: (504) 897-5775
Website: depaultulane.com/custompage.asp?guidCustomContentID=0AEF914C-
    9FB5-11D4-81F3-00508B1249D5
Type of organization: This teaching facility offers programs for children, adolescents, and adults. DePaul/Tulane Behavioral Health Center is well known for successfully treating difficult cases and accepting referrals from other facilities and therapists across the nation. The hospital offers free assessments and referrals twenty-four hours a day.

Louisiana Federation of Families for Children's Mental Health
PO Box 4767
Shreveport, LA 71134-0767
Phone: (800) 224-4010
Secondary phone: (318) 227-2796
Fax: (318) 227-2793
Type of organization: Parent advocacy group

Maine
Children's Behavioral Health Services
11 State House Station
Augusta, Maine 04333
Phone: (207) 287-4251
Toll-free: (800) 588-5511
TTY: (207) 287-9915

Community Health and Counseling Services
Big Red Redemption Center
12 Barker St.

Bangor, ME 04401-6408
Phone: (207) 947-0366
Type of organization: Residential treatment centers for children

Community Health and Counseling Services
42 Cedar St.
Bangor, ME 04401-6433
Phone: (207) 947-0366
Type of organization: Residential treatment centers for children

Maryland
North Baltimore Center
Children's Program
6999 Reisterstown Rd.,
2nd Floor, Ste. 7 and 8
Baltimore, MD 21215
Phone: (410) 585-0598
Type of organization: Multisetting mental health organizations

Regional Institute for Children and Adolescents—Baltimore
605 S. Chapel Gate Ln.
Baltimore, MD 21229-3999
Phone: (410) 368-7800
Type of organization: Residential treatment centers for children

Mental Health Association of Maryland
The Rotunda
711 W. Fortieth St., Ste. 460
Baltimore, MD 21211
Phone:(410) 235-1178
Toll-free: (800) 572-MHAM (6426)
Fax: (410) 235-1180
E-mail: info@mhamd.org

Massachusetts
DMDA—NE/Worcester
PO Box 2624
Worcester, MA 01653
Phone: (508) 842-0460

Fax: (508) 421-6556

Type of organization: Seeks to educate consumers, families, professionals, and the public concerning the nature of depressive and manic-depressive illness as treatable medical diseases; to foster self-help for consumers and families; to eliminate discrimination and stigma; to improve access to care; and to advocate for research toward the elimination of these illnesses.

Massachusetts Department of Mental Health
25 Staniford St.
Boston, MA 02114
Phone: (617) 262-8000
Website: www.state.ma.us/dmh/_MainLine/MissionStatement.htm
Type of organization: State mental health agency

Lutheran Mental Health
58 Centre Ave.
Abington, MA 02351-2228
Phone: (508) 626-1500
Type of organization: Residential treatment centers for children

Germaine Lawrence Diagnostic Center
18 Claremont Ave.
Arlington, MA 02476
Phone: (781) 648-6200
Type of organization: Residential treatment centers for children

Child and Family Service of Pioneer Valley
Easthampton Counseling/Mental Health Clinic
30 Union St.
Easthampton, MA 01027-1418
Phone: (413) 529-1764
Type of organization: Outpatient clinics

Michigan
DMDA MDSG—Grand Rapids
858 Reynard
Grand Rapids, MI 49507
Phone: (616) 246-0280

Type of organization: Seeks to educate patients, families, professionals, and the public concerning the nature of depressive and manic-depressive illness as treatable medical diseases; to foster self-help for patients and families; to eliminate discrimination and stigma; to improve access to care; and to advocate for research toward the elimination of these illnesses.

Community Mental Health for Central MI
Midland County Children and Family Services
3611 N. Saginaw Rd.
Midland, MI 48640-2384
Phone: (989) 631-2323
Type of organization: Multisetting mental health organizations

Eaton County Counseling Center
551 Courthouse Dr., Ste. 5
Charlotte, MI 48813-1054
Phone: (517) 543-5100
Type of organization: Residential treatment centers for children

Northpointe Behavioral Healthcare System
Bass Lake Home
3025 Bass Lake Rd.
Iron Mountain, MI 49801-9388
Phone: (906) 774-7809
Type of organization: Residential treatment centers for children

Minnesota

MDMDA—Minnesota
2021 E. Hennepin Ave., #412
Minneapolis, MN 55413
Phone: (612) 379-7933
Fax: (612) 331-1630
Type of organization: Seeks to educate patients, families, professionals, and the public concerning the nature of depressive and manic-depressive illness as treatable medical diseases; to foster self-help for patients and families; to eliminate discrimination and stigma; to improve access to care; and to advocate for research toward the elimination of these illnesses. They provide support to consumers and their families.

Wilder Foundation
919 LaFond Ave.
St. Paul, MN 55104
Type of organization: Children's mental health clinic

Washington Child Guidance Center
2430 Nicollett Ave.
Minneapolis, MN 55404
Phone: (612) 871-1454

Range Mental Health Center
624 S. Thirteenth St.
Virginia, MN 55792
Phone: (218) 749-2881
Type of organization: Children and adolescent center that deals with depression
    and mental illness

Mississippi
Mississippi Families as Allies for Children's Mental Health
5166 Keele St., Bldg. A
Jackson, MS 39206
Phone: (800) 833-9671
Secondary phone: (601) 981-1618
Fax: (601) 981-1696
Type of organization: Family support and advocacy organization. Provides
    respite services and some limited intensive case-management support. Also has
    family support and education programs.

National Alliance of Mental Health
411 Briarwood Dr.
Jackson, MS 39206
Type of organization: Focuses on adolescents with depression

Region VII
613 Marquette Rd.
Brandon, MS 39043
Type of organization: Focuses on children and adolescents with depression

Hiends Mental Health
969 Lakeland Dr.

Jackson, MS 39216
Type of organization: Focuses on children and adolescents with depression

Missouri
Missouri Department of Mental Health
1706 E. Elm
PO Box 687
Jefferson City, MO 65102
Phone: (800) 364-9687
Secondary phone: (573) 751-4122
Fax: (573) 751-8224
Website: www.dmh.missouri.gov
Type of organization: State mental health agency

Behavior Health Care
1430 Olive
St. Louis, MO 63103
Phone: (314) 206-3700

Truman Medical Center Behavioral Health
2211 Charlotte
Kansas City, MO 64111
Phone: (816) 404-5700

University Behavioral Health Service
601 Business Loop 70 W.
Columbia, MO 65201
Phone: (573) 884-1550

Montana
Mental Health Services Bureau
555 Fuller Ave.
PO Box 202905
Helena, MT 59620

KIDS Behavioral Health of Montana
55 Basin Creek Rd.
Butte, MT 59701-9704
Phone: (406) 494-4183
Type of organization: Residential treatment centers for children

Yellow Stone Boys and Girls Ranch
2303 Grand Ave.
Billings, MT 59102
Phone: (406) 245-2751

Partial School @ Deaconess Hospital
Deaconess Psychiatric Center
PO Box 37000
Billings, MT 59101
Phone: (406) 657-3900

Nebraska
Office of Mental Health, Substance Abuse and Addictions Services
PO Box 98925
Lincoln, NE 68509
Phone: (800) 254-4202
Secondary phone: (402) 479-5166
Fax: (402) 479-5162
Website: www.hhs.state.ne.us/beh/mhsa.htm
Type of organization: State mental health agency

Alegent Health Psychiatric Associates
16901 N. Seventy-second St.
Omaha, NE 68122
Phone: (402) 717-4673

Cedars Youth Services
640 N. Forty-eighth St., Ste. 100
Lincoln, NE 68504
Phone: (402) 461-3047
Website: www.lfsneb.org

Nevada
Nevada PEP Collaborating for Children Network
4600 Kietzke Ln., C-128
Reno, NV 89502
Phone: (800) 216-5188
Secondary phone: (775) 448-9950
Fax: (775) 448-9603
Website: www.nvpep.org

N. Nevada Mental Health Advisory Board
Building 1
480 Galletti Way
Sparks, NV 89431

Children's Mental Health Consortium
Division of Child/Family Conference Room
1572 E. College Parkway, Ste. 161
Carson City, NV 89706
Phone: (702) 388-8899

Nevada Mental Health and Developmental Services Division, Department of Human Resources
505 E. King St., Rm. 602
Carson City, NV 89701-3790
Phone: (800) 992-0900
Secondary phone: (775) 684-5943
Fax: (775) 684-5966
Website: mhds.state.nv.us
Type of organization: State mental health agency

Adolescent Residential Treatment Center
480 Galletti Way
Sparks, NV 89431-5564
Phone: (775) 688-1633
Type of organization: Residential treatment centers for children

New Hampshire
New Hampshire Division of Behavioral Health
State Office Park
S. 105 Pleasant St.
Concord, NH 03301
Phone: (800) 852-3345
Secondary phone: (603) 271-5000
Fax: (603) 271-5058
Website: www.dhhs.state.nh.us/DHHS/DHHS_SITE/default.htm
Type of organization: State mental health agency

DMDA—Nashua
PO Box 3761
Nashua, NH 03061

Phone: (603) 886-8520

Secondary phone: (603) 880-9225

Type of organization: Seeks to educate patients, families, professionals, and the public concerning the nature of depressive and manic-depressive illness as treatable medical diseases; to foster self-help for patients and families; to eliminate discrimination and stigma; to improve access to care; and to advocate for research toward the elimination of these illnesses.

Genesis Behavioral Health

771 North Main St.

Laconia, NH 03246

Phone: (603) 524-1100

Secondary phone: (603) 528-0305

Fax: (603) 528-0760

Website: www.genesisbh.org

Type of organization: Offers case management, therapy, psychiatry, groups, independent living, and medication management for children, adults, families, and seniors. Also provides emergency treatment and sliding-scale-fee services to low-income clients. Serves Belknap and lower Grafton counties.

NAMI New Hampshire

15 Green St.

Concord, NH 03301

Phone: (800) 242-6264

Secondary phone: (603) 225-5359

Fax: (603) 228-8848

Website: www.naminh.org

Type of organization: NAMI New Hampshire is a support and advocacy organization. They sponsor local support groups and offer education and information about community services for people with mental illness and their families.

Claremont Child and Family Center

West Central Behavioral Health

18 Bailey Ave.

Claremont, NH 03743-2704

Phone: (603) 543-5449

Type of organization: Multisetting mental health organizations

Riverbend Community Mental Health

Children's Intervention Program

3 N. State St.

Concord, NH 03301-4039
Phone: (603) 228-0547
Type of organization: Multisetting mental health organizations

New Jersey
DBSA—Mt. Holly
1337 Thornwood Dr.
Mt. Laurel, NJ 08054
Phone: (856) 234-6238
Type of organization: Seeks to educate patients, families, professionals, and the public concerning the nature of depressive and manic-depressive illness as treatable medical diseases; to foster self-help for patients and families; to eliminate discrimination and stigma; to improve access to care; and to advocate for research toward the elimination of these illnesses.

Division of Medical Assistance and Health Services, New Jersey Department of Human Services
PO Box 712
Trenton, NJ 08625-0712
Phone: (609) 588-2600
Fax: (609) 588-3583
Type of organization: State Medicaid agency

Woodbridge Child Diagnostic and Treatment Center
15 Paddock St.
Avenel, NJ 07001-1857
Phone: (732) 499-5050
Type of organization: Residential treatment centers for children

Ocean Mental Health Services
Ocean Academy for Children and Families
160 Route 9
Bayville, NJ 08721-1229
Phone: (732) 349-5550
Type of organization: Residential treatment centers for children

Family and Children's Services of Central New Jersey Mental Health Agency
223 State Rte. 18, Ste. 201
East Brunswick, NJ 08816-1913
Phone: (732) 418-7077
Type of organization: Outpatient clinics

New Mexico

Aspen Behavioral Health
3800 Osuna NE, Ste. 2
Albuquerque, NM 87109
Phone: (505) 342-2474
Secondary phone: (888) 912-7736
Fax: (505) 342-2454
Website: www.region5rcc.org
Type of organization: Aspen is a behavioral healthcare organization that provides quality mental health and substance abuse services for children, adults, and seniors. In addition, Aspen created and maintains a website with a comprehensive listing of behavioral health and social services in Bernalillo County for children, adults, and seniors, with funding from the New Mexico Department of Health.

DMDA — Albuquerque
PO Box 27619
Albuquerque, NM 87125-7619
Phone: (505) 889-3632
Website: www.dbsa4albq.org
Type of organization: Seeks to educate patients, families, professionals, and the public concerning the nature of depressive and manic-depressive illness as treatable medical diseases; to foster self-help for patients and families; to eliminate discrimination and stigma; to improve access to care; and to advocate for research toward the elimination of these illnesses.

New Mexico Behavioral Health Services Division
1190 Saint Francis Dr., Rm. North 3300
Santa Fe, NM 87502-6110
Phone: (505) 827-2601
Secondary phone: (800) 362-2013
Fax: (505) 827-0097
Website: www.nmcares.org
Type of organization: State mental health agency

Sequoyah Adolescent Treatment Center
3405 W Pan American Fwy. NE
Albuquerque, NM 87107-4786
Phone: (505) 344-4673
Type of organization: Residential treatment centers for children

University of New Mexico Children's Psychiatric Hospital
1001 Yale Blvd. NE
Albuquerque, NM 87131-0001
Phone: (505) 272-2890
Type of organization: Public psychiatric hospitals

Families and Youth
1320 S. Solano Dr.
Las Cruces, NM 88001-3758
Phone: (505) 522-4004
Type of organization: Multisetting mental health organizations

New York
Action for Mental Health
1585 Kenmore Ave.
Kenmore, NY 14217
Phone: (716) 871-0581
Fax: (716) 871-0614
Type of organization: Action for Mental Health is a consumer-based agency serving Erie County. They provide advocacy, civic education, and training and develop self-help groups to empower consumers of mental health services.

Behavioral Health Services North
159 Margaret St., Ste. 201
Plattsburgh, NY 12901
Phone: (518) 563-8206
Secondary phone: (518) 563-8207
Fax: (518) 563-9958
Website: www.bhsn.org
Type of organization: Affiliate of the NMHA. Also provides behavioral healthcare treatment services.

St. Catherine's Center for Children
40 N. Main Ave.
Albany, NY 12203-1481
Phone: (518) 453-6700
Type of organization: Residential treatment centers for children

Children and Family Mental Health Services
37 John St.

Amityville, NY 11701-2930
Phone: (631) 264-4325
Type of organization: Outpatient clinics

St. Mary's Hospital
Children's Mental Health Clinic
380 Guy Park Ave.
Amsterdam, NY 12010
Phone: (518) 841-7453
Type of organization: General hospitals with separate psychiatric units

North Carolina
Mental Health Association—Forsyth County
1509 S. Hawthorne Rd.
Winston-Salem, NC 27103
Phone: (336) 768-3880
Fax: (336) 768-3505
Website: www.mha-fc.org
Type of organization: The Mental Health Association provides services and information on mental and emotional problems and makes referrals to resources for help. The association has an on-site resource center.

Crossroads Behavioral Healthcare
200 Business Park Dr.
Elkin, NC 28621-0708
Phone: (336) 835-1000
Type of organization: Residential treatment centers for children

Crossroads Behavioral Healthcare
385 Timber Rd.
Mooresville, NC 28115-7855
Phone: (704) 660-1020
Type of organization: Residential treatment centers for children

Mental Health Association of Orange County
PO Box 2253
Chapel Hill, NC 27515
Phone: (919) 942-8083
Website: www.mhaoc.com

Type of organization: Affiliate of the North Carolina Mental Health Association. Promotes positive mental health among citizens of Orange County through advocacy, collaboration, education, and services.

North Dakota
Mental Health Association of North Dakota
PO Box 4106
Bismarck, ND 58502-4106
Phone: (479) 255-3692
Fax: (479) 255-2411
Type of organization: State affiliate of the NMHA

The Village Family Service Center (North Dakota)
1201 Twenty-fifth St. S.
Fargo, ND 58103
Phone: (701) 451-4900
Website: www.thevillagefamily.org
Type of organization: The Village provides a full range of services, including counseling programs, adoption, financial counseling, and mentoring programs like the Big Brothers Big Sisters Program. The Village has twenty offices throughout North Dakota and Minnesota. Thanks to United Way and donor support, the Village's services are available at a reduced fee for eligible participants.

North Dakota Division of Mental Health and Substance Abuse Services
600 S. Second St., Ste. #1D
Bismarck, ND 58504-5729
Phone: (800) 755-2719
Secondary phone: (701) 328-8940
Fax: (701) 328-8969
Website: lnotes.state.nd.us/dhs/dhsweb.nsf/ServicePages/MentalHealthandSub
stanceAbuseServices
Type of organization: State mental health agency

Ohio
Child and Adolescent Service Center
919 Second St. NE
Canton, OH 44704
Phone: (800) 791-7917

Secondary phone: (330) 454-7917

Fax: (330) 454-1476

Type of organization: The center provides mental health services for children and adolescents, family counseling, group therapy, individual counseling, and psychological services.

Thompkins Child and Adolescent Services

2007 E. Wheeling Ave.

Cambridge, OH 43725-2158

Phone: (740) 432-2377

Type of organization: Residential treatment centers for children

Eastway Behavioral Corporation

Community Living Center

2831 Salem Ave.

Dayton, OH 45406-2733

Phone: (937) 276-4167

Type of organization: Residential treatment centers for children

Oklahoma

Oklahoma Department of Mental Health and Substance Abuse Services

PO Box 53277

Capital Station

Oklahoma City, OK 73152

Phone: (800) 522-9054

Secondary phone: (405) 522-3908

Domestic Violence Safeline: (800) 522-7233

Fax: (405) 522-3650

Website: www.odmhsas.org

Type of organization: State mental health agency

Federation of Families for Children's Mental Health

PO Box 50370

Tulsa, OK 74150-0370

Phone: (918) 224-3476

Type of organization: Family support group that offers advocacy and education to families with children with behavioral or emotional disorders or mental illness.

Oklahoma Youth Center

320 Twelfth Ave. NE

Norman, OK 73071-5238
Phone: (405) 573-2222
Type of organization: State-run facility for children and adolescents with mental illness

Family and Children Services
3604 N. Cinncati
Tulsa, OK 74106
Phone: (918) 425-4200
Type of organization: Outpatient service that deals with children and adolescents with mental illnesses

Oregon
NAMI Oregon
2620 Greenway Dr. NE
Salem, OR 97301
Phone: (800) 343-6264
Secondary phone: (503) 370-7774
Fax: (503) 370-9452
Website: www.namioregon.org
Type of organization: NAMI Oregon is a support and advocacy organization. They sponsor local support groups and offer education and information about community services for people with mental illness and their families.

Oregon Department of Mental Health
500 Summer St. NE, E86
Salem, OR 97301
Phone: (503) 945-5763
Fax: (503) 378-8467
Website: www.dhs.state.or.us/mentalhealth
Type of organization: Assures that the rights of people with mental illness are protected. Assists counties and other providers in the delivery of services. Assures the provision of services close to home, as early as possible, and in the most normal setting to allow an adequate level of independence and to avoid disruption in the person's life. Assures effective care, treatment, and training in secure facilities or closely supervised programs for persons with mental illness who exhibit dangerous behavior.

Research and Training Center on Family Support and Children's Mental Health
Portland State University

PO Box 751
Portland, OR 97207-0751
Phone: (503) 725-4040
Fax: (503) 725-4180
Website: www.rtc.pdx.edu

Type of organization: The Research and Training Center on Family Support and Children's Mental Health conducts research on the child mental health service system and provides training and technical assistance to individuals and organizations working on behalf of children with emotional and/or behavioral disorders. The center's activities are based on the tenets of the Comprehensive Service System model, which stresses the importance of community-based, family-centered, and culturally appropriate services for children and their families.

Morrison Center Child and Family Services
Behavior Intervention Center
5205 SE Eighty-sixth Ave.
Portland, OR 97266-3199
Phone: (503) 916-5590

Type of organization: Residential treatment centers for children

Pennsylvania

DBSA Friends for Friends
4641 Roosevelt Blvd.
Philadelphia, PA 19124-2399
Phone: (215) 831-7809
Fax: (610) 525-3832

Type of organization: Seeks to educate patients, families, professionals, and the public concerning the nature of depressive and manic-depressive illness as treatable medical diseases; to foster self-help for patients and families; to eliminate discrimination and stigma; to improve access to care; and to advocate for research toward the elimination of these illnesses.

Horizon House
120 S. Thirtieth St.
Philadelphia, PA 19104-3403
Phone: (215) 386-3838
Fax: (215) 382-3626

Type of organization: Provides an environment in which individuals with mental health needs, developmental disabilities, homelessness, and substance abuse problems can develop the skills necessary to enjoy rewarding lives. Offers the following types of programs: (1) assessment/outpatient services, and (2) day programs, partial hospitalization, vocational services, education, social rehabilitation, homeless services, substance abuse services, specialized residential, intensive case management, and developmental.

KidsPeace National Centers
1650 Broadway
Bethlehem, PA 18015
Phone: (800) 8KID-123
Website: www.kidspeace.org
Type of organization: The national referral network for kids in crisis, KidsPeace is dedicated to serving the critical behavioral and mental health needs of children, preadolescents, and teens. Operates in ten states, including Pennsylvania, New York, Indiana, Maine, Maryland, New Jersey, Minnesota, Georgia, North Carolina, and Virginia.

Tioga County Department of Human Services
Clinical Services
149 E. Main St.
Knoxville, PA 16928-9788
Phone: (814) 326-4680
Type of organization: Residential treatment centers for children

Children's Service Center
Mental Health Group Home
137 E. Noble St.
Nanticoke, PA 18634-2803
Phone: (570) 735-7369
Type of organization: Residential treatment centers for children

Rhode Island
Mental Health Association of Rhode Island
500 Prospect St.
Pawtucket, RI 02860
Phone: (401) 726-8383
Fax: (401) 365-6170
Website: www.mhari.org
Type of organization: Affiliate of the NMHA

NAMI Rhode Island
1255 N. Main St.
Providence, RI 02904-1867
Phone: (800) 749-3197
Secondary phone: (401) 331-3060
Fax: (401) 274-3020
Website: ri.nami.org
Type of organization: NAMI Rhode Island is a support and advocacy organization. They sponsor local support groups and offer education and information about community services for people with mental illness and their families.

Parent Support Network
400 Warwick Ave., Ste. 12
Warwick, RI 02888
Phone: (800) 483-8844
Secondary phone: (401) 467-6855
Fax: (401) 467-6903
Type of organization: The Parent Support Network is an organization of families supporting families with children and youth who are at risk for or have behavioral or emotional challenges. Its goals are to strengthen and preserve families, enable families in self-advocacy, extend social networks and reduce family isolation, and develop social policies and systems of care. The Parent Support Network accomplishes these goals by providing advocacy, education, and training; promoting outreach and public awareness; facilitating social events for families; and participating on committees responsible for developing, implementing, and evaluating policies and systems of care.

Rhode Island Department of Mental Health, Mental Retardation, and Hospitals
14 Harrington Rd., Barry Hall
Cranston, RI 02920
Phone: (401) 462-3201
Fax: (401) 462-3204
Website: www.mhrh.state.ri.us

Valley Community School—Middletown
Community Counseling Center
60 Hammarlund Way
Middletown, RI 02842-5632
Phone: (401) 849-6981
Type of organization: Residential treatment centers for children, state mental health agency

Blackstone Adolescent Counseling Center
Community Counseling Center
475 Fountain St.
Pawtucket, RI 02860-1058
Phone: (401) 724-0535
Type of organization: Residential treatment centers for children

Blackstone Children's Home
Community Counseling Center
50 Walcott St.
Pawtucket, RI 02860-4111
Phone: (401) 729-1516
Type of organization: Residential treatment centers for children

South Carolina
South Carolina Department of Mental Health
PO Box 485
2414 Bull St.
Columbia, SC 29202
Phone: (803) 898-8581
Fax: (803) 898-8316
Website: www.state.sc.us/dmh
Type of organization: State mental health agency

National Alliance for the Mentally Ill
NAMI South Carolina
PO Box 1267
Columbia, SC 29202
Phone: (803) 733-9592
Toll-free: (800) 788-5131
Fax: (803) 733-9591
E-mail: namiofsc@logicsouth.com
Website: www.namisc.org
Type of organization: Maintains a helpline for information on mental illnesses and
    referrals to local groups. The local self-help groups have support and advocacy
    components and offer education and information about community services for
    families and individuals. For information about the alliance's affiliates and ac-
    tivities in your state, contact NAMI South Carolina.

Piedmont Center for Mental Health Services
Rainbow House/Day Program

900 W. Poinsett St.
Greer, SC 29650-1455
Phone: (864) 879-1088
Type of organization: Residential treatment centers for children

Piedmont Center for Mental Health Services
Greer Mental Health Clinic
220 Executive Dr.
Greer, SC 29651-1244
Phone: (864) 879-2111
Type of organization: Residential treatment centers for children

Piedmont Center for Mental Health Services
Clear Spring Home
108 Clear Spring Rd.
Simpsonville, SC 29681-4136
Phone: (864) 967-4432
Type of organization: Residential treatment centers for children

South Dakota
South Dakota Division of Mental Health
Hillsview Plaza
E. Hwy. 34
c/o 500 E. Capitol
Pierre, SD 57501-5070
Phone: (800) 265-9684
Secondary phone: (605) 773-5991
Fax: (605) 773-7076
Website: www.state.sd.us/dhs/dmh
Type of organization: State mental health agency. For more information about admission, care, treatment, release, and patient follow-up in public or private psychiatric residential facilities, contact the state mental health agency:

Kim Malsam-Rysdon, Director
Division of Mental Health
Department of Human Services
Hillsview Plaza
E. Highway 34
c/o 500 East Capitol
Pierre, SD 57501-5070

Phone: (605) 773-5991
Fax: (605) 773-7076
Toll-free: (800) 265-9684

Southeastern Behavioral HealthCare
Canton Office
112 1/2 S. Broadway St.
Canton, SD 57013-2225
Phone: (605) 987-2561
Type of organization: Residential treatment centers for children

Southeastern Behavioral HealthCare
Parker Office
400 S. Main St.
Parker, SD 57053
Phone: (605) 297-3699
Type of organization: Residential treatment centers for children

Southeastern Behavioral HealthCare
Salem Office
121 N. Main St.
Salem, SD 57058
Phone: (605) 425-2165
Type of organization: Residential treatment centers for children

Tennessee
Mental Health Association (I&R)—Memphis
1407 Union Ave., Ste. 1205
Memphis, TN 38104-3627
Phone: (901) 323-0633
Fax: (901) 323-0858
Type of organization: Offers information and referrals to local support groups. Provides public education and information forums on issues related to mental health, professional training, and seminars, as well as assistance in starting new groups and consultation to existing groups. Also offers facilitator training and speakers bureau.

Tennessee Association of Mental Health Organizations (TAMHO)
42 Rutledge St.
Nashville, TN 37210-2043

Phone: (800) 568-2642
Secondary phone: (615) 244-2220
Fax: (615) 254-8331
Website: www.tamho.org
Type of organization: TAMHO is a nonprofit organization of community mental
    health organizations in the state of Tennessee. Their mission is to improve the
    mental health care system in the state. They offer an opportunity for member
    agencies to network, and they publish the *TAMHO Membership Directory and
    Buyer's Guide*.

Tennessee Voices for Children
1315 Eighth Ave. S.
Nashville, TN 37203
Phone: (800) 670-9882
Secondary phone: (615) 269-7751
Fax: (615) 269-8914
Website: www.tnvoices.org
Type of organization: Family support organization

Child and Family Tennessee
Therapeutic Visitation
901 E. Summit Hill Dr.
Knoxville, TN 37915
Phone: (865) 521-5640
Type of organization: Residential treatment centers for children

Texas
American Society for Adolescent Psychiatry (ASAP)
PO Box 570218
Dallas, TX 75357
Phone: (972) 686-6166
Fax: (972) 613-5532
Website: www.adolpsych.org
Type of organization: ASAP supports research and provides a source of informed
    psychiatric opinion about adolescents. Members are psychiatrists with either a
    specialty or an active interest in adolescent psychiatry. ASAP conducts semi-
    nars and conferences. It is supported by dues.

Dallas Federation of Families for Children's Mental Health
2629 Sharpview Ln.
Dallas, TX 75228

Phone: (214) 320-1825

Fax: (214) 320-3750

Type of organization: The Dallas Federation is an advocacy service for families in need. They act as a liaison between professionals and families in need of specialized services for children with emotional/behavioral problems. They conduct trainings and workshops on national, state, and local levels regarding children's mental health.

Depressive and Manic Depressive Association—Amarillo/ Panhandle

1605 Parker St.

Amarillo, TX 79102

Phone: (806) 372-1023

Type of organization: Seeks to educate patients, families, professionals, and the public concerning the nature of depressive and manic-depressive illness as treatable medical diseases; to foster self-help for patients and families; to eliminate discrimination and stigma; to improve access to care; and to advocate for research toward the elimination of these illnesses.

Betty Hardwick Center

Adult and Youth Outpatient/Crisis Services

2626 S. Clack St.

Abilene, TX 79606-1557

Phone: (325) 690-5100

Type of organization: Outpatient clinics

Child and Family Guidance Center

8915 Harry Hines Blvd.

Dallas, TX 75235-1717

Phone: (214) 351-3490

Type of organization: Outpatient clinics

Utah

The Information and Referral Center—Salt Lake City

1025 S. 700 W.

Salt Lake City, UT 84104

Phone: (801) 978-3333

Fax: (801) 978-9565

Website: www.informationandreferral.org

Type of organization: Provides information and referral to local self-help groups in select areas. Also provides information on other local services and agencies.

Wasatch Mental Health Center
Heber City Office
135 S. Main, Ste. 206
Heber City, UT 84032
Phone: (435) 654-1618
Type of organization: Residential treatment centers for children

Wasatch Mental Health Youth Services
Park View School
1161 E. 300 N.
Provo, UT 84606
Phone: (801) 373-4765
Type of organization: Residential treatment centers for children

Wasatch Mental Health Center
Residential Supportive
280 E. 300 N.
Springville, UT 84663
Phone: (801) 489-8045
Type of organization: Residential treatment centers for children

Vermont
Vermont Association for Mental Health
PO Box 165
Montpelier, VT 05601
Phone: (802) 223-6263
Secondary phone: (800) 639-4052
Fax: (802) 828-5252
Website: www.vamh.org
Type of organization: Vermont chapter of the National Mental Health Associa-
    tion. Advocates for children and adults with psychiatric disabilities or sub-
    stance abuse problems.

Vermont Division of Developmental and Mental Health Services
Weeks Building
103 South Main St.
Waterbury, VT 05671-1601
Phone: (888) 212-4677 statewide
Secondary phone: (802) 241-2610
Fax: (802) 241-1129

Website: www.state.vt.us/dmh
Type of organization: State mental health agency

Vermont Federation of Families for Children's Mental Health
PO Box 607
Montpelier, VT 05601
Phone: (800) 639-6071
Fax: (802) 828-2159
Type of organization: Parent advocacy group for families with children that have mental health care needs

Howard Center for Human Services
Baird Center for Children and Families
1110 Pine St.
Burlington, VT 05401-5395
Phone: (802) 863-1326
Type of organization: Multisetting mental health organizations

Brookhaven Home for Boys
331 Main St.
Chelsea, VT 05038
Phone: (802) 685-4458
Type of organization: Residential treatment centers for children

Laraway Youth and Family Services
Laraway School
95 School St.
Johnson, VT 05656
Phone: (802) 635-2805
Type of organization: Residential treatment centers for children

Virginia

Federation of Families for Children's Mental Health
1101 King St., Ste. 420
Alexandria, VA 22314
Phone: (703) 684-7710
Fax: (703) 836-1040
Website: www.ffcmh.org
Type of organization: The federation is a national advocacy and support organization for families of children with mental, emotional, or behavioral disorders.

They sponsor parent advocacy groups across the country where parents can find support and learn about the children's mental health system and services in their community. The federation advocates for services on the national, state, and local levels and promotes family involvement in the mental health system. They sponsor an annual conference and publish a newsletter.

Mental Health Association in Fredericksburg (MHAF)
2217 Princess Anne St., Ste. 219-1
Fredericksburg, VA 22401
Phone: (800) 684-6423
Secondary phone: (540) 371-2704
Fax: (540) 372-3709
Website: www.fls.infi.net/~mhaf
Type of organization: MHAF is a nonprofit organization dedicated to addressing all aspects of mental health and mental illness through advocacy, education, and support services.

National Mental Health Association Information Center
2001 N. Beauregard St., 12th Floor
Alexandria, VA 22311
Phone: (703) 684-7722
Fax: (703) 684-5968
Toll-free: (800) 969-6642
TDD: (800) 433-5959
E-mail: infoctr@nmha.org
Website: www.nmha.org
Type of organization: The National Alliance for the Mentally Ill maintains a helpline for information on mental illnesses and referrals to local groups. The local self-help groups have support and advocacy components and offer education and information about community services for families and individuals.

Whisper Ridge Behavioral Health System
2101 Arlington Blvd.
Charlottesville, VA 22903-1593
Phone: (434) 977-1523
Type of organization: Residential treatment centers for children

Bridges Child and Adolescent Treatment Center
693 Leesville Rd.
Lynchburg, VA 24502-2828

Phone: (434) 947-5700
Type of organization: Residential treatment centers for children

Washington

Department of Social and Health Services
PO Box 45320
Olympia, WA 98504-5320
Phone: (800) 446-0259
Secondary phone: (360) 902-0790
Fax: (360) 902-0809
Website: www.wa.gov/dshs
Type of organization: State mental health agency

Ryther Child Center
2400 NE Ninety-fifth St.
Seattle, WA 98115-2499
Phone: (206) 525-5050
Fax: (206) 525-9795
Website: www.ryther.org
Type of organization: Ryther Child Center offers safe places for children to heal
and grow in residential settings and homes. Ryther helps children achieve better lives through high-quality and intensive mental health and chemical-de-
pendence services with compassionate concern for each child. These services
are provided by an energetic, devoted staff of highly trained professionals and
skilled child-care workers committed to continuous improvement and en-
hancement of the Ryther continuum of care.

Washington State Office of Children with Special Health Care Needs
(CSHCN)
Office of Maternal and Child Health
Department of Health
New Market Industrial Bldg. 10
PO Box 47835
Olympia, WA 98504-7835
Phone: (360) 236-3571
Website: www.doh.wa.gov/cfh/mch/CSHCNhome2.htm
Type of organization: The CSHCN program services children who have serious
physical, behavioral, or emotional conditions that require health and related
services beyond those generally required by children.

State Mental Health Agency
For more information about admission, care, treatment, release, and patient follow-up in public or private psychiatric residential facilities, contact the state mental health agency:
Karl Brimner, Director
Mental Health Division
Department of Social and Health Services
PO Box 45320
Olympia, WA 98504-5320
Phone: (360) 902-8070
Fax: (360) 902-0809
Toll-free: (800) 446-0259 (statewide)
Website: www1.dshs.wa.gov/mentalhealth

West Virginia
Family Support
The Center for Mental Health Services awards grants to statewide, family-run networks to provide support and information to families of children and adolescents with serious emotional, behavioral, or mental disorders. For more information, contact
Terri Toothman, Executive Director
Mountain State Parents, Children and Adolescent Network
PO Box 6658
Wheeling, WV 26003
Phone: (304) 233-5399
Fax: (304) 233-3847
Toll-free: (800) 244-5385 (statewide)
E-mail: ttoothman@mspcan.org
Website: www.mspcan.org

Region II Family Network
940 Fourth Ave., Ste. 321
Huntington, WV 25701
Phone: (888) 711-4334
E-mail: MSFA2003@aol.com

Mountain State Parents, Children and Adolescent Network
PO Box 6658
Wheeling, WV 26003-0906

Phone: (800) 244-5385
Website: www.mspcan.org

Wisconsin
Alliance for Children and Families
11700 W. Lake Park Dr.
Milwaukee, WI 53224-3099
Phone: (800) 221-3726
Secondary phone: (414) 359-1040
Fax: (414) 359-1074
Website: www.alliance1.org
Type of organization: The Alliance for Children and Families represents more than 350 child- and family-service organizations. The alliance formed in 1998 after the merging of Family Service America and the National Association of Homes and Services for Children.

Depression and Bipolar Support Alliance of Southeastern Wisconsin
PO Box 13306
Milwaukee, WI 53213-0306
Phone: (414) 964-2586
Type of organization: Self-help support group for individuals seventeen and older who have depression, bipolar disorder, or related illnesses. Services are extended to family and friends and include education and support in an atmosphere of confidentiality, trust, and shared experiences. Meetings are on the first and third Monday from 10 to 11:30 a.m. and on the second and fourth Monday from 7 to 9 p.m. Wheelchair accessible but call ahead for elevator services.

Northwest System
Northwest Counseling and Guidance Clinic
203 United Way
Frederic, WI 54837-8938
Phone: (715) 327-4402
Website: www.mentalhealth.samhsa.gov/databases/MappointLive/Location-Page.aspx?id=12809
Type of organization: Residential treatment centers for children

State Protection and Advocacy Agency
Each state has a protection and advocacy agency that receives funding from the Federal Center for Mental Health Services. Agencies are mandated to protect

and advocate for the rights of people with mental illnesses and to investigate reports of abuse and neglect in facilities that care for or treat individuals with mental illnesses. These facilities, which may be public or private, include hospitals, nursing homes, community facilities, board and care homes, homeless shelters, jails, and prisons. Agencies provide advocacy services or conduct investigations to address issues that arise during transportation or admission to such facilities, during residency in them, or within ninety days after discharge from them. Contact

Wisconsin Coalition for Advocacy
16 North Carroll St., Ste. 400
Madison, WI 53703
Phone/TDD: (608) 267-0214
Fax: (608) 267-0368
Toll-free: (800) 928-8778 (statewide—consumers and family members only)
Website: www.w-c-a.org

We Are the Children's Hope
2943 N. Ninth St.
Milwaukee, WI 53206
Phone: (414) 263-3375
Fax: (414) 263-1148
Type of organization: Parent advocacy group

Wyoming

Family Support
The Center for Mental Health Services awards grants to statewide, family-run networks to provide support and information to families of children and adolescents with serious emotional, behavioral, or mental disorders. For more information, contact
Peggy Nikkel, Executive Director
UPLIFT
PO Box 664
Cheyenne, WY 82003
Phone: (307) 778-8686
Fax: (307) 778-8681
Toll-free: (888) UPLIFT-3 (875-4383)
Website: www.upliftwy.org

NAMI Wyoming
PO Box 165
Torrington, WY 82240-0165
Phone: (307) 532-3290
Fax: (307) 532-3290
Website: www.wyami.org
Type of organization: NAMI Wyoming is a support and advocacy organization.
They sponsor local support groups and offer education and information about
community services for people with mental illness and their families.

Wyoming Department of Health: Mental Health Division
6101 Yellowstone Rd., Rm. 259-B
Cheyenne, WY 82002
Phone: (307) 777-7997
Fax: (307) 777-5580
Website: mentalhealth.state.wy.us
Type of organization: State mental health agency

References

American Academy of Child and Adolescent Psychiatry (AACAP). 2008. The depressed child. www.aacap.org/cs/root/facts_for_families/the_depressed_child (accessed October 22, 2008).

Anxiety Disorders Association of America (ADAA). Anxiety solutions. www.adaa.org (accessed April 20, 2008).

Hamelin, Jessica. 2007. PTSD in children and adolescents. U.S. Department of Veterans Affairs. www.ncptsd.va.gov/ncmain/ncdocs/fact_shts/fs_children.html (accessed April 20, 2008).

National Institute of Mental Health (NIMH). 2005. September. www.nimh.nih.gov/health/publications/depression/complete-publication.shtml. (retrieved April 21, 2008).

Voelker, Rebecca. 2003. Researchers probe depression in children. *Journal of the American Medical Association* 289: 3078–79.

Epilogue

Striking a Healthy Balance
between Safety and Overprotection

Writing this book, I (KW) found myself as a mom becoming quite paranoid about all of the dangers facing my young children. I became much more nervous watching them swimming in the lake or playing on the playground or riding their bikes. I was much more careful about how I did their seat belts in their car seats and fastened their helmets and life jackets. It's not that I wasn't careful or vigilant before, but I've found that writing this book increased my consciousness of these hidden dangers and increased my level of vigilance. We do hope that this book accomplishes the same for other parents, teachers, caretakers, and adults concerned about the welfare of the next generation—that it makes you all a bit more aware and a bit more careful.

While we hope to heighten awareness of some of these hidden dangers, we also hope that parents, teachers, and others do not become so fearful and overprotective that they do not allow children the full range of fun childhood activities available. The trick is finding the balance between safety and overprotection. Awareness of the dangers and knowing some strategies for keeping children safe in potentially risky situations can reduce the risk of farm. There are a few general rules for all caregivers that we would like to leave the reader with:

- Always know where your children (or the children in your care) are, what they are doing, and with whom they are doing it.
- Create the kind of relationship with your children or students in which they will tell you honestly what they are doing, as well as about their fears and concerns. Listen intently to what they tell you, and demonstrate that you care and want to help when necessary.

Be aware of these sometimes hidden dangers, and do what you can to protect your child or other children.

- Work with others — you don't need to do it alone. Caring for children is difficult, and nobody should have to do it alone.

If we all work together as adults, we can keep children safer and lead them into healthier futures. Then we can hope for a healthier, safer, brighter future for everyone.

About the Authors

Kimberly Williams received her doctorate from Syracuse University in foundations of education with a certificate in conflict resolution from the Maxwell School. She served as the principal investigator of the Syracuse University Violence Prevention Project—a subcontract of the Hamilton Fish National Institute on School and Community Violence. She then served on the faculty in the School of Education at the State University of New York's College at Cortland teaching courses in assessment and research methods. While at Cortland, she received grants to evaluate school health and safety programming—most notably serving as the local evaluator for the Syracuse City School District's Safe Schools/Healthy Students grant. After the State University of New York, she was a tenured associate professor in the College of Graduate Studies at Plymouth State University in Plymouth, New Hampshire. She spent nearly four years as a visiting associate professor at Dartmouth College in the Department of Education. Currently, she serves on the faculty as an associate professor at Hobart and William Smith Colleges in Geneva, New York. She has authored several books and articles on child and adolescent violence, drug abuse, prevention, and safety issues.

Marcel Lebrun has been an educator for thirty years. During that time he has been a classroom teacher, administrator, school counselor, and special education teacher. He was the director of a stress and anxiety clinic from 1994 to 2002 and a university counselor from 2002 to 2005. He is presently a professor at Plymouth State University in the Education Department, where he teaches classes in special education, behavior

.anagement, counseling, and educational methodology at the undergrad-
.1ate and graduate level. He has taught abroad and has traveled extensively
throughout the world. He has published several books on depression, sexual orientation, academic strategies, school shootings, and school violence, and has published a number of articles on behavior issues and mental health concerns in children. Currently he is on the leadership team for
the Positive Behavior Intervention and Supports Initiative in New Hampshire. He also provides consulting services to several school districts in
need of improvement, working mostly with school personnel around student issues in violence, aggression, functional assessment, and mental
health concerns. He has presented throughout the United States, Canada,
and Europe. Dr. Lebrun was recently honored with Distinguished Professor of the Year for 2008.